HOW
TO BE
SELFISH

HOW TO BE SELFISH

7 STEPS TO TAKING BACK YOUR POWER

SUZY READING

LONDON

VERMILION

UK | USA | Canada | Ireland | Australia
India | New Zealand | South Africa

Vermilion is part of the Penguin Random House group of companies
whose addresses can be found at global.penguinrandomhouse.com

Penguin Random House UK
One Embassy Gardens, 8 Viaduct Gardens, London SW11 7BW

penguin.co.uk
global.penguinrandomhouse.com

First published by Vermilion in 2025

1

Copyright © Suzy Reading 2025

The moral right of the author has been asserted.

The contents of this book are for informational purposes only and do not constitute medical advice. This book is not intended to be a substitute for, or replace, professional medical advice, diagnosis, or treatment. Always seek the advice of a physician or other qualified health provider with any questions you may have regarding a medical condition, and before following or relying upon any information in this book. Never disregard professional medical advice or delay in seeking it because of something you have read in this book. The author and publisher specifically disclaim any liability, loss, or risk, personal or otherwise, that is incurred as a consequence, directly or indirectly, of the use and application of any of the contents of this book.

No part of this book may be used or reproduced in any manner for the purpose of training artificial intelligence technologies or systems. In accordance with Article 4(3) of the DSM Directive 2019/790, Penguin Random House expressly reserves this work from the text and data mining exception.

Typeset in 10.5/14.5pt Bembo MT Pro by Six Red Marbles UK, Thetford, Norfolk
Printed and bound in Great Britain by Clays Ltd, Elcograf S.p.A.

The authorised representative in the EEA is Penguin Random House Ireland,
Morrison Chambers, 32 Nassau Street, Dublin D02 YH68

A CIP catalogue record for this book is available from the British Library

ISBN 9781785045295

Penguin Random House is committed to a sustainable future for our business, our readers and our planet. This book is made from Forest Stewardship Council® certified paper.

For any woman who has questioned her right to feel, to have needs, to take up space; may you stand tall in your abundant enoughness. May you fill the room. It is time to start living like you matter too.

CONTENTS

Introduction   1

Part One
Self, Selflessness and Selfishness

Chapter One: Getting to Know Yourself   15

Chapter Two: Healing Your Relationship with Self   39

Chapter Three: Breaking Free from Self-abandonment   71

Chapter Four: Introducing Your Toolkits for Reclaiming Self   93

Part Two
How We Can Think, Feel and Choose Differently

Step 1: I Reclaim My Mind   105

Step 2: I Reclaim My Attention   121

Step 3: I Reclaim My Body   145

Step 4: I Reclaim My Right to Feel   175

Step 5: I Take Back My Moral Compass   199

Step 6: I Prioritise Myself   221

Step 7: I Advocate for Myself   241

Next Steps   259

Further Reading and Listening	275
Notes	277
Acknowledgements	289

INTRODUCTION

Selfish.

Repeat the word a few times, roll it around in your mouth, and you can hear the venom with which this word is usually spoken. *Selfish.* Is there a harsher criticism? A less desirable trait?

We all know someone self-centred, uncaring, thoughtless, greedy or miserly.

Who in their right mind would want to be like them?

So let me stop you right there. That's *not* what this book is about.

The title of this book is not how to be *more* selfish. It's a book for those who couldn't be selfish if they tried. I have a giant heart too, the thought of being uncaring is abhorrent to me, and I share and celebrate those beautiful commitments to being a loving person.

But from the outset, let me invite you to reflect on selfishness. If you pause to think of the last time you felt selfish – I'm curious – were you truly putting your own needs above everyone else, or were you just allowing your needs to get a look in too? When I hear women talk about feeling selfish, time and again it's when they are resting, having spent all day tending to others, or when they are voicing their feelings, or an opinion, or just taking a few quiet breaths for themselves. None of these things are selfish, yet we have become so attuned to and fixated on the needs of others, and selfishness has become so demonised, that returning to self, even for a few snatched moments, feels shame inducing.

If you've lived a life of self-sacrifice, you'll know the depletion of people pleasing and overachieving, the loneliness of hyper-independence, the heaviness of hyper-responsibility, the resentment of martyrdom, the pain of invisibility, the ache of feeling lost and not knowing yourself, or the bottomless pit of 'not enoughness'. It's time for an alternative way to live your values, for something more than the hollowness of constant selflessness.

I will help you understand the brainwashing we're constantly being given about what it means to be a good human being. I will open your eyes to how we're immersed in a narrative that gaslights us. Once you recognise the pattern you can't unsee it: we must be resilient, we must be productive and strive, we must be convenient and conform, we must not burden others with our needs and emotions, we must also be loving, caring, kind and tend to others, and we must not be selfish. This is the sucker punch: we must be self-sufficient – but it's not OK to focus on self. We're raised in a culture that systematically distracts us from self, conditions us to be silent, criticises us for being needy while chastising us for attempting to meet our own needs, and then turns on us when burnout hits, proclaiming we should have taken better care of ourselves.

If just the title of this book makes you feel uncomfortable, this book is for you. The sheer fact that you worry about being selfish suggests *you are not a selfish person*.

I've been working in women's health for nearly three decades now, empowering my clients with nourishing habits and skills. After obtaining my master's degree in psychology, I spent my twenties working as a personal trainer, women coming to me to whip them into shape to meet ever-changing ideals. What I loved about that role was how soon those ideals became less of a driver, my clients relishing the opportunity to come home to themselves, to inhabit their bodies fully and to learn what it means to truly have their own back. In my thirties I focused on a therapeutic application of yoga, helping women to direct their attention inwards, to hear themselves and to cultivate a responsive, compassionate pace in their lives. In my forties, I reclaimed my psychological practice, supporting people through stress, loss and change, working with women to deepen their self-knowledge and skills in self-advocacy. I've drawn on all of these modalities in the practices in this book, so get ready to nurture yourself, and allow yourself to be nurtured by others, head, heart and body. The shifts I am going to tell you about are not just things that happen in your mind; you need to get all layers of your being involved.

Women often say that they don't have the time, energy or money for nourishing practices, but the truth is, they don't feel it's OK to direct attention inwards, to focus on self or prioritise self, which is seen as selfish and a distraction from our real job – to tend to the needs of others or to get on with being productive. I know this because my books are full of ways to overcome those barriers of time, expense and energy, and yet people are still not doing self-care, because when they get honest with themselves, the real barrier is feeling undeserving or unworthy of care. Tending to self feels selfish and even the desire to do it is shame inducing. Self is shameful so we deny ourselves the right to self. We confuse self-advocacy for selfishness.

What about you? Some questions this book will help you explore:

- How do you define selfishness? What does it mean to you?
- When do you feel like you are a selfish person? What are you doing when that pang of selfishness gets you in the guts?
- What would someone else be doing if you were to label them as selfish?

Reflection time: What makes you feel selfish?

Do you feel selfish when you do any of the following?

- Rest or relax
- Get an early night or otherwise prioritise your sleep needs
- Exercise
- Look after yourself too
- Voice your opinion
- Express your preference
- Protect your peace over keeping 'the peace'
- Allow others to support you too
- Ask for help
- Manage your workload, saying no to requests
- Manage your social calendar, declining invitations or changing plans
- Take time away from your family
- Leave your kids, even with their other parent
- Do something of your choosing
- Experience pleasure or joy

Which of these ring true for you? What might you add of your own? From here on, this book will encourage you to be on the lookout for those familiar feelings of selfishness. When they arise, grow your list to help you identify patterns.

If it resonates for you, think about what you weren't allowed to do as a child and see if these are the same things that come up when you think about what makes you feel selfish today (see the reflection time box). These are some common themes: asking for help, needing attention, expressing emotion, slowing down or making mistakes.

I hope that in holding these moments up to the light, we might be able to allow ourselves to take a closer look at why we feel selfish. Even just writing things down makes space for a different narrative to take hold. As you read through your list, consider whether you would label someone else selfish for engaging in these same behaviours, or whether you hold yourself to different standards. We might interpret other people's behaviour as forthright, direct, honest, even courageous, but feel bad when we engage in those same actions. Is it fair that you call yourself selfish in this moment? If it's OK for others, let's play with the idea that it is also OK for you. I will show you in the 7 Steps (Part II) how to sit with the disapproval you might encounter, with the discomfort this new action brings, but for now, let's at least entertain the thought. Go back to your definition of selfishness and ask yourself, are these actions truly selfish or can I allow myself greater freedom?

This is how our fear of being seen as selfish and our commitment to selflessness take shape: people pleasing, peace keeping, hyper-independence, hyper-responsibility, perfectionism, striving, martyrdom and feeling invisible or lost. I don't want to describe these as character types because we might engage in different behaviour across different settings and in different relationships, so let's just observe the various ways these patterns show up. I hope you feel seen, and I hope you feel understood, because you're not alone in this.

Can you also see these patterns play out in the lives of your friends or your mother? Can you have empathy for her? If you can see yourself in this woman and have empathy for her, why not for yourself?

Who this book is for

This book is for you if you have committed your whole life to being the good girl, the good woman, the good mother. You've tied yourself in knots trying to keep all the people happy, shape-shifting to accommodate their needs. In all that sensing and forecasting, you've become highly attuned, to the point you feel you're always on high alert. Maybe you identify with being a Highly Sensitive Person, like me, and you've been criticised for being too sensitive, for feeling too much. I hope you are ready to feel pride in your giant heart, knowing that you can be soft *and* strong. Perhaps you've made it to midlife and are feeling enraged that in this season of life, having given so much for so long, when you finally reach out for support, your needs are so often minimised, belittled or reasoned away. There's so much happening within you that it's simply not possible to keep facilitating all those around you like 'business as usual'. You are ready to have a turn. You're done with being that piece of elastic that just keeps getting stretched to service others, without reciprocity. You are ready to be seen, heard, known and championed for yourself, not just for what you do for others.

Full disclosure – I once walked out of a hairdressing appointment with a weeping, burnt scalp, without issuing a word of complaint ... I'm a kind person and I didn't want to hurt the hairdresser's feelings. I think I was partly in a state of shock too, but when I got home and realised the extent of the injury, I recognised I had a responsibility to let her know, so that she could learn from her error and never similarly harm another person. I was still prioritising the safety of other people over my own human needs. (Hairdressers, take note: don't use a hairdryer to expedite bleaching with foils.) I know I'm not alone in this kind of self-muting. A friend once told me she suffered in silence at the dentist when the anaesthetic failed. She was too busy protecting his feelings to advocate for herself.

I am still learning the art of self-advocacy. I can remember just this year, coming round from surgery under general anaesthetic in a ward with several other patients. One bed was empty, the patient's partner waiting for her return, and on seeing my eyes open he thought it was a good time to engage me in chat. After a few minutes of bleary-eyed conversation, placating his concerns, I remembered that I can be kind, giant-hearted and fucking boundaried too. This was not the time to navigate the needs of another patient's partner. You don't have to hold space for people, just because you can. Screw being selfless. Your health matters too.

I wonder where it all comes from, this desperate desire to be a good person no matter the personal cost to ourselves, and we are going to get crystal clear on that in the chapters ahead, but for now, let's plant a seed. Being a good human, what does that mean to you? I can remember my mum, who was and is the most incredible, loving support in my life, saying to me, 'Where has my good little girl gone?' Now, she was probably just trying to get me to put my shoes on so she could take me to school and go to work to provide for me, but this runs so deep, doesn't it? We all just want to be good. But perhaps it is time to let go of being a good human, and just be human.

The narrative of what it means to be 'good' is a roadblock to truly putting our needs first. Until we unpick the cultural messaging around what is expected of us, we will never feel enough, because we can never *be* enough to meet what is demanded of us.

Feel uneasy with the notion of dispensing with good and bad? I hear you. I am deeply committed to encouraging pro-social behaviour too, but ponder this: does labelling someone 'bad' achieve this aim? Accusing someone of being bad just invokes a feeling of shame, a hardening, doubling down, diminished self-esteem, or self-defence. Rather than 'What's wrong with you?' a more constructive question would be 'What happened to you?'

This book is not about robbing other people of your precious love and generosity, rather it is broadening these *to also include yourself*. I am inviting you to come home to yourself, to reclaim your right to personhood, to know, express, honour and finally be able to choose yourself too. This is fundamental to your health, and if that's not sufficiently galvanising, to the health of your relationships, and the health of future generations, your daughters *and* your sons. Because the truth is, time does not heal all wounds. The mere passage of time does not in itself mean that unhealthy beliefs and narratives are examined or challenged, or that our role in perpetuating them is held up to the light. Wounds that are unacknowledged, denied, hidden and allowed to fester will steal our life force and the damage will spread further as we uphold the same values that keep us trapped, judge others by the same measuring stick, praise ourselves and our kids for the righteous toil, the suffering, the subjugation, rather than seeing these behaviours for the toxic coping mechanisms we've been forced to rely on. If we want to heal, we have no choice but to see the wounds and participate in the healing process, no longer silencing or abandoning ourselves.

Your step-by-step journey through this book

This book will take you on a journey to being able to know yourself, choose yourself and advocate for yourself. It has two parts and you will be guided through each with regular opportunities to pause and consider what insight or action might be prompted for you.

In Part I we take a deep dive into your relationship with yourself and what's led you to your beliefs. We can't change what remains hidden and so we begin with bringing to light how you feel about 'self' and all that you associate with that, and we find room for fresh interpretations. You're invited to consider what selfishness means to you, so you can be on the lookout for those times when guilt taps you on the shoulder and stops you from prioritising yourself. We use a visualisation practice, and the support of a loved one, to help you give yourself permission to make fresh choices. We examine the multitude of cultural threads that have formed those beliefs and inner scripts, helping you see them for the untruths they are, so they no longer derail you.

You'll understand how you've been distracted from your inner experiences by the stimulation of modern life, disconnected from your needs and feelings by your rearing, gender conditioning, the medical system and societal norms, and you will be able to acknowledge with great compassion the ways in which you've had to abandon yourself to be the 'good girl'. We digest what science has to say about the dangers of selfishness and the health risks of selflessness, while also tenderly acknowledging the benefits of being a giver, because there is some gentle letting go required. By the end of Part I, you will feel reassured that it is time to honour yourself for the sake of your health, and the health of your relationships too, knowing that the discomfort you might feel is OK. I will help you feel safe to show up authentically, and to also know where it is safe to bring your whole self to the table. We will navigate it all together.

Part II is a gloriously practical framework of skills and rituals that will help you think and feel differently. This is where you'll take personalised action. You've done your fact finding in Part I and you'll feel ready for fresh choices. Part II is about getting clarity on what this means for you and setting that into motion. You'll meet the 7 Steps to Self-advocacy, a scaffolding of skills that will help you come home to self:

- Step 1: I Reclaim My Mind

    One by one we remove the roadblocks. This step will show you how to get your mind on side and deal with those self-limiting beliefs once and for all. We will awaken your inner elder to guide you along the way and develop your capacity to feel less pushed around by your inner critic.

- Step 2: I Reclaim My Attention

    You'll remember how to harness your senses and become alive again to your inner experiences, all those things you naturally excelled at in childhood.

- Step 3: I Reclaim My Body

    Get ready to feel acceptance, respect and compassion for your physical body like never before. Pleasure awaits!

- Step 4: I Reclaim My Right to Feel

    One toolkit at a time, you'll learn how to make space for all your emotions, moving through them in safe and healthy ways. This will be the validation and understanding you've been looking for your whole life long.

- Step 5: I Take Back My Moral Compass

    Having seen through the lies you've been told in Part I, now you get to choose for yourself what a meaningful life looks like.

- Step 6: I Prioritise Myself

    You will determine what your boundaries might look like, the key to start living like you matter.

- Step 7: I Advocate for Myself

    Now you know yourself and have resourced yourself, this step is all about building the confidence to represent yourself, so that you can voice your feelings and needs and finally *receive* the love and support you deserve.

How to read this book: A journey back to self

Let the ritual of reading this book be itself an act of rebellion – a chance to detach from tending to others and focus inwards. Leave your phone in another room, find a cosy nook, maximise your comfort and settle in to take a look at what's led you to this point in your life, and where you would like to go from this moment forwards. Just picking it up is an assertion of your worth. I encourage you to make an appointment with yourself if you find it hard to make space to read. Diarise it and make the commitment. Allow it to be a gentle and self-paced journey. One page a day can be enough; you get to choose. I hope it soon becomes a trusted companion, one that gets dog-eared and highlighted and annotated with 'aha' moments of your own.

This book isn't just meant to be read, it is meant to be shared. I hope that it feels like a dialogue between us and that you know I'm here, lending you a centre of abiding calm, sitting by your side as you make your own connections between the dots and digest the emotions that arise from those insights. You might also read it with a friend or book club, so you can talk about what you are learning and unlearning together, keeping each other honest in your new commitments to self. I love having exchanges in the comments on my Instagram posts, so please know you will find community and connection there. We were never meant to journey alone.

This book is not designed just to be read from cover to cover. It is intended as a guide that stimulates your independent exploration, something to be chewed on, with pauses to get up and take the nourishing actions that you feel called to do. A blank journal will come in handy to record your insights and commitments to self. Throughout the book there will be many opportunities for you to do some sifting and sorting of your own experiences. The practices I share are based on my training in Acceptance and Commitment Therapy (referred to by its acronym, ACT), an evidence-based approach that focuses on developing psychological flexibility and promoting values-driven behaviour change. Via the skills of mindfulness, acceptance and compassion, ACT teaches us to come into contact with our full experience, helping us identify current behaviour patterns and choose actions that are congruent with our values. ACT changes our relationship with our thoughts and feelings and empowers us to live a rich and meaningful life even in the presence of challenging experiences – it is the perfect approach to guide us in our journey to self-advocacy.

There will be all sorts of prompts in this book, such as thought exercises, timeline practices, visualisations, journaling inspiration, mantras and affirmations, as well as a whole host of physical practices including movement, breathwork and rituals of soothing touch. I hope it provides you with a smorgasbord of sensory pleasures, from which you can select the ones that speak to you, helping you feel safe in your own body and confident in your interactions with others.

I hope it is a book that you'll want to keep coming back to, to dip into for a fresh practice or to just be reminded just how far you've come in your journey back home to you. Take your time, darling. Let tenderness lead the way. It is an honour to walk the path with you.

We are living in a pandemic of 'not enoughness', and I believe the root of this comes from our aversion to being seen as selfish, that having needs means we are somehow being 'needy'. The drive to be selfless is going far beyond being meek and nurturing. It is leading us to self-erasure, and that denial of our right to feel and have needs is doing us great harm.

Here's to being ceaseless and tireless in our love, but let me plant this seed straight away: screw being selfless. You are not broken, flawed, lost or unworthy. The deficit was never yours. Return home, safely. Let the journey to self-advocacy begin.

PART ONE

SELF, SELFLESSNESS AND SELFISHNESS

CHAPTER ONE
GETTING TO KNOW YOURSELF

First, we need to get clear on how we're currently feeling in ourselves, and what we think and feel about self, selfishness and selflessness. Before we take our deep dive into learning how to prioritise ourselves, I invite you to take an honest look at what selfishness means to you.

I wonder whether you are already seeing how our idea of selfishness has become skewed. It's so distorted that the mere possession of self feels selfish, and identification with self generates shame. Instead of selfishness being an imbalance in priority, where there is too much focus on self and too little on other people, it's tipped us into self-denial. Maybe you feel like you don't have a right to be here, let alone take up space or use precious resources. Our own personhood can feel so prickly. I invite you to keep coming back to the understanding that it's not necessarily selfish to focus on self; it's selfish if we are *only* focusing on ourselves – but how often is this the case? Observe with compassion and let's see.

What is SELF?

As we journey through this book, I want you to reclaim your 'self', so we need to explore what that actually means. The dictionary offers a few interpretations: self is a person's essential being that distinguishes you from others; your own distinct individuality, character or identity. It also suggests your welfare, interests or pleasure. On top of this, it's the personal characteristics that make you unique – as in 'back to your old self' – and your conscious awareness of your own identity or being.

The 'self' I am referring to in this book is your sense of being your own independent person, of having the right to be a unique individual. I'm talking about you and your subjective introspective experience of life, the world and yourself – the sensations, emotions, thoughts, memories, needs, hopes, dreams and desires you possess as an autonomous human being. It includes your own being, knowledge, values and experiences of your inner and outer living, a self that is distinguishable from others. When I talk about coming home to your 'self', I am talking about reclaiming your right to personhood and standing firm in your own sense of being a unique and individual human being, in your own right to be here and to take up space.

Notice how we happily meet the energetic demands of our devices without maligning them as being selfish and yet our own human needs feel like a shameful personal deficit? It's time to embrace these things that make us uniquely human – our capacity to think and feel and to honour our needs.

How does 'self' make you feel?

When you hear the word 'self', what comes to mind? How does it make you feel inside? Do you notice any instinctive responses? Jot down without judgement what comes up for you.

Now write down all the negative associations you can generate for self. How about: selfish, self-centred, self-obsessed . . . Write down as many as you can think of.

Which words feel comfortable to you, which ones feel familiar? Are there some words here that you have a strong response to? Observe how many words you can generate. Does this give you any clues about your relationship to yourself or perhaps how you've been conditioned to feel about yourself? Are there some words that you're ready to move away from?

Take a good look at the list you've created – is 'self' a dirty word?

Take out a fresh piece of paper and let's switch things up. Now jot down all the words beginning with 'self' that have positive connotations. Let your mind run wild and free.

Once complete, reflect on your second list. How easy was it to come up with this positive list? Did you find more or fewer words than for your negative list? How do you feel about these words? Are there some that call to you? Listen out for that whisper from within; it might be really quiet at first.

Let me share the words on my negative list:

- Selfish
- Self-centred
- Self-obsessed
- Self-aggrandisement
- Selfie
- Self-important
- Self-promotion
- Self-denial
- Self-hatred
- Self-abandonment

- Self-harm
- Self-righteous
- Self-loathing
- Self-doubt
- Self-blame
- Self-disgust
- Self-distrust
- Self-conscious
- Self-pity
- Self-inflicted
- Self-punishment
- Self-destruction
- Self-defeat

And my positive associations:

- Selfless
- Self-soothing
- Self-regulation
- Self-belief
- Self-confidence
- Self-trust
- Self-esteem
- Self-respect
- Self-love

- Self-determination
- Self-forgiveness
- Self-advocacy
- Self-kindness
- Self-care
- Self-made
- Self-expression
- Self-assured
- Self-healing
- Self-satisfaction
- Self-compassion
- Self-approval
- Self-awareness
- Self-worth
- Self-control

Are there any words that are new to you, ones that didn't make it onto your list? Are there some that feel heavy, ones that you want nothing to do with? Do others feel light and bright? Do some pique your curiosity? Would you like them to become part of your inner road map, guiding you through your day? You're in the right place.

Permission to come home to yourself

I don't expect you to just take my word for it, that it's OK to be 'selfish', so I'm wondering if we can draw on the love and support of someone precious to you?

Take a moment. Give yourself time to become still, make any adjustments to find a position of comfort and let yourself soften into this moment.

Allow yourself to detach from doing, letting the busyness of your day drop from your shoulders.

Take a couple of relaxed breaths, feeling the sensation of your breath as it moves through you. Notice how your thoughts dart about, leaping to the future or digging around in the past. Every time you notice your attention wandering, just bring it back to feeling your breathing or your body sitting here.

No need for criticism, just bring your attention back to the here and now.

Now allow yourself to think about one role in life that is precious to you. It could be partner, parent, child, sibling or something career related.

Choose just one role that you care deeply about. Think about how you want to show up in this role – what does that look like to you?

What values do you want to bring to this role? How do you want to be experienced? What are the qualities that you want to model?

Imagine yourself acting in service of these values, showing up exactly as you aspire to, in this role that matters so much to you. Notice how it feels to see yourself taking this aligned action, to be in your body seeing yourself act with such integrity.

Now imagine that someone you love, someone who cares very much for you, walks into the room and takes a seat by your side. Imagine this person who you respect, who you know has your best interests at heart, says to you, 'Darling, it's OK to focus on yourself.' Imagine they tell you, 'It's OK for you to take up space. It's OK for you to have needs, and to have your needs met too.' Imagine they say to you, 'Your feelings are welcome, it's OK for you to express them all.' Imagine they even whisper in your ear, 'It's OK to be selfish.'

Notice how it feels to hear these words from someone who loves you. What narratives pop up in your mind? What does your body have to say? Just feel your response to the words. Sit with these feelings for a few breaths and then allow your attention to return to the room around you, wriggling fingers and toes. If this practice resonates for you, jot down what you observed.

There is no right or wrong here. Maybe what you felt was a melting pot of different emotions. Perhaps there was some relief at the invitation to allow your needs to be factored in. Maybe you felt a sense of joy, elation even, that finally someone was inviting you to share your desires and dreams. Perhaps you felt a sense of anger, a feeling of resentment that something so dear to you was being called into question, being compromised. Or maybe there was a sense of fear or dread at the thought of what might happen if you did turn your attention inwards, genuine worry about how this would be perceived and received, about the disappointment or disapproval this might unleash. Maybe there was a tinge of sadness, a feeling of panic at not knowing how to let yourself do things differently, a sense of loss of something so familiar and integral to the fabric of your life. Be gentle as you bear witness to all these different and valid responses.

You can be loving towards others, and you can also have your own needs met. You don't have to abandon yourself to uphold your value of kindness, nor abandon your commitment to kindness by allowing it to include yourself. We can be kind, loving people *and* reclaim our right to honour ourselves. The point of this exercise is to examine how we use our love and care, and to remember that we have permission to choose when, where, how much and for whom we care, and that you yourself deserve a look in too. I want to help you find a more flexible way of honouring your value of kindness, without having to put yourself last or deny yourself. You can be kind and loving without being selfless. More than that, it is OK to be 'selfish'.

Move over self-care, it's time for self-advocacy

I know how hard it is to care for yourself and arguably it's even harder to advocate for yourself. In truth, historically, I have been woeful at it. I can see that so much of my commitment to self-care was just another form of striving to conform, to fit the mould, to be good enough. I know all too well the anger and disappointment that come from unmet needs, and how this can wreak havoc on your health and poison relationships. My needs were unmet because largely they were unspoken. Writing this book has helped me better understand the ways that culturally I've been distracted and disconnected from myself and had to silence and abandon myself to cope. I've experienced firsthand the toll this has taken on me and those I love the most, and I've also seen how my life has bloomed as I've reclaimed myself and developed the skills of self-advocacy. I want to take you by the hand and share that journey with you now.

I remember lying in a hospital bed, post childbirth, time itself cracked open, feeling connected with all the birthing mothers before me. My father was lying in his own hospital bed, fighting for every breath. I voiced concern for how I was going to cope – when I looked at myself in the mirror, round belly like a baby myself, wearing a post-labour pad like a nappy – how could I tend to my baby when I felt so helpless? Later, a bearded man came in to assess me for the risk of self-harm, and harm to my baby. It was the antithesis of what I needed. I yearned for a grandmother figure to wrap me up in her arms, to gather up the fragments of me and help me come back to wholeness, to rock and soothe me and remind me that I'm not alone, that I can do this. She would whisper in my ear that I had every right to feel. I had every right to take up space. I had every right to be here. I had every right to have needs. I had every right to be cared for. She would help me come home to myself.

I want to be that voice for you, helping you reclaim those abandoned parts of you, helping you come home to yourself.

It wasn't until motherhood that I became truly aware of the fundamental need to advocate for myself. You learn fast that you have to get OK with the discomfort of speaking up on behalf of your children – whether that be among well-meaning family members, in the playground, at school or in the medical system. It goes against our conditioning to rock the boat, to question authority, to ask for help, to be the squeaky wheel, to be direct and let others know when they're overstepping your boundaries, but you do it anyway because you know your kids are relying on you. It is your job to advocate for them and protect them. You learn how to say no; you learn that it's not only OK but necessary to prioritise your kids, regardless of the feathers this will ruffle.

In learning to advocate for my kids, I began to see myself as an extension of their needs, knowing that I had to protect my own health as their mother, to be able to best nurture and look after them. I began to see the implications of me modelling selflessness. If I presented as a woman without needs or feelings, how could I raise compassionate children with an awareness of the needs or feelings of others? What kind of future was I setting my kids up for by modelling the negation of my own needs and desires? If I didn't want that for my kids, I had to show them how it is done. Of course, the opportunities for self-expression vary according to the seasons of motherhood. In those early months it's not as if you can roll over at night when your baby cries and say 'not now'. We need to be responsive, but as our children grow and become more self-reliant, we can allow ourselves more time and space for our needs and desires. It is an integral part of my professional practice too – I have to walk my talk if I want to practise in my field as a psychologist with any authenticity.

It took me many more years to learn that I had a right to my own needs and desires simply as an autonomous human being. In losing my father gradually to motor neurone disease, my grief journey deepened this learning. To survive that chapter of my life,

I had to get 'selfish'. Life was so challenging that I couldn't add to my burden with trash talk or self-denial. I had to get on my own side, and it's a commitment I make to myself daily. Life changed infinitely when I made that decision – to respect self.

And now the gift of perimenopause. I see it as the fire of transformation, burning away all the dross in my life. There is so much going on beneath the surface that I have no tolerance for bullshit, including my own. I have no capacity to dance to society's ideals and can finally see them for the untruths they are, enabling me to drop the people pleasing, the endless questioning of my worth, and the futile self-sabotage and self-neglect. This is a season of our lives when we need to receive care and it is enraging that, after a lifetime of tending to the needs of others, it's so hard to have our own needs met – or worse, they are negated. That rage galvanises us to stand firm, to take no shit and to advocate for ourselves with vigour, embracing the true transformative power of perimenopause.

It is painful looking back at the ways I have felt silenced, and have silenced myself – and I am an able-bodied, heterosexual white woman. I want to acknowledge how blessed I've been with educational opportunities and a family who supported me, and yet I still felt so unworthy of my own attention . . . my heart goes out to those who have had so much more to contend with than I, and I sincerely hope this book can be a catalyst in your life.

Risks and benefits of selfishness

We are social animals, relying on one another for collective survival, and so the aversion to being seen as selfish is rooted in our DNA. Historically, all tribe members were required to contribute to be accepted and protected by the group. Fear of selfishness promotes harmony in the group; we behave lest we be cast out and have to fend for ourselves, alone. While we're no longer living in tribes, we still rely on one another for support and those drives to be accepted are still very much present today.

Selfishness can be defined as 'acting excessively or solely in a manner that benefits yourself even if it disadvantages others'.[1] Signs of selfishness, in the true sense of the word, include the following: a sense of entitlement at the expense of others; little or no regard for how one's behaviour impacts other people; consistently acting in one's own best interests rather than factoring in the needs of others; little empathy for the suffering of others; no remorse for wrongdoing; manipulating or taking advantage of others for personal gain; accepting kindness but rarely reciprocating; and when kindness is extended it comes at a cost, either motivated by wanting to look good, or with respect or praise demanded in return, or it's about exerting control or creating a feeling of debt. We can see how all this differs vastly from what so many women construe as selfish when they are evaluating their own behaviour.

People who engage in true selfishness run the risk of becoming social pariahs. Selfish people will constantly feel let down by others who don't meet their unrealistic expectations, and they'll be disappointed when life doesn't magically live up to their standards, as they believe they so deserve. Their lack of empathy makes it hard to connect with others and their refusal to take ownership of their mistakes and rejection of criticism or feedback stifles personal growth. Being seen as a taker can lead to conflict with others, poor relationships and relationship breakdown. Takers churn through friends, with people distancing themselves after feeling used, manipulated or left waiting for an apology, and often wind up feeling alienated and lonely. Over time, repeated selfish behaviour can damage your reputation, being seen as greedy, inconsiderate, uncaring or callous.

Research also shows that selfish motivation leads to not only diminished psychological wellbeing but poor physical health.[2] Preoccupation with image is associated with depression and anxiety,[3] less emotional clarity and increased emotional confusion.[4] Excessive focus on self can lead to exaggerated worry about health and social anxiety, particularly where people are highly motivated to manage the impressions that others have of them.[5] Fixation on acquiring material goods – another typically selfish trait – is associated with negative self-appraisals such as higher self-doubt,[6] and dispositional greed – an insatiable desire for more, whether possessions or power – is linked with greater envy and lower life satisfaction.[7] Giving that is motivated by selfish reasons is associated with greater psychological distress.[8]

Selfish motivations are also shown to impact negatively on physical health, with a robust link between self-presentation concerns and risky health habits such as drinking, smoking and reckless driving[9] and failure to seek medical treatment and substance abuse.[10] The effects of selfishness on physical health might also be a result of the loneliness that selfish people often experience. People with selfish motivations tend to provide poorer support to their partners and to be ineffective in meeting their partner's needs, to the detriment of their partner's wellbeing and the health of their relationship.[11] People preoccupied with self-image tend to be less responsive in relationships[12] and provide less support,[13] leading to greater interpersonal conflict[14] and decreased relationship stability.[15]

The exception to this is a grandiose narcissist who reports high life satisfaction, wellbeing and self-esteem,[16] but they may have an unwillingness to disclose negative assessments of their wellbeing or relationships, because they are trying to maintain a positive self-view and protect their image. It may also be that they care less about the quality of their relationships and feel less affected by the negative consequences of their selfishness than other people do. Research shows that narcissists do have difficulty maintaining their relationships[17] and the satisfaction of their relationship partners declines over time.[18]

While selfish people might secure more resources for themselves and keep their time for their own purposes, there are few benefits to *being seen as selfish*. So why am I inviting you to be selfish? I am inviting you to maintain your care for other people, but to become more boundaried in the way that you show up for others, and to also allow yourself to *receive* care. What I am proposing I have seen described as 'healthy selfish', but I'd prefer to express this more accurately as 'self-advocacy'. Let's first acknowledge the benefits of being seen as selfless, because there is some letting go required here, and then explore the costs it incurs.

Benefits and risks of selflessness

It doesn't just feel good to give of yourself, there are some serious health benefits to being a giver too. Research shows that giving our financial support boosts our happiness[19] and, similarly, gifting our time promotes our happiness and wellbeing.[20] Being of service to others is also known to decrease loneliness[21] and provide a protective buffer against depression.[22] Giving to others also has physical health benefits, with research demonstrating links with cardiovascular health (specifically lower blood pressure)[23] and prosocial behaviour even linked with a lower predicted mortality risk.[24] Giving promotes the health of our relationships, boosting closeness, quality of connection[25] and relationship satisfaction.[26]

But there are also costs to giving and the research suggests that in some circumstances it can be damaging to our quality of life and longevity. Research on caregivers shows that caregiver stressors are related to symptoms of depression[27] and lower subjective wellbeing.[28] Giving of ourselves can take a physical toll, as shown by caregivers experiencing slower wound healing,[29] higher stress hormones and a lower antibody response than non-caregivers,[30] and the negative physical health consequences can be long lasting.[31] The health implications for older caregivers, particularly those who feel burdened with responsibility, are even more serious, with a 63 per cent greater risk of mortality compared to non-caregivers.[32]

So what makes giving in some circumstances good for our health and in other scenarios so damaging? It's possible that focusing on others can distract people from their own issues, and the act of giving itself can enhance a sense of meaning in life, a feeling of being competent, needed. The praise that many people get for their self-sacrifice can be very affirming, boosting self-esteem. Giving support deepens our bonds and we feel better about ourselves when we can see the difference we are making. People turning to us for our strengths not only helps us feel needed but also boosts our feeling of agency, whereas people asking for help that lies outside our remit can make us feel lacking. Our capacity to give what's being asked of us has a huge impact on how we feel about that sacrifice, and our freedom to choose has a bearing too, as does the support we have available for ourselves.

For giving to have health benefits it needs to be freely chosen, in keeping with the giver's strengths and current resources, and the giver needs to be well supported themselves. When caregivers give more than they receive, it often comes at the expense of meeting their own human needs.[33] When they are well supported, they tend to experience more of the health benefits of caregiving,[34] but when their giving is at the cost of their own social connection, the risk of loneliness renders them vulnerable to poor psychological wellbeing and physical health outcomes.[35] Even perceiving that emotional support is available boosts wellbeing.[36]

Research aside, let's take a closer look at some of the dangers of selflessness that the studies can't quite capture. Caring for others might distract us from our own problems, but if this comes at the constant expense of our own needs and feelings, it is a recipe for illness and burnout. If there's anything I have learned in navigating my own life challenges, it is the wisdom of taking action at the whisper, rather than waiting for the shout. If you are so immersed in your giving that you are neglecting cues from your own body, it's likely that ill health will stop you. Pushing on is often a false economy – we think we're saving time, being productive, but the intervention that a 'shout' requires is far more labour-intensive and time consuming than attending to the 'whisper'. Deny yourself long enough and you're looking at stress, anxiety, depression, exhaustion, overwhelm, burnout, injury and physical illness. Suppression of our emotions has some major health consequences.

How supressing your emotions can harm you

There is an energetic charge to emotions. When you stifle a laugh or hold back a tear, the energy doesn't just dissipate, it gets stored in the body, waiting to be released. Anger in particular mobilises us to take action. You can feel the surge of survival energy that comes with it and there are consequences to denying your right to feel it, pushing it down or twisting away from it. Unexpressed, unresolved emotions such as anger and sadness often have a corrosive effect, eating away at our peace, manifesting as stress, apprehension, agitation, anxiety and, if they are left to fester long enough, depression. Anger turned inwards leads to shame.

When you don't allow yourself to feel your feelings it has a negative effect on the whole body.[37] Emotional suppression alters how our nervous system functions,[38] disrupts the health of our immune system,[39] reduces the diversity of our gut microbiome,[40] disrupts sleep quality,[41] increases inflammation in the body,[42] reduces pain tolerance and increases the intensity of pain and the distress caused by it,[43] and is a risk factor in the development of chronic pain conditions.[44] Self-silencing emotions can predispose us to a host of chronic illnesses and diseases including cancer,[45] coronary artery disease,[46] carotid atherosclerosis[47] (when plaque reduces the flow of blood through the carotid artery, associated with higher risk of heart attack), irritable bowel disease,[48] depression[49] and eating disorders.[50]

There are social costs to emotional suppression too, reducing our feeling of closeness to each other, our feeling of being supported and the joy we get from social interaction.[51] The strategies that people use to numb or distract themselves from feeling – excessive screen use, excessive exercise, turning to drugs, alcohol or food for comfort – all have their own health consequences.

Let's take a look at the gender differences in disease rates and you'll see what self-silencing is doing to women. Today, women account for 80 per cent of people experiencing autoimmune diseases,[52] they are twice as likely as men to die after having a heart attack,[53] they experience PTSD[54] and depression[55] at twice the rate of men, and anxiety disorders are not only more prevalent but also more disabling in women than in men.[56] Anorexia nervosa occurs nine times more often in females.[57] Women are at a greater risk of suffering from the debilitating conditions of fibromyalgia,[58] insomnia,[59] irritable bowel syndrome,[60] migraines,[61] long Covid[62] and chronic pain.[63] There are damaging consequences not only for health but also for longevity and quality of life. Darling, it is time to give yourself permission to feel.

Selflessness often gets woven into who you think you are as a person. If it's what you value about yourself, your worth might become dependent on being needed, being of service and how little you yourself take. But we know how achievable and sustainable that is. Praise for altruism can become addictive and it can skew motivation from it being a true act of selflessness to a self-sacrifice driven by a selfish need for recognition. You are likely to feel guilt and shame when you're forced to tend to yourself and a sense of failure when you are not able to meet others' needs all the time. But if you turn down their support, your loved ones miss out on the warm, uplifting feelings of providing care and may feel superfluous to needs or not trusted. Selflessness can lead to inequity in relationships, creating unfair burdens, and also resulting in people feeling rejected when they are not welcomed to contribute. Continue in these patterns long enough and martyrdom emerges.

Martyrdom explained

Do any of these internal scripts sound familiar? 'I have to do everything.' 'No one appreciates me.' 'I can't accept help; I can't trust anyone else to do it properly so it's better to just do it myself.' A martyr is someone who sacrifices their own needs or happiness for the sake of others, but it's a sacrifice made with a sense of obligation, duty or resentment that tends to make those on the receiving end of the gesture feel guilty or 'less than' as a result. Martyrs often don't let others help because of their own lofty standards but then complain about their burden, or make others feel inadequate, and they are committed to the narrative that they are a victim. The help martyrs offer doesn't feel good because it comes with a price – the selfless act isn't as selfless as it appears because it locks others into a position of the lazy, underperforming one, when they had no choice in that. Martyrdom is generosity that leaves you with a feeling like you've done something wrong, and often effusive praise or thanks is demanded in return for the kindness you never asked for in the first place.

People might think they're being selfless but really they are inflicting unreasonable expectations on others, perhaps the same austere standards they were raised with. Childhood experiences of deprivation can sometimes make people stingy, miserly, cold, unempathetic, demanding and ultimately impossible to please. People can fall into the role of the martyr when they've been praised for being selfless or shamed for expressing themselves, particularly pain, or when their emotions haven't been tolerated. When people are thrust into responsibility at an early age or have self-sacrifice modelled for them, they can find themselves falling into the same behaviour patterns in adulthood.

The question is, when you martyr yourself, who do you demonise? When you deny yourself the right to speak up and voice your needs and feelings, you tend to begrudge others the right too. You begin to see their normal, healthy expression as needy and selfish. You might get snarky and nasty, you might belittle or shame them. This doesn't serve the martyr, leaving them perpetually disappointed in others, and vulnerable to resentment, bitterness and burnout, and it also wounds the self-esteem of the people they sacrifice themselves for. It's painful to always come up wanting compared to exacting or plain impossible standards. It's exhausting wearing the disdain and giving endless recognition.

Martyrdom results in hurt feelings, alienation and potentially relationship breakdown and depression.

How can we break free from martyrdom?

If you're concerned that you are tipping into martyrdom territory, remember that your desires might be crystal clear in your own head, but if you fail to speak them and resentment breeds, your self-denial is a trap for everyone. It is OK to prioritise your needs too, and we're going to look at how to do this in Step 6, I Prioritise Myself (page 221). Perhaps in friendship you tend to go with the flow even when you don't enjoy it and then later complain about inequities. Become skilled in letting people know your preferences up front and co-create plans you can all agree on. Your interests matter. Perhaps you are there for your friends but you don't reach out for support and then feel disappointed about imbalances in your relationship or unfairly criticise people for not being there for you. People are not mind readers; you need to let them in. Communication skills are key, making honest requests for help while also tweaking your standards to enable others to get involved with less friction. Healthy boundaries will help you avoid overextending and feeling bitter about it later. Allow your good deeds to come from a place of genuine care rather than in exchange for praise or other debts. Check in with your motivations and ask if they are healthy for all involved.

Perhaps you're reading this and feeling like there are parts of martyrdom that fit and others that really don't. Sometimes we have asked for help many times over and help hasn't been forthcoming, or we've been chastised for asking, or the help that was offered came with a price and it was safer for us to stop asking, to just carry on in silence and do it ourselves. Sometimes we have to pick up slack where others were genuinely neglectful of their responsibilities. Sometimes we've had no choice but to do it all ourselves. If this is you, I am sorry you had to be so strong. I am sorry you had to do it all on your own. Please be gentle with yourself and give yourself space to acknowledge disappointment. I have a toolkit for this waiting for you in Step 4, I Reclaim My Right to Feel (page 175). Unvoiced disappointment turns into resentment, and it can be so toxic for our health and those we love. Give it voice, let it shift, and I am wishing you all the reciprocity. Perhaps you're still waiting for someone to share the load with you. Please keep reaching out.

Martyrdom aside, selflessness can lead to inauthentic relationships and makes genuine connection impossible. How can we be in true relationship with someone who doesn't honestly communicate their needs or share their emotional life? Every time you reply to the question of 'Are you OK, is everything alright?' with a 'Yes' when you feel no, this is a lie, and it has potential consequences. Selflessness means that we often don't bring our full self to the conversation or interaction, so how can people really know us?

The trouble with selflessness is that it doesn't leave much room for boundaries and we need those for the health of ourselves and our relationships. It's an unrewarding experience all round, characterised by a feeling of disconnection, misunderstanding, confusion, conflict and potential relationship breakdown. You run the risk of being taken advantage of, taken for granted, overlooked and unappreciated – your sacrifices that aren't even seen, let alone thanked. This is just as relevant in the workplace as it is in our personal relationships.

If you think you're being selfless by being 'easy going' in group decisions, recognise the burden this places on other group members to generate ideas or call the shots. It can be deeply irritating for other people if you are constantly responding with 'I don't mind'. It's social loafing, and shirking your responsibility means someone else has to carry your load.

Being selfless means acting from extrinsic motivation – doing what you think you *should* aspire to, or what other people want you to do. When you live like this, you miss out on the juice of intrinsic motivation. Research shows that you're more likely to find the staying power to last the distance when you are acting in service of intrinsic goals – what you want for you, anchored in your strengths and values. You get more satisfaction and pleasure from achieving these intrinsically motivated goals.[64] It's OK to ask 'What's in it for me?' This is another reason why selflessness sets us up for failure – if those extrinsic goals never give us enough puff to see them through to completion, we fail and then wind up feeling bad about ourselves. Constantly pursuing aims that are not truly ours drains our willpower reserves, and that has an impact on the quality of all our decision making, in everything that matters to us. The fatigue is real!

Selflessness also leads to a denial of pleasure and joy, and far from being frivolous, you need these experiences to help shift you out of the stress response. A life lacking in pleasure denies you of the feeling of safety that comes with joy, delaying healing and robbing you of the opportunity to re-energise and resource yourself.

Why selflessness isn't working for us

I hope you are beginning to question how selflessness is working for you. I invite you to look at the personal costs in your own life. What does your aversion to selfishness prevent you from doing or receiving? I think it is abundantly clear that our relationships with ourselves need urgent repair. Consider, for example, the following telling stats:

- In 2019, an estimated 280 million people, or 5 per cent of the world's adults, had depression,[65] while the most common mental disorder globally was anxiety, affecting 301 million people in that year.[66]

- In 2021, 296 million people across the world were estimated to be using drugs, an increase of almost one quarter (23 per cent) over the last decade.[67]

- Autoimmune diseases are also on the rise, cumulatively affecting 5-10 per cent of the industrial world population.[68]
- Loneliness is a global public health concern with 24 per cent of people in a 2024 Meta-Gallup study reporting they felt 'very' or 'fairly' lonely.[69] This research is echoed by the worldwide estimates from the WHO Commission on Social Connection suggesting that 1 in 4 older adults experience social isolation and 5-15 per cent of adolescents experience loneliness.[70]

Disconnection is clearly contributing to these health trends and given the messaging that we've been raised with about not expressing needs and feelings, it's little surprise that the quality of our connection is compromised. Even in the company of others we can still feel lonely and long for understanding, but how can we be seen and understood when we are masking our true self, when our fear of being seen as selfish stops us from being open and from receiving? It's not just disconnection from each other that's contributing to these worrying trends, it's disconnection from self.

What does self-advocacy look like?

The world needs you to continue in your beautiful capacity to care, to notice the struggles of others and act to help them avoid or alleviate their difficulties; but for you to do that effectively, you also need to prioritise your own health and allow yourself to *receive*. You need the support of others to resource you, so that you can keep being a compassionate agent. For you to show up in your relationships with integrity and authenticity, you need to be honest about your human needs and feelings too, making space for them to be met by you and by those who love you. In honestly representing yourself you are better placed to do anything and everything that really matters to you. You need the skill of self-advocacy: the ability to speak up and act on your own behalf. In moving towards self-advocacy, you are embracing:

- Awareness of your feelings and needs
- Permission to nourish and take care of yourself
- Permission to prioritise yourself too – your hopes, dreams, pleasures and preferences – and speaking up on your behalf so you can act on these desires
- Honouring healthy boundaries with yourself – self-respect and commitment to habits that support your health and wellbeing
- Honouring healthy boundaries with other people and not tolerating those who might try to exploit you
- Balancing the needs of self and others, allowing both to factor into your decision making
- Knowing when to give and when to take
- Knowing when to work and when to rest
- Allowing others to also care for, nurture and support you – allowing yourself to receive

Reflection time: how to be more ME

What does taking back your self mean? See if any of these ideas resonate:

- Knowing myself
- Understanding myself
- Accepting myself
- Trusting myself
- Respecting myself

- Forgiving myself
- Living my values
- Speaking my truth
- Expressing myself
- Seeking my own approval
- Valuing myself
- Honouring myself
- Being more unapologetically me

Let's finish our examination of self, selfishness and selflessness with one more thought experiment. Ponder this prompt to get you thinking about wiggle room in your life.

If I was selfish I would . . .

What might you choose to do if you allowed yourself a little more freedom of self-expression? What might this allow you to say or feel? How might it benefit you? Is this really selfish? Does this actually transgress your moral code? Other than selflessness, are there any values that this action allows you to uphold? Does it truly detract from your ability to care for others?

Let's take it a step further, is there any way this 'selfish' action could even benefit the people you love so dearly? What difference might this make in your life? What is the smallest 'selfish' action you can take today? Can you do it now? Enjoy!

CHAPTER TWO

HEALING YOUR RELATIONSHIP WITH SELF

Well done! You have acknowledged how you are feeling about selfishness and selflessness, and connected with a readiness to address these imbalances in your life, but before you can take action, you need to know what has led you to your current ways of thinking and acting. There is some unpicking to be done before you'll feel free to make new choices.

If you want to understand why you find it so hard to focus on yourself, to know yourself, to prioritise yourself in the confidence that your feelings and needs matter, and to speak up for yourself secure in your worth, you need to see how you've historically been represented, perceived and treated. You need to see all the ways you've been distracted, disconnected and silenced. Let's begin with an opportunity to reflect on your own personal experiences.

Your timeline of selfishness

Before we dive into an exploration of the cultural influences on how we collectively feel about selfishness and selflessness, I invite you to do some reflection on your own personal history, with the purpose of getting to the bottom of how you feel about self and your right to advocate for yourself. This timeline exercise will help you understand why you are afraid of being seen as selfish and why you hold on with white knuckles to the value of selflessness.

Let's take a gentle look at the story your mind is holding onto about your right to prioritise yourself and the different narratives shaped by shame, fear, disapproval, rejection or 'not enoughness' that you've been led to believe. We're going to enquire into how old this story is and where you heard it. We'll observe how you learned that you needed to self-sacrifice to be a good human and get clear on what that sacrifice entailed. This exercise will help you pinpoint the various ways you learned this story that it is bad to be selfish, and what you did to cope.

Find a blank piece of paper and let's map it out together. Towards the bottom of the page, on the left, write the heading 'Childhood'. Beneath the heading, write down what you heard about this story when you were a child. Ask yourself: Were you ever shamed for being yourself or for taking up space or resources? What specific messages were you given about this? Who gave them? What did your mind tell you about your right to have needs and to express yourself? Which emotions were acceptable and which ones were off-limits? Can you remember what you did in response to this message that it was not OK to honour yourself? How did you change your behaviour? Did this story have an impact on how you felt about yourself then?

Above this section, write the heading 'Teens'. Beneath it jot down what you were told about selfishness when you were a teen. What messages about selflessness did you absorb and from where? What narratives about your worth were you told? In your teens, what did your mind tell you about the story of your self-worth and how did you mould yourself to cope?

Above this, write down the heading 'Twenties'. What messages did you hear about your right to personhood in this stage of your life? What did your mind tell you about the need to self-sacrifice and how did you manage this story?

Depending on your age, please complete a section on your page for every decade of your life, outlining the message that you were told, the source of this information and how you shaped yourself to manage the story.

Look back over your timeline of this story about selfishness and selflessness. Can you see how old it is and how many different threads there are? Can you identify where the messages came from? Did you hear them at home, at school, in the media, in your romantic relationships, in your friendships or in the workplace? Did the story change over time? What did you do to manage it? What ways did you contort or abandon yourself to meet these societal demands? How did that impact your relationship with yourself? How does it make you feel about yourself now?

By looking with curious compassion at these historic influences and patterns in our behaviour, we can begin to reclaim those parts of ourselves that we've discarded or hidden out of shame. I hope you can see how these beliefs have shaped your sense of self, your values and your actions and that in seeing, you now have greater power to choose differently. And darling, I hope you are beginning to be able to choose your 'self'. When we see the story we have been told, it allows us to make a pivot. We don't have to remain trapped in this fundamental rejection of 'self' and we don't have to repeat the same behaviours. We can see there have already been shifts in the story and in our response to it over time, so there is malleability. We can change. And if things still feel sticky, it's OK. Step 1, I Reclaim My Mind, will support you in dealing with tenacious self-limiting beliefs.

If this practice has brought with it feelings of loss, shame, guilt, sadness or grief, you're not alone. You did not deserve this story. You did the very best with what you had at the time to cope with what you were told and how you were made to feel. These acknowledgements are painful and there is a deep grieving that comes with this territory but please know that this is where the healing begins and we will do it together in Step 4, I Reclaim My Right to Feel.

You are not alone in how you feel for a very good reason. Let's now look at why we *collectively* feel as we do – we're going to bring this pattern gently to light and then we can't unsee it. In being able to see all these common threads in the landscape of modern life, we can better understand how and why we feel as we do. From this clarity comes the possibility of making fresh choices, establishing new ways of being and moving through the world, and finally feeling differently – more *ourselves* again.

How the world distracts us

In our desire to find our way home to ourselves, to be able to know and prioritise ourselves, it's helpful to see the myriad ways in which modern life takes us away from our own inner experiences, feelings and needs. One by one, we can address these distractions, dial down the noise and tune in again. Making change in your life is not always about doing something new; it can mean simply swapping or avoiding an existing toxic habit or influence.

Our attention is constantly being pulled away, our energy being depleted, our eyes drawn to comparison; it's no wonder we are separated from ourselves. When you recognise the sheer number of ways in which we are distracted from ourselves in modern life and the volume of those disturbances, you will marvel that we can even hear ourselves think . . .

Information overload

I can remember poring over encyclopaedias as a kid. I'd dip into a single reliable source to deal with one school assignment at time. In later school years, it was a trip to the library and a few different trusted resources to leaf through to find the answer. And now, hello internet. The experience is vastly different, and the information overload is real. It's not just the volume that's a problem, it's the challenge of trying to find information that is accurate and safe for us to consume. We can't unsee what's shown to us on the internet and one sloppy search can leave us vulnerable. There is so much knowledge available, but while it's brilliant to be able to find solutions and facts so swiftly, I am sure at one time or another we've all experienced the dangers of consulting Dr Google. It's one epic rabbit hole to navigate.

If you're wondering what this has to do with our ability to honour ourselves, how much sleep have you missed by getting sucked into web searches, message boards or watching *just one more* TikTok video? Remember when channels went offline at night, and there were only three or four to choose from? TV never sleeps now. We don't need to wait till next week for the new episode, we can sit there and binge the entire series in one go . . . we become so distracted, we don't even notice the passing of time or any of our internal cues of fatigue. And tomorrow, after a hard day's work, we reward ourselves in the same way all over again and the distraction and depletion continue.

All this information creates a certain DIY culture, putting additional pressure on us. In times gone by, when the pipes went awry, you'd call your plumber; now we google online tutorials and have a go ourselves. Again, knowledge is power and it's a great advantage to be able to upskill ourselves, but it can fuel our hyper-independence and the pressure to strive. Watching the Insta experts makes us think we should be excelling in all areas of life. We can't be all things to all people and attempting that is the perfect recipe for burnout. You don't need to bake like the chefs. You don't need to exercise like the personal trainers. You don't need to create like the artists. You don't need to garden like the horticulturalists. You don't need to counsel your kids like the psychologists. It's OK to stay in your lane and know that YOU are enough. Our online culture sets us up to consume information and the expertise of others constantly, shifting the goalposts with changing standards and poking at our insecurities along the way. It encourages us to keep imbibing more knowledge, delaying us from taking action because we never feel good enough, we never feel ready compared to the experts, or we have so many open tabs we just don't know where to start. We don't need another university degree, we don't need another course or workshop, we don't need to watch another YouTube tutorial. My concern is that if we are constantly deferring to the experts, we get distracted from our own wisdom. Information overload is squeezing out room for inner knowing and if we lose touch with that, how do we ever trust ourselves?

Perhaps the most insidious of all causes of the modern information overload is the news. We are privy to a constant onslaught of suffering with no buffer, and the impact on our nervous system is tangible. It's on our radios, on our TVs, in our inboxes and all over our social media feeds, whether we want it or not. Of course we need to be informed, but this constant consumption of news fuels our sense of being selfish for focusing on self, for not being grateful in the midst of all this suffering, and it has us minimising our struggles in comparison. I am all for healthy perspective, appreciation of our blessings and supporting those in need, but please let's allow space for our own humanity and health in the process.

Communication overload

When I was a child – we're talking just 40 years ago – we had mail delivered once a day (weekdays only), there was a landline (often in the bloody hall where everyone could hear your conversation) and some select few had a fancy fax machine. Mail, phone and fax, that was it. And there were real boundaries when it came to using those means of communication. It was a 'no-no' to call during dinner time and only in the case of emergencies would anyone phone after 9pm. Can you hear the silence in that world? The space? Can you remember it yourself? If you've never experienced that kind of pace of life, can you even imagine it?

Fast-forward to today. Some of us still have a landline; most of us don't know the number and unplugged the handset after receiving countless spam calls at all hours. We don't need it anyway, we have our mobile which we carry with us in our pockets or on our wrist wherever we go, making us contactable 24/7. On that personal device we have access to calls, emails which people send around the clock, whether it suits us to receive them in that manner or not, as well as text messages, WhatsApp and all the social media apps where you respond not only to comments on posts but also to direct messages, all these communications piling up from people we treasure and complete strangers alike.

Four decades ago we might have had to contend with the odd glossy pamphlet posted through our door, but now our inbox is inundated with junk advertising material about products and services we never signed up to hear about. One mention of school correspondence will have every parent groaning. It's not just the weekly newsletters and PTA bulletins, it's the parent WhatsApp groups with the endless concerns and queries about fancy dress days and home learning to wade through. School admin is a full-time job. We're drowning in communication yet feel less connected than ever before.

Modern life doesn't have to be 24/7. You have permission to switch off, but let's acknowledge how difficult this can be. There is the delicate balance of allowing yourself time to decompress set against the fear of the emails accumulating in our inbox for when we plug back in. Sometimes it's impossible to keep on top of it all. Look at how our expectations of response time have changed – we'd have given ourselves days to reply when we relied on mail; now we expect instant turnarounds. We can't take time away from our desk lest the communication pile up and we are not seen to be 'responsive'. What we're talking about here is a culture of urgency and it's not just distracting, it's incredibly depleting.

This culture of immediacy is created not just by evolving modes of communication but is also fuelled by the nature of the content that we are consuming. Take one look at the videos we watch on social media, with all the natural pauses removed. It is all 'now, now, now', so no wonder we feel we can't take a momentary breath, no surprise we can't delay gratification. Take notice of this relentlessness and, where you can, cultivate a more compassionate pace. Choose the content you imbibe carefully. If you don't know where to start, please don't be concerned; I will gently guide you in Step 2, I Reclaim My Attention. We will do it together, one nourishing choice at a time.

Choice overload

Go to the supermarket and just look at how many options there are for milk alone. Shopping online involves wading through the same choices and just try getting to the checkout without pages of 'suggestions' first (more on that shortly, page 47). Think of all the variations you have to choose between when you pick up a coffee. Can you see why we are so overwhelmed? Add up the number of choices we face in a day and it's no wonder we can't think straight. And the choices are everywhere, from what we eat and drink to what we wear, where we live, how we move around, and the studies and careers we pursue. Infinite choice, endless decisions, much of which takes us away from our inner experience. We're so busy totting things up in our heads to even notice what's happening below our necks. In the midst of all these incidental alternatives, how is there any brainpower to deal with the real open tabs, the difficult decisions, the life-altering ones?

Comparison overload

In bygone eras we'd send the odd postcard and take holiday snaps for ourselves, or maybe we'd bore everyone with a slide show of our far-flung adventures – it was much rarer in those days. Today, we're exposed to an endless stream of the best bits of total strangers' lives, completely skewing our perception of what normal existence looks like. We used to just notice the neighbour's grass looked greener, now via social media and 'reality' TV we get to see the glamorous interiors and gourmet meals of countless people we don't even know. Remember this: 'reel life' is not real life. The perfect images served up on social media are not a fair representation and the attempt to keep up with the Joneses makes us even more distracted from ourselves and what matters to us as individuals. Instead of giving you the shot of inspiration you're after, subscribing to all the aspirational social media accounts might just be feeding your stress levels and, especially for the high achievers among us, encouraging never-ending competition with an infinite string of experts and celebrities. Don't let comparison steal your peace of mind. It's easier said than done, but in coming home to yourself, you can learn to dial down all this external noise.

Temptation overload

Consumerism is constantly tugging at our attention and poking at our insecurities. Influencer promotions, product placement that you're not even aware of, TV ads, print media ads, billboards everywhere, invitations to buy landing in your inbox daily . . . temptation is everywhere you look from the moment you open your eyes to the minute you clock off. It takes huge effort and energy to resist it. A mere mention of a product or place will lead to a cascading of fresh ads in our social media feed. All this temptation knocks us off centre and makes it so challenging to stay anchored in what is personally meaningful.

Sensory overload

Maybe we still use flip charts, but the blackboards are long gone. The world has gone high tech and so many processes and interactions are now digitised and screen based. We rely on screens for work, play, social connection, entertainment, downtime, education, life admin, communication and relaxation. Tally up how much of your day you spend on screens and there's no wonder you're cut off from your body and your senses need a rest.

It's not because you're doing anything wrong. The fact is our minds and bodies can't keep pace with the evolution of technology and the volume of communication, information and decision making that is impacting us. Please make time and space for rest to compensate for the stimulation of modern life. It's not weak or lazy, it's smart; one big reset overnight is just not enough. And yet, it is *selfish* to rest . . . see the bind? We will break free, together.

How our rearing disconnects us

We're now going to take an honest and courageous look at the way our upbringing has infiltrated our thinking, beliefs and identity, and left us all perpetually questioning our worth. Just think about the number of times you've been shamed for feeling, needing or wanting, and asked *How could you be so selfish?* Right from the way we talk about 'goodness' in babies and children, through to gender conditioning and the all-pervading celebration of resilience, gratitude and productivity, you will see how we have been systematically disconnected from our feelings and needs and denied the right to express ourselves. You'll be able to understand why we feel so compelled to be selfless, and are so fearful of being seen as selfish, and why we all feel this gaping hole of not-enoughness within. The beautiful thing is, our true self can never be sullied, there is no deficit and we can rediscover her in her wholeness by peeling back these extraneous layers, one by one.

Think about how kids were treated historically and, while we may have moved on from 'children should be seen and not heard', a good child is still conceptualised as one that doesn't talk back to adults, so you may question just how far we've come. Pause for a moment and consider how we talk about children. What makes for a 'good' baby? A good baby is one who doesn't cry, doesn't trouble their parents, sleeps well and is easy, pliable and malleable, depending on how well it fits with the needs and preferences of other people. A baby who has trouble digesting is labelled 'fussy'; they are not 'good' . . . Can we hold up to the light how ridiculous this is – the notion of a 'bad' baby?

How easy we are as babies does not determine our worth and yet this is exactly the message that is perpetuated throughout our entire childhood and beyond. Infants are celebrated for attaining their developmental milestones in this endless push to independence, praised for being able to self-soothe, sleep independently, feed themselves and toilet alone. Let's examine the pressure around self-settling and sleeping alone. Why do we expect our kids to sleep alone when most adults co-sleep?

Reflection time: What did you learn in childhood?

It's time to take back our bodies and our minds, to know in our bones the truth that our feelings matter, that our needs matter, that we matter. It's time that we redirect our attention, reconnect and reclaim our bodies, our voice, our power, our pride, our courage, our confidence, our worth. That's exactly what we will do together in Part II with our 7 Steps to Self-advocacy. But for now, I invite you to reflect:

- What did you as a child wish that others had seen, heard or believed?
- What weren't you allowed to feel or do?
- What experience was dismissed, minimised or denied?
- What ways of expressing yourself did you learn were unacceptable?

Please be gentle with yourself as you reflect.

Girls must uphold the rules. Boys are welcome to be unruly, assertive, opinionated and wilful – these things can even be seen as admirable – but if little girls are anything other than kind, nice and compliant, they are demonised. Boys can be angry and domineering, but they mustn't cry, incurring boys a wound of their own. Look at suicide rates in young men to see the harm this cultural stereotype causes. Girls are permitted to cry, but they mustn't be angry or contrary. A domineering girl would be labelled bossy, a girl sure of herself is 'Too big for her boots'. She must not sing her own praises because 'No one likes a show off'. The good-girl conditioning is tenacious. She knows 'You catch more flies with honey than vinegar'. She must be agreeable and unassuming, it is her job to please and facilitate others, disappointing others is a 'no-no' and she mustn't make a fuss. To be all these things she must put her own needs and feelings last and our unswerving commitment to selflessness is born. But that's not all. In addition to learning that her emotions and needs don't matter, she's taught that she must meet everyone else's needs, and the relentless striving and hypervigilance begin. The question shifts from 'Am I OK?' to 'Is everyone else OK?', and we lose connection with self.

From the moment we enter this world, the gender conditioning begins – blue for boys, pink for girls, trucks and trains for boys, dolls and fairies for girls. Little girls wear garments featuring kittens and rainbows, little boys wear clothing emblazoned with slogans about bravery and symbols of strength and power. This conditioning is woven into our language, showing us how this message seeps from childhood into adulthood. Google synonyms for 'manly' and you'll see brave, courageous, bold, valiant, fearless, plucky, macho, intrepid, daring, lionhearted, heroic, gallant, chivalrous, adventurous, resolute, determined, stalwart, Ramboesque, gutsy, ballsy, hardy, strong, robust, sturdy, muscular, brawny, powerful, self-reliant, noble . . . and the opposite of manly is effeminate, cowardly and – wait for it – weak! It's just fact that females are the weaker sex: boys portraying female qualities are a sissy and no one wants to be told that they 'play like a girl'. These days, it's OK for a girl to be a tomboy – those masculine traits can be strengths for us too, even though we are born to be kind and nurturing, right? Women are natural multitaskers too. This is all just in our DNA, it's said – a rather convenient explanation to keep us in our caregiving roles. In fact, there is no neuroscientific proof for gender differences in the brain making women better at nurturing or multitasking.

Let's see what the dictionary has for us as alternative descriptions of 'womanly'. Surely, we will see a celebration of our strengths and virtues too? Apparently to be womanly is to be feminine, womanlike, girlish, ladylike, maidenly, matronly, maternal, motherly, girly, effeminate, unmanly, voluptuous, curvaceous, shapely, ample, opulent, full-figured, well formed, Rubenesque, buxom, full-bosomed, luscious, curvy, busty, plump, rounded, chesty and sexy. Being womanly isn't associated with any character traits to take pride in, such as courage. It's just a stage in life – we are either a maiden, a mother or a crone – and not only are we reduced to just a body, we better be a body that is pleasing to the eye depending on the version of female beauty currently in vogue, so we can be a vessel for men's enjoyment.

It's not just being nice, though; the demands run deeper. We must be quiet and keep ourselves small. We're taught that 'Good things come to those who wait', but the last time I checked, most human beings are poor mind readers, and I think it would be fairer to say that *Great things come to those who ask*. This is a pattern I see frequently in my work with women, a propensity to keep our desires and opinions hidden at all costs, and it sets in early. Harvard researchers L.M. Brown and C. Gilligan found that even girls who'd been outspoken in their childhood stopped sharing their true feelings and thoughts in their teens, for fear of being the odd one out or being seen as too honest, too direct.[1] How many young men are referred to as 'little boys'? I still encounter 'little lady' in my late forties! Social standards have most women trying to shrink themselves, diverting so much of their precious energy into taking up less space. Dieting, weight concerns and body dissatisfaction have all been reported in girls as young as age five.[2] Think of how much of our time and resources we have spent trying to get smaller, thinner, achieve that thigh gap, while men are encouraged to stand tall, grow bigger and command the room with their physical presence. Small and quiet: women must not rock the boat, we must not ruffle feathers, we must self-sacrifice and keep the peace. We must cooperate, compromise and comply and above all else we must be satisfied with our lot. It is certainly not ladylike to be seen to be wanting, desiring, seeking our own pleasure. Our anger is conveniently pathologised, keeping us disempowered.

Despite changes in our traditional gender roles, the basic assumption we've been raised to believe is that men's time is more valuable than women's. This is still evident in men being paid more outside the home for the same work as women, and in the fact that women are still carrying a disproportionate amount of the emotional, mental and physical load. At work female members of staff are still expected to make the cups of tea, remember the birthdays and take on responsibility for any emotional issues, while women still do the bulk of the domestic labour, from cleaning to cooking to child-related admin. We're set up to see ourselves as the facilitators for the men to do their important work, our value dependent on external approval, on how successfully we keep all the people happy all the time. This is how we learn not only to revere selflessness but also to fear being seen as selfish. In our aversion to being seen as greedy, self-centred and uncaring, we silence our wants and desires and feel shameful for having them. We feel lacking for needing any help in achieving our aspirations. Just look at how women are labelled as needy for expressing a desire for emotional intimacy in relationships. At best in this paradigm we are just passive recipients of life, with no sense of agency because 'Silence is golden' . . . but is it, really?

Alternatively, we shun it all and become a strong, independent woman accepting no help, because we're told we can now have it all. But I think we all know how that's working out for us. One human being might be able to do it all, but no one can do it all at the same time.

In films, books and on TV, women are often portrayed as untrustworthy, self-serving and gossipy. Our natural forms of connection are often denigrated – we overshare, we nag, we complain, we whine or we moan. We're busybodies. We talk too much. Whereas the heroes, the men, are the 'strong and silent' type. Even the good girls are surrounded by a gaggle of disloyal, jealous, bitching, backstabbing frenemies. Patriarchy doesn't just affect how men view women, it shapes how women view themselves and each other. We're taught to doubt ourselves and distrust each other, to view each other as competition, and to police each other for rule breaking. We're disconnected from ourselves, and we're disconnected from each other; in this way patriarchy keeps us divided and conquered. Part of reclaiming ourselves is reclaiming trust in other women, and faith in female friendships.

Women are at a significant financial disadvantage to men, and not just because of the gender pay gap (which in the UK in 2024 stood at 6.9 per cent, meaning that the average salary for a woman was 6.9 per cent lower than the average salary for a man).[3] In some countries it's possible to defer repayments on student loans while on maternity leave, but while you can pause repayments, debts are still indexed, which means we pay more for the same education than our male counterparts.[4] Women graduates can expect to face student debt for 16 years while men are likely to be able to square things off in just 11.[5] This is just one example of what's known as the 'motherhood penalty', which refers to the many ways women are effectively financially penalised for having children. The gender pension gap brings home women's disadvantage in terms of lifetime earnings. A 2024 report found that in the UK today, women retire on average with pension savings of £69k compared to £205k for men. To close this gap, a girl would have to start saving for her pension at just three years of age to retire with the same amount of money as working men.[6]

There's yet another double standard to examine. Women are also assessed according to our sexual history, and in exploring the mixed messages we are given about sexual activity, we can better understand our inner conflict, our devotion to selflessness and our fear of being seen as selfish. Look at the stark contrasts between how male and female pleasure are culturally viewed. Men *need* to sow their seed, while historically women were instructed to save themselves for marriage. Self-pleasure, because it's a need for men, is totally normal, but it's dirty for a woman – she's 'that' kind of girl. 'Boys will be boys' and that's more than OK, but for girls, innocence is a virtue. Promiscuous boys are labelled studs, they're given kudos for the notches in their belts, they're respected and admired, celebrated even. Promiscuous girls are labelled sluts and they're shamed; a few decades ago, this would've just been whispers behind backs and foul inscriptions in the toilet blocks, but now it is taken to a whole new insidious level with the circulation of nude images on smartphones and public humiliation via social media. No wonder girls have to hide their feelings and carefully police themselves. But equally girls are shamed for being frigid if they don't put out, so we really can't win. We must be chaste but mustn't be prudish. It seems we should appear virginal but meet all men's wildest fantasies in the bedroom. How do many people learn about sex? Via porn. And who is the vast majority of porn created for? Men. We've acknowledged the gender pay gap and the pension gap, but can we take a moment to also recognise the orgasm gap? Research has shown that approximately 95 per cent of heterosexual males say they usually always orgasm when sexually intimate compared to only 65 per cent of heterosexual females.[7] Yet another way women are losing out. Consider for a moment the impact that the 'good girl' and 'selfless woman' narratives have had on your sex life. Ladies, it's about time we reclaimed our right to have not just human needs but *pleasure*.

Patriarchal society has served us up the 'perfect mother' ideal. She is selfless, she must prioritise the needs of others over her own, she must be present, attentive and endlessly patient. She must never be selfish and she must never, ever be angry. Being the perfect mother became even harder when 'gentle parenting' emerged in the 1930s. While it was a necessary correction to the harsh authoritarian parenting practices of the Victorian era, when the norm was using punishment to discipline kids, and children were to be seen and not heard, it put the onus of providing 'attachment parenting' on the mother, for whom correct child rearing meant maintaining constant proximity to the baby, 24/7. This shift in child rearing, while well intentioned, placed huge demands and unrealistic expectations on mothers and shaped our current problematic understanding of what it means to be a 'good mother'.

You don't have to be a perfect parent. In our messy moments, we give our children permission to be human. We demonstrate that it is OK to make mistakes and that no one gets it right all the time. We can model how to resolve conflict, repair, make apologies and forgive ourselves and others. These are gifts that last a lifetime. It's not our job to raise perpetually happy children; instead, let's prepare them for life, for feeling joy in the good and sadness in loss. Parents, it's OK for your kids to see you cry. Remind them that we cry tears of joy, love and pride too. Parents, take the pressure off; it's more than enough to be their safe place. But how hard it is to tolerate emotions in others that were not tolerated in us, and that we don't give ourselves permission to feel or express. You see? This is why we need to reclaim the right to feel our own feelings, to meet our own human needs. We need to model how it's done, and we need to do it so that we are resourced enough to show up as a parent according to our own moral compass. Can you see how selflessness is the very thing that interferes with our ability to parent as we aspire to?

You might notice here that I have shifted from using the term 'mothers' to 'parents'. This switch in language is vital. If we are always referring to the 'motherload', how will it ever be anything other than the mother's load? The fact is some fathers still refer to parenting as babysitting. They're excelling if they're present for bathtime – that's just expected of mothers, and if they're not there, they're deemed less of a mother. If Mother's Day means waking naturally and a break from cooking meals, then every day feels like Father's Day for some mothers. We are not there yet when it comes to gender equality.

Thank goodness we are now having more open and honest conversations about parenthood, but let's take a closer look at how many of these are heard. Some of my favourite podcasts focus on mothering and parenting, talking about the very real and gritty experiences we face raising kids, but look at the majority of guests – they are either experts or celebrities. Even here we are consuming a skewed perception of parenthood – the experts have tools and a depth of understanding not available to the ordinary parent, and similarly the celebrity will often have means of support not at the disposal of most. Where are the voices of the everyday mother? Where do we see her story? We may see snippets on Instagram or catch moments at the school gate, but most often the experience of parenthood is presented to other women via a distorted perspective. I hope you feel seen and understood in the pages of this book.

How resilience contributes to our fear of selfishness

When Positive Psychology rose to prominence 20-something years ago, I found it thrilling. As a psychologist who specialised in human performance, motivation and behaviour change, I was excited to see psychology move away from the study of mental illness and a focus on what isn't working to understanding more deeply what does serve us. Positive Psychology made the commitment to exploring the building blocks of happiness and wellbeing, examining the foundations of a well-lived life. The paradigm shift that occurred in the early 2000s was so enlivening and life giving: we saw fresh concrete practices emerge, backed by rigorous scientific research. It was encouraging to see that adversity didn't necessarily mean that we would flounder; research showed us that quite often people would grow as a result and in time those upheavals could be seen as life lessons that brought about something profoundly meaningful. We saw how gratitude and other skills such as growth mindset, mindfulness and savouring could help us get the juice out of life. But fast-forward to today, and more and more I am seeing these constructs used as a whip to beat ourselves and each other. There is undeniable value in these skills and practices, but when crudely applied, overused or suggested in the wrong moments, the ideals can silence our self-expression and shame us for having a tough time.

I hear these things in just about every single coaching or counselling session I hold – do you say them to yourself? 'I should be stronger.' 'I should be more resilient.' 'I should be able to handle this on my own.' 'I should be coping better.' 'I should stop feeling sorry for myself, other people have it so much worse.' 'I have nothing to complain about and I should be grateful.' 'I must find the silver lining, because everything happens for a reason.' 'I just have to think more positively.'

Maybe these are things that you say to yourself, or maybe, when you get brave and share your vulnerability, these are things that you've been told. Maybe you've heard from other generations, 'It was good enough for me growing up, what's wrong with you?' Resilience has been bastardised and rather than helping us cope, our attempts to be strong shut down our ability to voice our feelings and inadvertently keep us stuck.

What does the world tell us about resilience? We know it is prized by society – look at all the praise we see for resilient kids, resilient adults, people who can just get on with it regardless of what life throws at them. I wonder how resilient these kids really are – perhaps they just don't have the words to describe how they feel, or they're too frightened to voice their concerns, and we assume their silence is an absence of struggle. (Just look at the message that our children receive about rest and healing time via the fixation with school attendance.) Yes, we should be proud of our ability to weather tough times. But rather than congratulating you on how strong you've been, which only amplifies society's toxic preoccupation with resilience, I am more inclined now to say, 'I am sorry it's been so tough, and you've had to be so strong. Darling, you deserve a break.' Lands differently, right?

In our times of heartbreaking loss and change, we had no choice but to be strong, and rather than just applauding resilience, maybe an invitation to not have it all together all the time would be welcome, maybe a pair of hands to lighten the load might have been longed for. I'm all for celebrating our tenacity and staying power, but let's not silence ourselves or shame ourselves for needing support. All the praise can make people feel like they have to maintain this appearance of strength and keep shouldering their load alone. It doesn't encourage them to reach out and it makes them feel weak for not being able to sustain this superhuman level of performance.

If you want more clues as to why we revere resilience so much, look to how the world views sensitivity. Maybe these are things you've also heard: 'You're too sensitive.' 'Don't take things so personally.' 'You're too emotional.' 'Why do you have to make a fuss?' 'Just relax and stop worrying.' 'Just push through it.' Heightened awareness of the emotions of others, an ability to sense threats and other changes in one's surroundings, and a capacity for deep thinking and deep feeling all tend to be met with frustration and interpreted as weakness, and when it comes to children are often seen as adding to the inconvenience for the caregiver. Yes, it might be more work raising a sensitive child, but that's not because our sensitive child is weak; in fact, it takes great courage to move through life as if we don't have skin, privy to other people's energy and feelings. So many highly sensitive people (HSP) have been told they just need to toughen up and get on with it. Toughening up in this context essentially means stop talking or thinking about it.

Toughening up doesn't work, but more than that, it doesn't serve us, and it doesn't serve humanity as a whole. We don't toughen up our nervous system by just pushing through; that results in sensory overload and emotional overwhelm. We don't need to dial down our beautiful capacity to sense and feel, but we do need a container for such big awareness. We need understanding, validation and care. We can gently grow our capacity to cope by expanding our comfort zone in self-directed ways, led by what matters to us as human beings and making sure that we are compassionately pacing ourselves. You will learn exactly this in Step 2, I Reclaim My Attention. Sensitive people need a break from sensory stimulation, time to process and restore, perhaps more rest and sleep – yet rest and sleep are frowned upon as lazy. We don't want to 'toughen up' HSPs, those sensitive souls who play a vital role in our communities by providing a safe place for others to express themselves, who radiate care and understanding, detect sources of danger and find creative solutions to protect ourselves and our environment. Think of the meerkat keeping watch at the top of the burrow; you *want* that scout to be an HSP because your survival relies on their ability to notice danger and alert you! Our sensitivity, when nurtured and supported, can be a superpower, and one that I hope one day will be cherished.

If you close your eyes, what does resilience look like to you? What words or images come to mind? How do you feel about it as a quality? How do you feel about your ability to be resilient?

Resilience does not mean that we are unaffected by stress, loss and change. It does not mean that life's blows don't hurt. It does not mean that we are immune from challenging thoughts and difficult feelings, or from grief, depression and anxiety. It doesn't mean that our health and our energy levels are unchanged. It most certainly doesn't mean an absence of struggle. Resilience doesn't look put together all the time; in fact, a more accurate representation could be someone curled up in a little ball, howling it out, then that same person asking for a hug, resting and then emerging to engage in everyday life again at a tempered pace.

Demystifying mental and emotional health

I invite you to pause for a moment and consider what you think of as mental and emotional health? Just like we tend to assume that resilience means we have our shit together, and coping means that we are trucking along, people commonly see mental health as the absence of difficult thoughts, and emotional health as feeling good or happy.

In fact, mental health refers to our relationship with our thoughts, our ability to manage them. Rather than feeling identified with and pushed around by our thoughts, mental health is the ability to step back from our inner experiences and choose for ourselves where we place our energy, attention and meaning. It is understanding that not all our thoughts are facts, knowing that thoughts are not necessarily a prediction or a prophesy. It's about having a healthy relationship with our thinking, not about thinking positively or even necessarily thinking constructively *all the time*. You'll get these skills confidently under your belt in Step 1, I Reclaim My Mind. Even the most even-keeled person with all the mental coping strategies will still have toxic, destructive thoughts; we will still catastrophise, but we notice when we're doing it and gently shift our attention back to something more helpful, balanced and aligned with our values. A healthy mind is one that helps us take care of ourselves and treat ourselves and others with respect, kindness and compassion, but can you see how this is at odds with society's expectation that we be selfless?

Similarly, emotional health is not perpetual happiness, and the aim is not to avoid or eliminate unpleasant feelings. Emotional health refers to our capacity to understand and feel all our feelings, to be at ease with them, and to manage and move through them in safe and healthy ways. We will explore emotions in greater depth in Step 4, I Reclaim My Right to Feel, but for now, let me explain it as this: emotions help us navigate the landscape of life – what's happening outside us and within us. They are cues, messengers or signals, alerting us to ways we can keep ourselves safe, or promote the health of our relationships. They all have their place, even the dark and murky ones, the ones that really don't feel good, such as anger, guilt and anxiety. We need them all to keep us safe, so emotional health is certainly not limited to feeling happy, but is about being able to identify and articulate how we feel and determine the action we might need to take to meet our needs in the moment. Emotions give us clues to what we need to keep us safe and healthy – read that again. *Emotions give us clues to what we need to feel safe and healthy.* They all have a purpose. If you think about how emotions were handled in your childhood and the messaging you've received about 'positive' or 'negative' emotions, or which ones are OK for you to express . . . can you see how fundamentally limiting this is? I am so looking forward to rewriting the script when it comes to 'healthy emotions' with you in Step 4 but for now, let's make friends with them all. You have a right to feel them all. You need them all for your health.

Resilience means that we get back up again, we bounce back, but it doesn't mean that we're not bowled over by life in the first place and it doesn't mean that we emerge unscathed. Coping doesn't look like a shiny steam train that never pauses. It can also be an ebb and flow. It can be a period of retreat, when we allow ourselves to get messy and feel the feelings, giving ourselves time to process, digest, release and replenish, so that we can make sense of things and carve out a new, more compassionately paced or aligned path forwards, even a new sense of self. The things that we normally associate with being weak or unproductive such as sadness, loss, anger, needing to take a break from socialising, rest and sleep are all essential parts of the coping and healing process. It is totally normal to struggle in response to a tough time and someone else's burden does not negate your own. Permission to feel, my friend. How would any human feel?

The thing that frustrates me the most about our cultural preoccupation with resilience is that when we also acknowledge the demand to be selfless, we can see the vice we are held in. What does it take to be able to bounce back from adversity in life? It doesn't just require mental fortitude, it's not something that just happens in our heads. Resilience requires *nourishment*. To be resilient we need good sleep, and decent nutrition and hydration. We need time to rest, an opportunity to move our bodies, and to connect with Mother Nature and kindred spirits. Society demands that we be resilient but not selfish, and yet all these things that stoke our ability to cope require time and energy via focus on self! Resilience is also a function of social support, but you can see how our fear of burdening others gets in the way of us reaching out for the very thing that helps us heal.

Society says we must keep ourselves together, but resilience requires emotional expression. The work of grief is to feel the feelings, and we don't just grieve when we're bereaved. We grieve any ending, any loss; even when it is chosen and desired, there is still a grieving. Grief isn't an emotion but a response to loss that may include sadness, loneliness, confusion, rage, resentment and shock, as well as awe, appreciation and love. The feeling is the healing! Falling apart is not the failure that we've been led to believe. It allows us to move through our emotions, to carve a new identity in response to the changing circumstances of life.

The cultural glorification of resilience celebrates our ability to put a lid on our emotions and get on with it without burdening others. It reinforces the message that we must be self-sufficient, we shouldn't be messy, and that we are only lovable when we hold it together on our own. We work so hard to be a good corporate citizen, and resilience just hammers further home the notion that emotions are bad, needs are bad. But resilience is only one piece of the puzzle now there is this overweening emphasis on positivity, gratitude and growth.

How toxic positivity disconnects us

I'm sure you've heard the following suggestions: 'Chin up', 'Cheer up', 'Good vibes only', 'Stay positive', 'Where's your positive mental attitude?' 'What doesn't kill you makes you stronger', 'You grow through what you go through'.

Stiff upper lip isn't new, but now we've got to plaster on a 'permagrin' and this message of 'Trauma makes you stronger' suggests that we should be grateful in the midst of our suffering. I am all for seeing things with perspective and acknowledging our blessings, in fact my ability to appreciate is probably one of my most sustaining skills, but not at the expense of feeling my feelings. I agree, let's fine-tune our eyes to spot glimmers of hope and joy, while also giving ourselves time to grieve our loss. There are real dangers to excessive positivity and gratitude, or positivity and gratitude in the wrong moments. Being pushed to identify the silver linings before we're ready can be harmful; there's a feeling that it's not enough to be able to cope with challenging life events, now we have to come out stronger. The pioneers of 'posttraumatic growth'[8] went to great lengths when sharing their research to say that people should not feel pressured to find the gifts in their suffering, but this message seems to have gotten lost in the cultural wash.

What we're talking about here is toxic positivity, which is what we experience when we're told to buck up, think positive, get over it or, worse, be grateful for it . . . how many times has someone else's 'At least . . . ' diminished our struggles: 'Yes, your boss is toxic, but *at least* you have a job.' 'Yes, it's sad you've lost your mother but *at least* she lived a long life.' 'Yes, it's hard raising teens, but *at least* you've got kids.' Toxic positivity is something we do to ourselves, too, when we compare our troubles to someone else's, when we negate our burden and feel we don't have a right to struggle.

Toxic positivity is the excessive overgeneralisation of an optimistic mood state across all circumstances and while it might be well intentioned, the consequences can be deeply damaging. Being told to look on the bright side or be grateful effectively shuts down honest conversation, preventing people from receiving the validation and understanding they need, and piling on an additional load of judgement, blame and guilt. When sad things happen, the human response is to feel sad. When our values are violated, the natural response is to feel angry. If those words 'Everything happens for a reason' have you scratching around in the rubble of your life, asking yourself what that reason could possibly be, permission to let it go, my friend. Sometimes unthinkable things happen to the most kind-hearted people, and they don't deserve it, nor should they feel pressured to grow or feel grateful. Sometimes it's just plain shit and, darling, I am so sorry.

Perhaps you've come across the social media trend 'lucky girl syndrome'. This highlights the potential dangers in excessive positivity and brings home just how harmful these sentiments can be to people experiencing adversity in suggesting that our struggles are because of our own deficit. 'Lucky girl' takes manifesting to the next level . . . Manifesting is where we get clear on a vision we want for the future and we consciously direct our energy, thoughts and actions, allowing that vision to come to fruition. It involves clarity on our desires, a feeling of belief that they are possible, supportive self-talk, and dedicated action to bring that desire to life. The concept behind the lucky girl trend is that you reflect on all the luck you've had, repeatedly affirm to the universe how fortunate you are, expect good luck, and lo and behold you manifest more and more good luck. You'll find countless privileged people extolling the virtues of this practice, without sparing a thought for the message this sends to people who have been afflicted by tragedy; that somehow they haven't thought themselves lucky enough to escape the barbs of life. It's harmful and callous. The last thing people who've suffered adversity need is a sense that they are to blame for their own misfortune. You just didn't manifest it right, you didn't want it enough, or darling, you got in your own way . . .

But you didn't fail at manifesting when your company made you redundant. It's nothing to do with manifesting if you're still single. If you can't afford your own home, it's not because you haven't tried hard enough to manifest it. You're not to blame if you couldn't will away chronic illness.

Reading *The Secret* while expecting my first child was a mistake; in fact I soon put it down. With the normal and natural flurry of maternal concerns, I did not need the message that 'Our worries are a prayer for what we don't want.' I didn't need the burden of 'My thoughts are creating my reality.' It is totally human to worry, it is completely natural for the mind to generate worst-case scenarios, and while we don't want to wallow around in negative thinking, we also don't need to invest such power in those negative thoughts. They are just a passing state! All your thoughts are OK. I look forward to taking a deeper look at how we can make peace with all our thoughts, while also shaping our self-talk to support us in our pursuits and help us weather the hand we are dealt. We will do this in Step 1, I Reclaim My Mind (page 105). But please let me leave you with this: we cannot just think ourselves happy, healthy, resilient, selfless or anything else. Yes, let's massage our self-talk so we're on our own side, but there are other variables at play. There is such healing in the words 'It wasn't your fault.'

While in the right moments, there is great solace in an awareness of our blessings, and being open to life's beauty can change the lens through which we see our day unfold, another danger of the overemphasis of gratitude is that it can potentially stifle desire. Is this something you've noticed? People feel such guilt for wanting more. 'Why am I not satisfied?' But what's wrong with aspiring? It doesn't make you *ungrateful*. Maybe it's OK to want, it's OK to desire, it's OK to seek ways of creating more alignment, more peace. We can have a good life and still want more. Yes, let's stay anchored in perspective, let's be deeply mindful of our blessings, let's be committed to helping those less fortunate, but let's not stem the flow of desire, of authentic self-expression. Who knows what good we can bring to the world when we truly allow ourselves to dream?

I hope these explorations of resilience, gratitude, positivity and growth create a little more wiggle room in how we view them and how we use them. Please, can we stop celebrating people's silence and their ability to weather shit alone? Can we stop making these demands of ourselves? I'm sorry that society hurries your healing in the name of resilience and then coerces you to find the silver lining in the name of gratitude. I'm sorry your suffering has been compounded by these compassionless pressures. Why not try saying, 'I am so sorry you experienced that', and 'Thank you for letting me in. I'm here for you and we'll face this together. You don't have to do it on your own.' Vulnerability and honesty take courage. Let's applaud that. We see the price in hiding vulnerability and staying strong and silent in the suicide and self-harm rates. I love that author Elizabeth Lesser, in her myth-busting book on origin tales, *Cassandra Speaks*, offers a fresh alternative to strong and silent – brave and open. She calls us to move away from the identification of power with masculine traits, from language peppered with war and sport metaphors, to something more regenerative, celebrating softness, nurturing, openness and understanding. We are still living in a gendered value system. Here's to moving towards a society that reveres feminine values too.

The relentless hustle of capitalism

Let's now explore how capitalism has shaped our understanding of what it means to be a worthy human. If you feel a fundamental aversion to rest, or are addicted to productivity, this will help you understand why. The vilification of rest goes back a long way. Look to the Bible for the origin of these sayings: 'No rest for the wicked'[9] and 'Idle hands do the Devil's work'.[10] These messages were very handy for mill and factory owners to get more graft out of their workforce, given that being unproductive was a sin for which they'd be sent straight to hell. No wonder we feel uncomfortable with the notion of rest. And this is nothing compared to the messaging that's passed on in the blueprint of the nervous system of descendants of the oppressed people, enslaved people, for whom the ability to keep going was necessary for survival. It literally doesn't feel safe to rest.

Growing up in a capitalist society we know our primary motive is to make a profit. We're taught that 'Time is money' and 'Cash is king'. We're told we can do anything we set our minds to, if we work hard enough. We have to strive to climb the ladder, work hard to be the best, because the top is the only place to be and if we're not at the top, we're missing out. But we can see that there are a limited number of places at the top and this sets us up for relentless competition, for not stopping lest someone else gets ahead. We can't say no, because that might suggest we're not committed or we're not loyal. Maybe someone else will get that promotion ahead of us. We can't pause to rest because there is another project to complete. Meanwhile, the emails just keep piling up.

But I'm wondering whether you've noticed this too – the only reward for getting work done is more work! The feel-good hit of a promotion fades so fast and we are already busy 'nexting'[11] ourselves – the next shiny toy, the next ambition, the next accolade. It is never enough. We are never enough. We can always see that other person ahead of us, or sense that colleague hot on our heels, and it's a full-time job keeping up with the Joneses in our personal lives. The Puritan work ethic combined with capitalism is a deadly cocktail of toxic productivity, perseverance and grit. It is thriving today, as seen in the 'girl boss' messaging, 'hustle culture' and the 5am club. There is a glorification of doing over being, and a complete conflation of self-worth with productivity. There is no time for rest; hell, there's not even time for sleep. Richard Branson only needs five hours of sleep, so I'll make do with four.

And then let us add consumerism to the pressure cooker. We have to work hard not only to be good human beings, but also because it's so damn expensive forking out for all the products and services we need to be 'whole' individuals. Our material wealth is a measure of our worth. We must keep acquiring to show our status and the goalposts of what it means to be successful and 'beautiful' are conveniently always moving. We're encouraged to keep splashing that cash because it feels good, and it is so needed because consumerism is forever poking at our insecurities and manufacturing new ones left, right and centre.

Take beauty and fitness culture; track how the perfect eyebrow has morphed over the decades, look at how the perfect figure has changed over the years. Remember the 'circle of shame' in *Heat* magazine where a celebrity was 'papped' and their offending body parts ringed and ridiculed? How many women were shamed with these photographs of a completely normal-looking part of their body, and how many female readers were terrorised into buying some useless antidote to that unsightly cellulite. Women are constantly told what they should look like by advertising, films, magazines and social media. Now we compare ourselves to ideals that aren't just that one-in-a-million stroke of genetic luck – now, with the advent of AI, they don't even exist. Filters, airbrushing, posing and digital manipulation . . . in reality, the people we aspire to emulate don't even look like the images we see of them. Consumerism is always ready to pounce on new emerging markets – you can't miss the explosion of products catering for the menopausal woman. Do we really need scorched almonds specifically for our hormone health?[12] Please. Ladies, nor do our private parts need a specific wash. We are not dirty. I can't wait to share Step 3 with you – get ready to reclaim your body!

How convenient that we are forever at war with ourselves rather than with the structures that ensnare us. Consumerism sets us up for constant distraction from our values, hopes, dreams, feelings and true needs. And in a culture that frowns upon neediness and insecurity, yet plucks at our vulnerabilities and sets impossible and ever-changing standards, we are stuck on a treadmill of consuming to address the gaping artificial hole that we can never fill. We're caught in this impossible bind of 'Don't be selfish, don't be needy, but darling, you simply must do something about that muffin top, buy this product to fix yourself.' No wonder the guilt is paralysing. We can't just extricate ourselves from the economic system we are embedded in, but we can overcome the pressures of consumerism and capitalism by trusting in our inherent worth irrespective of our productivity, performance, pay check, size of following or physical appearance.

There is so much unpicking to be done. Let's begin it together, now.

Maybe you don't need to try harder, maybe you need a rest.

Maybe you don't need to strive more, maybe you need some fun.

Maybe you don't need to be more resilient, maybe you need a break.

Maybe you don't need a new stress-management technique, maybe you need a hug.

Maybe you don't need a new coping tool, maybe you need hands-on support.

Maybe you don't need to manage your time better, maybe you need a reasonable workload.

Maybe you're not too sensitive, maybe the world is too much.

Maybe your giant heart is not a weakness, maybe it's a superpower to be celebrated.

Maybe you don't need to be tougher, maybe you just need understanding.

Maybe you don't need to keep it together, maybe you need a safe place to let it all hang out.

Maybe you don't need to keep going like this, maybe it's OK to pause, reassess and do things differently.

Maybe you don't need self-improvement, maybe you need consumerism to bugger off and stop creating endless artificial needs.

Why do we always assume the deficit is ours? How can we ever reach out or speak up when we are desperately trying to be selfless and self-reliant? Maybe it's just too much for any one human. Darling, we were never meant to do it all alone. But selflessness keeps us trapped on our own. It's time to reimagine what it means to be worthy and we will get beautiful clarity on that in Step 5, I Take Back My Moral Compass. *Selflessness was always just a coping mechanism.*

CHAPTER THREE

BREAKING FREE FROM SELF-ABANDONMENT

We've seen how we have been distracted and disconnected from our true selves; in this chapter we are going to observe how we've been silenced historically and how we are still fighting now to be heard and respected. We'll take a whistlestop tour of women's rights, reminding ourselves that many of the milestones in reclaiming our voice are in very recent history – the right to vote, the right to financial independence and the fight for body autonomy. We will see that gender inequality is rife in our religions and that similar messaging still permeates our medical system, evidenced by gaslighting terminology and a neglect of women's health. It's evident, too, in how we respond as a society to sexual and domestic abuse. We also turn our attention to childhood, to see that even well-intended praise can set our kids up for a lifelong debate about their worth as human beings, and we learn that some children are thrust into caregiving roles from an early age, or are taught by their narcissistic parents that they must tend to the needs of others before considering their own, and we acknowledge those living in abusive homes, where it's better simply to be invisible.

In this chapter we understand that for many people, it is not just about a fear of being seen as selfish, or an adherence to the value of selflessness; they have learned that it's just not safe to be seen or heard or have needs at all, they've had to abandon themselves to survive. The selflessness we see here, the complete subjugation of needs, the painful splitting off from self is clearly not something to revere. It's something that deserves deep compassion and urgently needs healing and delicate untangling, and until we have done that, we will stay stuck in our fury, our decision-making paralysis, our inauthentic relationships, our bone-aching depletion, our autoimmune diseases. I know this chapter is a harrowing read, but once we've seen the patterns, once we've identified the painful costs, we won't deny ourselves a moment longer. We will be ready to get 'selfish' and take back our peace and our power.

What has religion and mythology told us about ourselves?

I remember as a child attending our weekly church service and dutifully repeating the confessional prayer – 'We are not worthy even to gather up the crumbs from under your table'.[1] I can still feel now the shame this invoked in me as a small girl. It felt so big, so damning and so all-encompassing. I wondered what we'd done that was so wrong and what it was going to take to wash myself clean of it. While no human is worthy, there is special disgrace reserved for women. Look to the origin stories of mankind. Eve was the temptress that deceived Adam into taking a bite from the forbidden fruit that led to the fall of man. The Bible has this gem for us: 'In pain you shall bring forth children, woman, and you shall turn to your husband, and he shall rule over you ... You are the Devil's gateway.' We also read, 'No wickedness comes anywhere near the wickedness of a woman. Sin began with a woman and thanks to her we all must die.'[2] In the biblical work Ecclesiasticus we are told, 'A gift from the Lord is a silent wife, and nothing is so precious as her self-discipline. Charm upon charm is a wife with a sense of shame, and nothing is more valuable than her bound-up mouth.' The ancient texts live on in modern times with this pithy offering from Martin Luther: 'If they become tired or even die, that does not matter. Let them die in childbirth, that's why they are there.'[3]

It's not just the Christians; the Jewish faith has similar messages for women. Orthodox Jewish men recite the following daily prayer: 'Blessed be God King of the universe that Thou has not made me a woman.'[4] There is this, from the Mishnah: 'To the woman He gave nine curses and death: the burden of the blood of menstruation and the blood of virginity; the burden of pregnancy; the burden of childbirth; the burden of bringing up the children; her head is covered as one in mourning; she pierces her ear like a permanent slave or slave girl who serves her master; she is not to be believed as a witness'[5] ... and so the gaslighting begins.

Ancient Greek mythology is no different, with women being portrayed as deceitful, manipulative and essentially a scourge to man. Pandora, like Eve, ruined it all. Not only was she created as punishment for the wrongdoing of man, she then against strict instructions went on to open the goddamn box and became the harbinger of all evil in this world. Aphrodite, known for her beauty and promiscuity, taught men that they couldn't trust any woman's character and that the safest way to curb her wandering ways was to keep her busy with childrearing and domestic tasks at home, distraction from her lustful desires. Despite men being active participants in Aphrodite's extramarital affairs, they were absolved of fault; it was her beauty and feminine wiles that were exclusively to blame. The legend of Helen of Troy, renowned to be the most beautiful woman in the world, follows a similar theme. According to some versions of the story, she abandoned her husband and family for a younger lover, and the entire blame for the war that ensued landed squarely on her shoulders. Helen and her beauty were the cause of every warrior's death.

These origin stories and myths tell us that we should be silent and if we do speak up, that we are not to be trusted. We are to be scorned, punished and not even allowed to be the experts on our own inner experience – the hysterical woman was born in ancient times. Against the backdrop of these messages, we can see why women through the ages have felt they had no choice but to atone by enduring barbaric practices, such as the Victorian corsets that restricted the very air they breathed, or the binding of feet in China, making sure they stayed small and the women were kept subordinate. This is just the woman's lot. We've been told that we are the 'origin of all sin', that we are inherently wrong and that we must spend our whole lives repenting. We must be monitored and we must self-police because we ourselves can't be trusted. Perhaps you've noticed how we even silence ourselves to avoid judgement by other women.

You might look at the biblical tales and wonder how relevant they are. Well, this kind of misogynistic thinking is very much alive and kicking in many circles. Women can become ordained priests in the Church of England, but it's still forbidden by the Catholic Church. You won't have to look far to find anti-women hate on social media – just read the comments on female-empowerment posts. The popularity of people such as Andrew Tate, dubbed the king of toxic masculinity and a self-described misogynist, is alarming. Misogyny lives on strong in what some men call harmless banter. In 2023, James Cleverly, the UK Home Secretary at the time and the man responsible for law enforcement and protecting women from violence, suggested that the secret to a long marriage was to keep your wife sedated. He was reported to have shared this funny little quip: 'a little bit of Rohypnol in her drink every night' was 'not really illegal if it's only a little bit'.[6] This was on the same day that a new policy on drink spiking was announced.

It is sickening that drugging women can be treated as a laughing matter. No wonder we don't feel safe.

Let's look at the recent timeline of women's rights to see just how long it has taken for us to take back our voice, and perhaps how far we still have to go. If you're wondering why I am sharing these historic facts and figures, remember that to be able to advocate for ourselves, we need to know ourselves, trust ourselves, prioritise ourselves and speak up for ourselves. When you see how recent these historical markers of rights and legal protection are, I hope it helps you understand why self-doubt can be so gnawing, why we so often second-guess our capability and strength, why we question our right to own and possess, why we doubt our own authority, our worth as human beings, even our right to be here.

The more shocking information given below will bring home why we still may hesitate to use our voice. Through history it hasn't been safe for us to express our needs and emotions, let alone our desires or discontent, and that fear lives on in our nervous systems to this day.

Timeline of women's rights

The right to vote

Before 1918 no women were allowed to vote – no say, no direct power. Without the right to choose who governs us, we were effectively silenced. In 1918 the Representation of the People Act was passed in the UK, giving some women the right to vote, provided they were aged over 30 and either they or their husband met a property-ownership qualification. The Parliament (Qualification of Women) Act was also passed in 1918, allowing women to stand for Parliament and 1919 saw Nancy Astor, the first female MP, take her seat. It wasn't until 1928 that all women in the UK over the age of 21 got the right to vote – staggering to acknowledge that this was less than 100 years ago. In the US, the 19th amendment was ratified in 1920, granting women the right to vote, but not all women. It wasn't until the Voting Rights Act was passed in 1965 that African Americans were enfranchised in the US. In 1971 Switzerland became one of the last European countries to grant women the vote at national level, and it wasn't until 2015 that women were allowed to vote in municipal elections in Saudia Arabia. Women may now have a say in who is elected to power but are we truly represented by the people who are making the legislation? Let's look to the percentage of women in government in the UK. How many women are actively shaping our legislation? After the 2024 general election in the UK, Keir Starmer's cabinet is the most gender-balanced in history with 46 per cent female members[7] and Rachel Reeves became the first female Chancellor ever. Despite this increase in female representation, ethnic representation has fallen.[8] Of the 24 top jobs in Donald Trump's 2025 cabinet, women hold just 8.[9]

The right to earn

Without the means to earn, we are financially dependent and limited in our choices. Prior to World War I, women's jobs were traditionally domestic – our place was in the home.

Of the small proportion of women in paid employment, their opportunity to work was limited to the industrial workforce, mainly concentrated in textile manufacture. The first female civil servants were employed in the UK in 1870, when the Post Office took them on as clerical workers, albeit at a considerably lower rate than their male counterparts.[10] Until 1946 only unmarried women or widows could work for the Civil Service and unmarried women had to resign on marriage. The Marriage Bar of 1921 stated that 'Women working in the Civil Service are not prevented from getting married, but they are not retained in established capacities after marriage except with the consent of the head of their Department and of the Treasury.' In the 1920s, professions such as teaching and medicine were also opening up to women, but only if they remained unmarried.

World War I allowed women to enter the workforce en masse for the first time, filling the gap left by a lost generation of military men. Instead of their work focusing on clerical tasks, women stepped into broader roles, working in factories, as drivers and in the police and becoming skilled in mechanics and engineering. Even though the labour provided by women was in desperate need during the war, childcare was in short supply. In response to the urgent demand for women to produce munitions, the government provided some funding towards the cost of day nurseries and by 1917 there were more than 100 across the UK. Unless you were a munitions worker, however, there was no childcare provision and women had to rely on family and friends to help care for their children while they were working. We only saw financial provision made for maternity leave in the UK in 1975, and it took until 2003 for a paid two-week paternity leave to be introduced. Despite these new opportunities and their growing skill base, women were still being paid less than half of what men were earning for the same jobs and it wasn't until 1970 that the Equal Pay Act made it illegal to discriminate against women by paying them less for equally skilled work. In January 2010 UK fathers were finally given the right to take a statutory six-month paternity leave while their partners returned to work, in effect taking the place of the mother at home.

The right to financial independence

We may have had the right to earn but the right to possess material wealth with autonomy lagged well behind. While married women could inherit thanks to the Married Women's Property Act of 1882, it wasn't until 1975 that women could open a bank account in their own name. As recently as the mid-seventies, single women still needed a signature from their father to apply for a loan or credit card in their own name, even if they earned more than he did, and working women were also refused mortgages in their own right without the signature of a male guarantor. In the light of these facts, which show just how recently women have been discriminated against and disempowered, films such as *Muriel's Wedding* make more sense. I can better understand now why historically women felt such an urgency to wed. How else could they gain power and financial security? These fears take generations to leave our consciousness. Managing finances has also traditionally been seen as a man's domain, so I think it's fair to say that many women feel they are playing catch up when it comes to knowledge about finances, investment and wealth management, and even in feeling the right to receive financial abundance. It just wasn't modelled for many of us growing up. There is significant inequality in relationships where we are financially dependent and this is still a problem today. Financial dependence takes our power away and even though our avenues to gain financial freedom are increasing, the gender pay gap and motherhood penalty show there is a long way for women to go. The struggle for flexible working conditions for parents goes on, with great adaptability shown during the Covid-19 pandemic, but many organisations are now returning to more rigid practices.

At this point, you might be thinking, *Yes I have a job, I have my own bank account, I have access to credit and I'd love to be selfish, but I can't afford it!* And you would be absolutely right. This is a social justice issue. The cost of living makes financial freedom out of reach for many. It costs money to get the education you want, to rent or buy property so you can live in a safe, life-giving environment. It costs money to attend that gym, buy those supplements or have that physio appointment. It costs money to raise children. It even costs money to leave an unhealthy, unhappy relationship. Many people have to compromise their self-expression because they can't afford to live life on their own terms. The people that *have* must keep advocating for the people that don't. We must also check our privilege when we're talking about responsibility for our own health and wellbeing – not everyone has equal access to a nourishing way of life, we don't all have the same 24 hours in a day, and this inequity needs to be recognised and addressed.

The right to body autonomy

Women in the UK may have ceased being the property of their husband in 1882, but you might be shocked to learn that it wasn't until 1991 that the UK abolished immunity for marital rape, while it took until 1993 for marital rape to be outlawed nationwide in the US. It wasn't until 2003 that there was a statutory definition of consent. Prior to 1857 a divorce could only be obtained by a private act of Parliament and most of those granted were initiated by the husband. In 1878 changes in law made provisions for those in violent marriages, enabling them to obtain separation orders, and from 1923 new laws allowed women to also seek a petition for divorce, but this was based only on the grounds of their spouse's adultery. It took until 1937 for grounds for divorce to extend beyond adultery to include desertion, cruelty and incurable insanity, and this was only broadened in 1969, allowing for 'marital breakdown' to be cited as a valid reason for divorce. When you look at the medical gaslighting women experienced (see below), this is all the more shocking. I wonder how often a woman's anger was pathologised as a means to seek a divorce.

It is telling that in the US states that adopted divorce reform, making it easier for people to seek a divorce without the consent of their spouse or demonstration of a marital fault, female suicide dropped by 20 per cent.[11] Unilateral divorce (first legalised in California in 1969, and in the majority of states by 1985, with New York being the last state to adopt it in 2010) also led to a large decline in domestic violence for both men and women, and a decline in women being murdered by their partners.[12] People who bemoan the degradation of the family unit are conveniently forgetting the high female suicide, domestic violence and absence of female financial autonomy in the era prior to the acceptance of no-fault divorce.

In 1973 the first UK Rape Crisis Centre was established, providing support for women and girls. In 1976 laws were passed giving legal protection to victims of domestic violence, enabling women to obtain court orders against violent husbands without divorce or separation proceedings already being in place. Laws were put in place in 2015 to criminalise coercive control, recognising that humiliation, intimidation and subordination could be as harmful as physical abuse, and acknowledging that trauma experienced by victims of psychological abuse can have a more significant lasting impact than physical abuse. Forced marriage only became an offense in 2014.

How the medical system neglects and gaslights women

If you wonder why you have trouble advocating for your needs in general or more specifically feel uncomfortable speaking up about health concerns, pay special attention to this next section. I think it is fair to say that women have been let down by the medical system and, worse than that, have been gaslit and abused. Medical terminology is rife with offensive language, heaping blame on the bodies of those already suffering with health and reproductive challenges. Here are just a select few to chew on: 'geriatric mothers' refers to an expecting mother aged 35 years or older, 'barren woman' or 'inhospitable womb' refers to a woman with fertility challenges, and then we have an 'incompetent', 'shy' or 'unfavourable' cervix, 'lazy' ovaries, 'hostile' or 'irritable' uterus. 'Poor maternal effort' is really just slowed labour, 'failure to progress' and 'failed pregnancy' feel barbed too. 'Spontaneous abortion' suggests it was some kind of choice. Imagine experiencing recurrent miscarriages and being labelled a 'habitual aborter'. Even after birth there are harmful terms such as 'artificial feeding' for babies who are not breastfed or 'insufficient milk supply'. Kids get it too – 'birth difference' feels very different to 'birth defect'. Slow growth is labelled 'failure to thrive' – surely they should have tried harder. For a whole glossary of outdated terms and their modernised alternatives, see www.peanut-app.io/blog/renaming-revolution-glossary.

We've seen the ancient threads of 'women should suffer', 'they should be silent' and, when they do speak up, 'they are not to be believed' in biblical texts, but the same stigma *still* pervades the medical system. Debilitating period pain? It's just part of your lot. IUDs (intrauterine devices) are routinely fitted without the offer of pain relief. Why is this pain just considered normal . . . the Bible told me so. Women with crippling symptoms of endometriosis are told that they just need to wait to get pregnant and it will all sort itself out, or worse, it's all in their head. This is after it's taken, on average, nearly a decade for them to get a diagnosis[13] – if these problems were experienced by men, surely research would have yielded solutions sooner. Erectile dysfunction is a case in point. Medical treatment was being given to men way before hormone replacement therapy (HRT) was widely available for women. Consider the imbalance this potentially created – men in midlife stoked by libido-boosting drugs while their female partner struggled with her own fluctuating hormones unsupported, often resulting in vaginal dryness and low sex drive. And I'm curious, are CBT and antidepressants recommended as regularly for men with low sex drive as they are to women in perimenopause?

You might wonder where the term 'hysterical woman' came from. It predates Freud and can be traced all the way back to Hippocrates, the 5th-century BCE founder of modern medicine, who coined hysteria from *hystera*, the Greek word for uterus. The ancient Greek interpretation was that the uterus was sad when it wasn't sexually active or bearing children, so naturally, the treatment for hysteria was sex. While this might seem laughable, it was also a treatment for women in Victorian times in both the US and Europe via a vibrator that induced hysterical paroxysm (orgasm). Symptoms of hysteria included anxiety, fainting, hysterical emotions, insomnia, weeping, excessive or lacking sexual desire (we can't win either way), irritability, inability to conceive or fulfil mothering duties or a 'tendency to cause trouble for others' (perimenopausal women, beware!). When you cast your mind back to the lack of financial independence, the lack of body autonomy and the abuse that women have been subjected to through the centuries, the symptoms make sense. Too right, women were fucked off. If the vibrator didn't work, women were sent off to insane asylums or forced to undergo surgical hysterectomy. The American Psychiatric Association dropped the term 'female hysteria' in 1950, only to replace it with the Freudian 'hysterical neurosis', which stuck around until 1980.

It's no wonder that generations of women stayed silent rather than reach out for support for health issues. While the diagnosis of 'hysterical woman' or 'angry woman' might no longer stand, women are still being ignored and abused by the medical system. The 'whiney woman' label still exists; it might not be written down in medical notes but it's a verbal code among doctors used for women with multiple complaints, aching bodies, sleep issues, brain fog.[14] Sounds like menopause, right? 'It's all in her head' is reflected in the fact that women are still more likely to be offered antidepressants than the HRT that can alleviate so many of the concerns she is raising. Instead, she's likely to be running around in circles trying to sort the myriad of issues individually – the dentist for gum problems, the specialist for her frozen shoulder, the orthopaedic surgeon for the arthritis in her feet, the psychologist for memory, brain fog and sleep issues . . . all the while feeling she is being a nuisance and a burden.

What does a breakdown of the funding for women's health research tell us? The vast majority is spent on fertility and pregnancy, with just a tiny percentage reserved at present for menopause, although this is something *every* woman will face if she lives long enough. It all just reinforces this notion that women have a 'best before' date, perpetuating these ancient myths that our worth depends on our ability to reproduce. We're so used to being undervalued, dismissed and shut down, no wonder it's hard to trust ourselves and find the confidence to give voice.

Sexual abuse and victim blaming and shaming

If you need yet another reason why women silence themselves, look at these statistics. You will soon see why it's often not safe to speak up, why we are frightened and shamed into silence and why we often abandon ourselves to avoid the pain. We can't always just pipe up and prioritise ourselves; there are times when we need to keep invisible for our own safety.

- 1 in 4 women experiences domestic abuse in her lifetime,[15] and 1 in 5 kids in the UK will have lived with an adult perpetrating domestic abuse – either witnessing it or experiencing it themselves.[16]

- On average, a woman is killed by a partner or ex every five days in England and Wales. Abuse escalates for pregnant women, and it is estimated that around 3 women a week die by suicide as a result of domestic abuse.[17]

- A report by Femicide Census showed that of the women killed by a former partner, 37 per cent were reported to have separated or taken steps to separate from the men who killed them, revealing that women need more protection in leaving a violent relationship.[18]

- 41 per cent of UK girls aged 14 to 17 in an intimate relationship experienced some form of sexual violence from their partner.[19]

- A study by academics at Lancaster University found that domestic abuse increases by 38 per cent when the England men's football team lose a major tournament, and by 26 per cent when they win or draw.[20] There is a campaign raising awareness about domestic violence and football, #nomoreinjurytime.

And here's one more. In 2024, Screenshot, a digital media company, went out into the streets of London to film a video segment in which they put a single question to random women passing by – 'Would you rather be stuck in the forest with a man you don't know or a bear?' The answers and the internet response to this viral video are telling; the vast majority of women polled selected the bear. As one respondent reasoned, 'If I said a bear attacked me, I'd be believed, and no one would ask me what I was wearing or how much I had to drink.'[21] Within days the TikTok video had amassed over 14 million views, 2 million likes and more than 65,000 comments. It's not just that the threat of male violence is real, it's the fear of how you'll be treated if you do speak up.

If you follow the news in the UK, you'll understand the reluctance to reach out for police support and report crimes. The Sarah Everard case is just one chilling example – the very people who are meant to be protecting us are committing the kidnap, the rape and the murder.[22] Other police officers have been caught taking degrading photos of murdered women's bodies.[23] Strangers, police officers, even our own husbands. In September 2024 it came to light that Gisèle Pelicot had been drugged and raped by 73 men, organised by her own husband, who admitted getting satisfaction from seeing other men rape his wife of 50 years. These men didn't just want their woman silent; they preferred her unconscious. What's so disturbing about this case is the number of men who saw the ad placed by her husband, who had conversations with him about it, who came to the house and saw what was happening, and who did nothing to stop it. Many – not just the perpetrators, but the public – said they didn't think it was rape because her husband condoned it. How many colleagues turn a blind eye to the questionable attitudes and behaviour of their misogynist police officer workmate? It's not all men, but it's frightening how many men hate and heinously harm women, and even more distressing how many *more* men don't report them, intervene or talk about these issues publicly.

So who are we meant to turn to? And when we are brave enough to come forward, the counter-claims are ferocious: women labelled as liars, attention-seekers, fame-hungry, trying to make a quick buck, man-haters. Talk about suffering wound upon wound. In 2013, just days after giving evidence at the trial of her abuser, Frances Andrade committed suicide. During the rape trial, she had been called a 'fantasist' by the defendant's barrister.[24] After such trauma, who has the stomach for character assassination? Especially when, at the end of the day, just 2 per cent of rapists are ever convicted.[25]

Look at the online abuse women receive when they speak out about women's issues. Feminist campaigners like Clementine Ford being told that she is 'unrapeable'. If we give voice, we are complaining, we're too sensitive, we're weak, we're exaggerating, we're hysterical, we're mentally unstable. It is dangerous to speak up. I am sure there are plenty of women who feel they would love to be more 'selfish' but it's simply not safe for them to be. Women and girls are constantly navigating a world where self-expression must be carefully weighed against their safety, and for victims of sexual and violent crimes, the traumatic aftermath can be one where it's simply too painful to connect with self. Silenced, denied the right to represent ourselves, denied the opportunity for self-determination, we cut ourselves off, we abandon ourselves.

Emotional abuse

Emotional abuse is such a painful subject, and it has so many people scratching their heads, wondering whether it was all in their imagination. It's an insidious thing and sometimes it is easier to recognise a bruise or a broken bone than it is to detect the wounds of emotional neglect. Many people could look back on their childhood and proclaim that it was largely happy – a normal upbringing – and still be victims of emotional abuse, still carrying the scars. If this speaks to you, my heart goes out to you. I am so sorry. It was not your fault. And so many of you will as adults have courageously shared your experiences with other people, only to be met with shock that you have turned your back on your ageing parents. You will be asked, 'How could you do it? How selfish are you?' The question we should be asking is, 'How could a parent ever treat their child like that?' I am so sorry; you didn't deserve that wound either. It is so painful to be misunderstood and maligned when you have every right to protect yourself.

Let's look at what emotional abuse and emotional neglect are, and what you might have experienced if you were raised by emotionally immature parents. Emotional abuse is any act that makes a child feel worthless, unloved, alone or afraid. It can manifest in constant criticism, humiliation, direct threats, name calling, teasing, sarcasm, hurtful jokes, bullying, being yelled at, character insults, blaming, shaming, scapegoating, being made to perform degrading acts, being prevented from having friends or other means of social support, not being allowed to express your unique identity, being controlled, being pushed too hard, being told you're too much, a burden, a mistake. It can be experienced in adulthood, too, and be just as harmful.

Emotional neglect is different to emotional abuse but still constitutes a form of abuse. It is a failure to act: failure to safeguard, to protect, to care, to provide support, to promote social development, to be present, loving and available. Emotional neglect results in a child feeling ignored, unvalidated, uncared for, unappreciated and disregarded, and if unaddressed can make people feel invisible and worthless their whole lives long. Some caregivers might be inconsistent or unreliable in their response to their child's emotions; they may be attentive to particular emotional needs but not others, for example, and approval is conditional with only some emotions tolerated. Other caregivers completely neglect their child's emotional needs by being indifferent or unresponsive. Examples of emotional neglect include giving the silent treatment, dismissing, belittling or denying your experience, withholding or not showing affection, lack of emotional support especially during challenging life experiences or illness, not protecting you from domestic violence or other abuse, and not advocating for you or intervening on your behalf.

I've been privy to many recollections of clients who were verbally punished for being defiant, for expressing anger. Some were even physically restrained during emotional outbursts. Children learn here that they should be not only afraid of their caregivers, but fearful of emotion itself. Feelings become unsafe because they just make the child vulnerable to more trouble, pain, disappointment, judgement or punishment. It is safer to cut themselves off from their feelings and so the self is abandoned. That fundamental distrust of emotion can feel so frightening to overcome, but we can learn to tolerate emotion again.

And, sadly, kids don't just suffer when they're being 'disobedient'; they are also attacked for being exuberant, happy, sad or for just being themselves. They're told they're being manipulative for trying to get their own way. Where 'self' has been demonised and self-advocacy is interpreted by parents as being disrespectful, they are denied the right to suggest preferences or be self-selecting, and repeated attempts are met with punishment. These lessons run so deep, and many people are left asking if they're being manipulative when they are just trying to assert or represent themselves as any human deserves the right to. If children have had their perspectives belittled or requests invalidated, it leads them to question their own reality, and many people find it hard to trust their own instincts, sensations, feelings and memories. These childhood experiences are incredibly destabilising and confusing. So many adults in my consulting room learned as children that they were not allowed to have needs, or that being needless resulted in praise, or that being needy meant more abuse, so they quickly learned to shut themselves down. These habits are hard to break. We might feel so estranged that we can't even be honest with ourselves, let alone honest with other people, but we can come home to ourselves and trust again.

Perhaps it doesn't feel fair to label your parents as emotionally abusive or neglectful, but their needs eclipsed your own, so it might be kinder to suggest they were emotionally immature. If as a child you had to navigate a parent's mood swings, you may have been too busy forecasting your parent's emotional needs for your own to get a look in. Maybe when you were young, a parent had a chronic health issue which thrust you into a caring role when it was you who needed to be cared for. Focusing on others can then become a coping mechanism, distracting you from your own pain. Maybe due to financial constraints or family breakdown, you had to tend to the needs of your younger siblings or provide for them financially. Sometimes, for this reason, siblings can have very different views of family life, and even when those responsibilities were 'gladly' born as a child (most often because we are trying so hard to be good and therefore lovable), resentment can surface later in life and this can lead to fractures that other family members find hard to understand. Please remember, they were just a child; and if this resonates with you, please gently acknowledge *you* were just a child.

Maybe all your basic physical needs were met but there was a distinct lack of emotional tending, and your requests for more were rejected as superfluous. Perhaps you have a close relationship with your parent but that also involved you being your parent's cheerleader, their confidant, their therapist. Those secrets shared so young can be such a burden, and perhaps they are still wanting to know every last detail about your life now, as if having a private life means you are being secretive. Perhaps you were privy to more than you wanted to be and you were expected to mediate in family arguments, to keep the peace. Maybe your parents wanted so much for you, but it was a projection of their own hopes and dreams, not your own. You might have felt like their self-worth hinged on your success and so you've spent your whole life knowing you couldn't screw up! Perhaps your parents gave their heart and soul to rearing you and now demand that your life revolves around them, frequently guilting and shaming you for not making enough effort or simply making a choice that's good for you. We can look to our relationships with our parents and feel loved but also feel so damn enmeshed, like that love comes at a great price – our freedom. I know how challenging navigating these boundaries can be, but together we'll find clarity and confidence in Step 7, I Advocate for Myself.

Maybe it's not oversharing that's a problem; maybe your parents undershared. Perhaps they loved you so much they went to great lengths to protect you from worry, shielding you from the realities of life, hiding conflict, never showing you how to have a healthy argument, always with a smile on their faces, leaving you wondering why you find adulting so fucking hard. Perhaps they cared so deeply for you that they prevented every imagined danger and, having kept life so small, you're forever feeling unsafe and unsure of your capability to cope. Maybe your parents thought it was their job to keep you perpetually happy and when things got tough, as they do for everyone, and you showed up authentically, they felt they were failing and you had to bear the burden of their disappointment too.

Even when you think you've had a 'normal' childhood, there can be many ways in which your relationship with yourself can be affected. Time doesn't heal all wounds and we need to address the core beliefs we formed as a result of our childhood experiences. How do you prioritise yourself when you've learned that you don't have a right to self-expression or needs? It can take much healing to feel safe to have needs and to speak up and represent yourself. We need to reclaim our right to personhood to be able to be 'selfish'.

Please know that any caregiver's or parent's inability to love us, care for us, support us, protect us, validate or comfort us is not our deficit. Their inability to bear witness to our feelings does not mean we're unlovable or that our feelings are not OK. The deficit was never ours.

Your needs, your feelings, are not the problem – the problem comes for us in suppressing them and resisting them, yet for so many of us, and for women throughout history, it hasn't been safe to share them. Let's work together to create a feeling of safety in your body. We'll explore a toolkit for doing that in Chapter 4 (page 93), and also identify people and places where it is safe for you to bring your whole self.

> ### Reflection time: In what ways have you been silenced?
>
> Please use these questions to reflect gently on how you may have been silenced and know that speaking up for ourselves is a skill we can reclaim, just as we can reclaim all those hidden parts of self. We will do just that in Part II, by following our 7 Steps to Self-advocacy.
>
> - Throughout your life, have you been afraid of being honest, or afraid of any other form of self-expression?
> - Where has voicing your needs or feelings been welcome and where hasn't it been safe to do so?
> - How has your anger been received?
> - Can you think of a time when you felt dismissed, minimised or silenced, in the past or more recently? What happened, why did you feel it wasn't OK to speak up and what were the consequences?
> - Can you also identify a time when you were courageous and spoke up? What were the consequences – what were the benefits and costs?
> - Reflecting on these experiences, are there parts of you that you feel have been denied, cut off or pushed away? What might you feel drawn to reclaiming?

- How have these experiences shaped your propensity to give voice or your feelings about your ability to advocate for yourself?

To round out this exploration of why we revere selflessness and feel so afraid of being seen as selfish, revisit the timeline you created in Chapter 2 (page 39). Having digested the historical and current threads of distraction and silencing, consider if there is anything that you would add to your map in terms of what you have encountered in your life and what you did to cope. While Part I might have been uncomfortable reading, I hope it has fuelled you to make some changes in your life – changes of your choosing. It's time to take yourself back.

CHAPTER FOUR

INTRODUCING YOUR TOOLKITS FOR RECLAIMING SELF

You understand now why you've felt the need to be seen as selfless, not selfish. Well done for questioning those cultural norms that have kept you small, silent and stuck. By observing this conditioning, which was not chosen by you and is not contingent with your values, you can decide what you adhere to from this point forwards. You will also be painfully aware of the costs of self-sacrifice, but I hope you can see now what gifts await you and your loved ones when you allow yourself to be 'selfish'. You finally know why it is OK for you to advocate for yourself and realise that loosening your commitment to selflessness doesn't mean moving away from what matters to you. When you commit to stop abandoning yourself, you have greater access to all the qualities that you hold dear.

You are not becoming less principled; this commitment means you are better placed to show up as you aspire. I hope now that you are feeling ready to let your needs, feelings, hopes, pleasures and dreams take centre stage. So how do we do it? We take it step by step and we do it together.

I want to acknowledge that even when we know we want to create change, it can feel really difficult taking the first steps. Telling someone to prioritise themselves after years of people pleasing, or that it's OK to trust and rely on others after being hyper-independent for so long, is like telling someone who is anxious to 'just relax'. *It doesn't feel safe.* Selflessness, people pleasing, hyper-independence, hyper-responsibility, hypervigilance, perfectionism are all coping mechanisms we have employed in our response to our conditioning and life experiences. We can't just stop being selfless and it doesn't feel safe to advocate for ourselves, depend on others, take up space, be seen, heard and known. I understand how hard this is, and I want you to know that we will go gently here, finding ways to feel differently and make different choices.

Throughout the rest of the book, I will offer a range of practical toolkits for you to use in different situations to support you in your journey to self-advocacy, giving you techniques to vent without being toxic, sit with difficult emotions, navigate grief, break free from self-sacrifice and many other challenging situations. There are also many step-by-step plans and much other practical guidance. I have left some little love notes for you, too, which are more meditative in nature. I hope they will offer some warm encouragement if you find yourself flagging.

I would like now to introduce you to the first toolkit.

Your toolkit to feel safe

It is hard to feel safe as an adult if you didn't feel safe as a child – even the sensation of relaxing can feel strange and unfamiliar – but, my darling, it is something you can reclaim.

Sometimes we need to cultivate a feeling of safety in relationship with others, rather than trying to soothe ourselves on our own. See page 255 on how to cultivate trust to work out who you can lean on here. The gift of a skilled therapist is to lend their calm, abiding centre as you learn how to feel accepted as you are, safe enough to be vulnerable and share your inner life.

Even if you feel you had a happy childhood, of all the toolkits in this book, this one might be the one you turn to most frequently. It is hard to speak up for ourselves and act in our own interests in a world that demonises selfishness and there will be many times that you'll need support when that pang of guilt about disappointing others zaps you. It feels genuinely scary to be 'selfish', to challenge the scripts that have been whittering away in our ears our whole lives long! Go gently and let this toolkit soothe you so it feels safe to take bold action and make different choices. What you'll find here is a topline introduction to practices that soothe the nervous system; we will explore these more fully as we journey together through Part 2.

Summary: What to do when anxiety arises

1. When anxiety pops up, welcome it and thank it for trying to keep you safe. If you're an HSP please don't berate yourself for being so attentive – we want to hug that little meerkat keeping her troop safe, not give her grief! If hypervigilance has been a necessary coping mechanism in the past, again say your gentle thanks but remind yourself that things have changed and it's OK to come down from high alert.

2. Once you've made space for the anxious thoughts or feelings, identify the source. What is bringing the feeling of threat? Is it real? If it is, what can you do to protect yourself? Take the necessary action. If the imagined threat is not a true risk, you can still validate

the feelings but also remind yourself that you are safe and move on to soothing your nervous system. If there are lifestyle factors that are contributing to this feeling of being on edge, take note and make some changes. Sleep deprivation, hunger, dehydration, stimulants such as coffee, sugar and screens, and depressants such as alcohol can all rob you of your sense of peace.

3. Try out the different practices in this toolkit to feel safe and make a note of the ones that speak to you, adding any of your own favourites to the mix. Refer to this soothing selection whenever you need a little pocket of peace.

Breathwork

- When we breathe in a spacious, relaxed way, we shift our nervous system out of the stress response and into 'rest and digest' mode, which we will explore in greater depth in Step 3, I Reclaim My Body (page 145). As a general rule, aim for nostril breathing, unless you're congested, and aim to make your exhalation longer than your inhalation.

- One long candle breath can be enough: inhale through your nose and exhale through gently pursed lips as if you are cooling a cup of tea.

- If you'd like a breathing exercise that feels more galvanising, opt for 'mountain breath'. Stand tall, feet hip width apart and gaze directed forwards. As you breathe in, raise your arms out wide to the side, filling the room, and touch your palms together above your head, looking up. As you exhale, slowly lower your hands to your heart and gaze forwards. Enjoy this ten times, growing taller and more resolute with every repetition. This can also be a good alternative if breathing in stillness exacerbates anxiety – move with your breath instead.

Tender touch

- Try the 'face hug', cradling your chin in your hands, or place your hands on your heart, or hold one thumb in the other hand (doesn't matter which). Feel how these somatic holds bring you comfort.

- 'Massage your horns' by making two fists and pressing the bony base of your thumbs into your forehead where you would have two imaginary horns. Press firmly for five breaths and feel how this releases your eyes and jaw and slows your rate of breathing down.

- Open your mouth wide like a goldfish and make a pitter-patter action on your cheeks with your fingertips. Open and close your fish mouth during the self-massage, releasing all the things you didn't say and all the facial expressions you haven't shown.

Tension-relieving movement

- Run your tongue around your top row of teeth, ten times one way, ten times the other. Feel how this relaxes your tongue and softens your jaw.

- Try a tongue stretch to release your throat, jaw and eyes, particularly useful for an emotional letting go. Start by securing the skin on the left-hand side of your neck with your left hand, feeling as though you are sliding your left fingertips slightly back behind you. Keeping your head still, open your mouth and stick your tongue out to the right as far as possible and simultaneously take your gaze to the left, in the opposite direction to your tongue. Hold and feel the dynamic tension between your tongue and eyes moving in opposing directions. Release and repeat on the other side, securing the skin of the right-hand side of your neck with your right hand, taking your tongue to the left and looking to the right. Notice the freedom this creates in your face. Bask in the glow before re-entering your day.

- Don't dismiss the therapeutic power of a simple walk around the block, training your eyes to spot anything that piques curiosity or awe.

Grounding techniques

- Where possible, enjoy going barefoot and getting acquainted with your feet. Wriggle your toes and, when grounding them, fan them out as if you are splaying your fingertips wide.

- Rolling your foot over a spiky ball will also help you reclaim dexterity in your toes, helping you feel more grounded.

- Massage your feet to stimulate blood flow and add magnesium oil for a stress-relieving ritual with real anti-inflammatory properties.

- Place your hands on the countertop or press them into the wall for a sense of containment and security.

- When you're drinking a glass of water, ground yourself by doing so with a hand on your heart.

- Rock from side to side as it feels good to you or make some hip circles, like you are working with a giant hula hoop.

- Try some alternate heel lifts, just feeling the stability of the earth beneath you.

- Play with calf raises, sweeping your arms forwards and upwards and raising your heels as you breathe in. Breathe out, lowering your arms back down as your heels descend. Let this one connect you with a sense of humour, anchoring you not only in your environment but in the present moment – any exercise involving balance will make it virtually impossible to think about anything else at the same time, which can be a welcome relief from overthinking. While there is no need to run from your thoughts, sometimes we need a break!

- For a more effortless method of feeling grounded, receive comfort from a weighted blanket. Snuggle in and be held.
- Relax with your pet and enjoy the weight of its body and the beating of its heart, just watching it breathe.

Lubricating posture moves

- Alignment of your head and spine will help you hold your body in a way that cultivates confidence and calm. As an antidote to the forward head posture that screen time creates, try the 'turtle neck'. Sitting or standing tall, breathe in and glide your chin forwards as if you are a turtle poking its head out of its shell. As you exhale, slide your head back as if you are drawing your head back into your turtle shell. Make this lubricating movement ten times. To finish, nestle your chin ever so slightly back, lengthening the back of your neck and lifting the crown of your head skywards.
- As an antidote to a round-spine position which lowers mood and energy, make some 'chicken wing shoulder rolls'. Fingertips on shoulders, breathe in and raise your elbows forwards and up, and as you breathe out, slide them back and down. Try 5–10 rolls and enjoy the poise this cultivates.

All the kind words

- This is not optional. Every practice above is rendered obsolete if coupled with harsh, punitive words of self-criticism. Don't allow your words to be a form of self-harm.
- Talk to yourself as if you are your favourite baby animal. Who could trash talk a kitten?

I hope some of the practices above can calm your nerves and create a feeling of security as we look ahead to what we will work through together in the remainder of the book. Pause and come back to them as needed.

Introducing the 7 Steps to Self-advocacy

Welcome to the action part of this journey! These 7 Steps will show you how to take back your peace and your power. I suggest you address them in order because they provide a scaffolding of awareness and skills, each step building on the previous one. This is how we avoid overwhelm and feel safe to create change.

- Step 1: I Reclaim My Mind

  We will begin with renegotiating your relationship with your thoughts, learning where your control lies and how to get out of your own way.

- Step 2: I Reclaim My Attention

  We will use your senses to learn how to direct your focus, helping you reconnect with yourself. This step provides the foundation for you to be aware of your needs.

- Step 3: I Reclaim My Body

  Welcome home to your body as a means of getting in touch with your emotions and learning to feel safe when you are challenging old behaviour patterns and building new habits. This step builds your capacity to soothe your nervous system and reclaim your right to experience pleasure, which is key to healing and energy management.

- Step 4: I Reclaim My Right to Feel

  Having grown your capacity to direct your focus and connect with your body, this step is all about your emotional health – reclaiming your right to feel all your emotions and gaining the skills of moving through them in healthy ways.

- Step 5: I Take Back My Moral Compass

    In this step you deepen your knowledge of your values and what matters to you most. It is fundamental to your ability to trust and prioritise yourself.

- Step 6: I Prioritise Myself

    This step is all about your relationship and boundaries with yourself. You need to learn how to honour yourself before you can begin to assert yourself in relationship with other people. Here you will learn how to prioritise yourself and meet your own needs.

- Step 7: I Advocate for Myself

    Here we focus on your relationship with others and your right to advocate for yourself. We develop the concrete skills of articulating your needs and feelings and honouring your boundaries with other people. This step will empower you with the ability to speak up on your behalf and manage relationships with other people, at home, in the workplace and in the doctor's office.

I will take you one step at a time, helping you grow your courage in being seen and heard, gain the confidence to make requests and voice your desires, become comfortable with trusting and leaning on others, and develop the ability to be direct, honest and stand your ground. We will practise together how to get comfortable with vulnerability and feel safe to share your emotional life, so that you can connect authentically with other people.

PART TWO

HOW WE CAN THINK, FEEL AND CHOOSE DIFFERENTLY

STEP 1
I RECLAIM MY MIND

One of the biggest barriers we face in our journey to prioritising ourselves is our own mind. I'm curious, how many times a day does your brain beat you up for being selfish? 'I can't rest, that would be selfish.' 'I am a bad mother for not playing with my kids.' (While you're trying to prepare dinner for them . . .) 'I shouldn't be feeling low, other people have it so much worse.' The thoughts drone on and so often stop us from taking the nourishing action we know we need. The very first place we need to start is reclaiming your mind and by this I mean coping with unhelpful thoughts, questioning self-limiting beliefs and learning to cultivate supportive self-talk. Challenging, yes, but we all have the capacity to do it.

Getting your mind on side, does this appeal to you? But it might be a little different to what you're imagining. The number one problem that brings people to my therapy room is the desire to get rid of a particular thought. Have you noticed how impossible this is? And how, when we attempt to eradicate a certain thought, this backfires and it becomes even stickier and louder? I don't know about you, but I've spent an awful lot of time trying to get rid of unhelpful thoughts and I can categorically state that I have failed. Perhaps you've experienced this too. It doesn't mean you are doing something wrong! Darling, I have good news: you don't have to get rid of your thought that it's bad to be selfish – or whatever phrase stops you from speaking up for yourself – all you have to do is change your relationship with the thought. Let me show you another way. Are you up for a couple of thought experiments?

Changing your relationship with your story

What's your story? 'It's selfish to focus on myself. I'm not enough. I'm not worthy. My needs don't matter.' Let's try an experiment with these words to see if there's some wiggle room in how we experience them, feel about them and how they make us feel about ourselves.

Choose the statements your mind needles you with often, the words that stick out most for you, and write them down on a piece of A4 paper. You can let them be so large that they fill the page, like a shout, or you can jot them down in small lettering if you prefer. It is totally up to you but do notice the difference this makes in how you feel. Now let's manipulate this piece of paper containing our story and see what we can do with it.

Bring to mind a role in life that matters to you and imagine yourself moving through your day in this role – imagine it playing out before your eyes. Now hold up this piece of paper in front of you – this is what you are doing when you invest your identity in this thought, allowing yourself to wallow in it, amplifying it. Notice how distracting it is, how it obscures your vision of what's happening during your day. You can only see the periphery of what matters to you. This story, when you fixate and ruminate on it, gets in your way of responding and tending to what's important. Notice how much effort it takes for your hands to hold this story up like this. The energy it takes when we feed it with our attention is not only distracting, it is depleting. This story is stopping you from interacting with life in ways that are deeply meaningful to you.

You might be tempted to try to get rid of this story once and for all, or to hide it away and keep it secret, but let's see what happens when you attempt to do that. This story that we tell ourselves, contained here on this piece of paper, let's try to squash it right down. Screw it up into a tiny ball using all your strength. Spend a good minute crushing it and notice what happens. Can you see that this is also distracting you from the important things that are unfolding right in front of you? Can you feel how tiring this is? How it makes your hands ache? And despite all the effort, the story remains, the distraction remains, the depletion remains. It's like a beach ball that just won't be submerged. Try with everything you've got, but the damn thing is going to keep popping back up!

Let's try another option. Open and flatten out the piece of paper containing your story and rather than wrestling with the thought, identifying with it, trying to get rid of it, how would it be to rest this paper gently in your lap, freeing up your hands? It takes next to no effort to allow it to be in your lap, just letting it be there, not trying to fix or eradicate it. Notice how you are now free to look up at what's important to you and nothing is obscuring your vision. You can give your full attention to what matters to you, even in the presence of this story. It can be there without getting in your way, without it being part of who you are, just something you experience, like the weather. Its presence has no bearing on your worth as a human being, it's just a passing state. Just by making space for it – it doesn't have to go away completely – can you feel you have greater capacity for being present and responsive to your life? Does this gentle acceptance help you feel calmer?

This practice shows us that these stories we've been told don't have to be eradicated. We can hold them up to the light for the untruths they are and feel less pushed around by them. They are not who we are and we don't have to waste precious time and energy disposing of them. We can notice them and carry on with what our soul decides is valuable.

While we don't need to eradicate this story, I think there is value in challenging a habitual one that sabotages us by identifying a truthful statement that counters it. Let's try another experiment. This time, please select a small piece of paper about the size of a Post-it note. Write down your pesky phrase of not enoughness. Let's deliberately choose small font this time, to remind yourself that you can let these thoughts be, but they don't need to dominate you. Now, on the other side of the paper, write down the words, 'I see you, this story I've been told. Thank you for trying to keep me safe but I have permission to choose now.' Think of a statement that counters your story, such as, 'I have every right to take up space. My feelings matter. It's OK to have needs. I honour myself. I choose myself.' Please jot down whatever you find galvanising. Every time this thought of worthlessness pops up, you can flip it over and see a fresh perspective. It will help you greet the story with less resistance and less fear, and remember your truth.

Let me be clear, and I hope you find this liberating, we are not trying to control our thoughts or eliminate difficult ones. Thinking well does not mean an absence of shitty thoughts, it means that we have a healthy relationship with our thoughts and we don't invest our identity in ones that aren't aligned with our values. We need to develop a new relationship with our thoughts, understanding that not all of them are true, not all of them are facts, not all of them are predictions or prophesies, and that ultimately we are not our thoughts. Who you are as an individual is distinct from your thoughts. Thoughts come to us. They happen to us. We do not consciously choose them; so from this perspective, can you see how futile it is to try to manipulate them? Where we do have power is how we *respond* to our thoughts – our self-talk. Our sphere of influence lies in how we deliberately interact with that thought that randomly pops into our heads. In a nutshell, we cannot change, stop or control our thoughts, but we can choose how we respond to them.

At this point you might be thinking, I've tried the whole 'kind self-talk' thing and I just couldn't do it. It can feel like your self-talk is automatic, and while it is a habit, I promise, you are capable, and it is something that you can influence and shape. What we are dealing with here is the *belief* that you can't change your self-talk. So let's explore beliefs in greater detail first, before we move on to strategies to cope with the thoughts and inner chatter you'd rather not have.

How do you alter your beliefs?

Beliefs are assumptions we make about ourselves, others, situations and the world. They are something we believe to be true, shaped by our family, geography, society, culture, the media, and our own learnings and values. You can think of beliefs as thoughts you've invested your identity with. Some examples of how our thoughts become fused with identity are:

- 'I can't change my self-talk.'
- 'I must be selfless to be worthy.'
- 'I am a bad sleeper.'
- 'I am punctual.'
- 'I have poor willpower.'
- 'I'm skilled in the kitchen.'
- 'I'm not good enough.'
- 'I have to look a certain way to be acceptable.'
- 'It is better to give than to receive.'
- 'It is wrong to display anger.'

- 'It is selfish to prioritise yourself.'
- 'The world is a dangerous place.'
- 'When I make a mistake, I must be tough on myself.'
- 'I am capable.'
- 'I am too sensitive.'
- 'I can learn and grow.'

You can see how some of these beliefs are supportive and some of them will derail you, like invisible barriers disrupting your efforts to advocate for yourself.

I invite you to make a mind map of your beliefs about your right to honour yourself. In the centre of the page, write the words 'what it means to be a good human' and add spokes like a wheel to record all the associations that come to mind. You can use words, images or colour and highlighting – whatever helps you express yourself and organise your beliefs. What are the beliefs that get in the way of you prioritising yourself and taking care of yourself? What are the ones that galvanise you to speak up? Think of all the stories you have been told about being good, not disappointing others, keeping the peace, making mistakes, rest, being productive, being responsible for the feelings of others, having to do it all on your own, your right to feel, your right to receive and your right to be here. Cast your mind back through the chapters where we've looked at how we've been distracted, disconnected and silenced. Remember that these messages are not the truth and that you can choose where you invest your identity and future. Religion told us we are not worthy. Capitalism told us our worth is contingent on our material wealth and productivity. Consumerism told us we had to buy that product or look a certain (ever-changing) way to be worthy. Patriarchal society told us we must shrink ourselves and put the needs of others first. Modern messaging tells us we must be strong, grateful, self-reliant and selfless. Relationships may have taught us that it's not safe to be our true self. Jot down the phrases that come to mind when you think about being selfish, what you associate with being a good human being, or you could use the prompt: *I am only worthy if* . . .

Let this be an ongoing practice. Add to this mind map when another belief pops into your head.

Looking at all the beliefs on your mind map, ask yourself if these statements are true. Where is the evidence for them? What else could be true and where is the evidence for that? Even if you struggle with refuting some of these statements, ask yourself, do these beliefs help you live the life you want to lead? Do these beliefs serve you? What impact do they have on what really matters to you? Can you trace them back to their origin – did they ever really belong to you? At what cost do you keep investing meaning and your identity in these statements and allowing them to influence the direction of your life? What might it look like to think and feel differently?

Highlight the beliefs that serve you. Scrub out the ones that sabotage you and write out an alternative that makes space for your growth. Instead of the belief that you must always be selfless, switch it for 'I can be kind and generous and also include myself.' If one of your beliefs is that you should never show anger, try the phrase 'I am allowed to express my anger in safe and healthy ways.' If you've been led to believe that you're too sensitive, swap it for 'I have a giant heart that deserves protection.' Switch your belief that you're only worthy when you're pleasing others for 'I can seek my own approval.' Change up the belief that you must always be self-sufficient for 'People need people and it's OK to ask for help.' In this process you are still making space for that initial thought while also reframing it into something more constructive. We will explore concrete strategies for coping with persistent self-sabotaging thoughts shortly.

We *can* modify our beliefs. For the ancient people who believed the world was flat, could you imagine how mind altering it would be to see pictures of Earth from space; that's what I hope the snapshots of how we've been distracted, disconnected and silenced will do for you. They can help dissolve those hardened beliefs that keep us stuck and isolated. Once we see through them, we have an opportunity to articulate our own values, but at the same time we will need strategies to soothe our nervous system because it can be deeply unsettling to dispense with the coping mechanisms we've relied on our whole lives long.

Beliefs, while they feel set in stone, are all malleable. We just need to bring them to light, roll them around in our mouths, say them out loud and see whether they support or hinder us. Challenge them, and find new ways of expressing them that bolster your confidence and ability to act in service of your values. Repeat your new beliefs out loud and feel how getting familiar with them helps them take root. The process of unlearning can be challenging to the point of feeling like an existential threat. These things that we have told ourselves to be true were the foundation of who we thought we were. They helped us feel secure and make sense of the world, so shaking them up rocks our faith in our discernment. If we question this, what else might unravel? We have to admit that we got it wrong and that can be so painful, but darling, permission to be human, permission to make mistakes.

It might even feel easier to stick with the familiar and avoid the confusion, fear and grief of losing the certainty and security that came with those old beliefs. It is uncomfortable to disrupt them but at what cost do we not? Use your toolkit to feel safe (page 94) to help you create this shift in your core beliefs. We can cultivate fresh stability with new beliefs that lovingly tend to the person that we are becoming. We can give ourselves permission to try and permission to be beginners! We can do hard things. We can evolve. We can choose. We can learn to do things differently. We are worthy. Let's begin with an unquestioned belief in our worth as human beings. You exist, therefore you are worthy. If you are constantly telling yourself you're not worthy, don't worry, the next section will support you. Please also remember that you don't have to feel deserving to take care of yourself – the feeling of worth comes *from* the nourishing action.

OK, so we know that we are not our thoughts, we know that it's OK to have all our thoughts, that we don't choose them and don't have to try to eradicate or fix them. We know it's helpful to take a look at thoughts that have hardened into beliefs and challenge the ones that sabotage us, but if they linger, it's also OK! We can just see them as passing thoughts, although they may be ones that keep coming back like a pesky fly. We need strategies to help us cope with them as they arise, and to learn how to generate kind self-talk in response to them. That's what we will address next.

How to cope with difficult thoughts

When you are trying to unhook from self-limiting beliefs or feel bombarded by recurring thoughts, try this process. Remind yourself that the purpose of this exercise is not to eradicate this thought, it's to help you feel less pushed around by it.

1. Call to mind the thought or old belief that stops you prioritising yourself. Choose just one. Something like, 'I'm not good enough. I'm not worthy. I can't focus on me.'

2. For the next minute think about this thought, taking it to be true, repeating it and giving it your full attention. Just sit there and do nothing but mull over that thought. Notice how this feels in your body and how you feel about yourself after that minute.

3. Next, we're going to tweak that phrase slightly. For the next minute, please repeat the words 'I am having the thought that . . . ' and notice what this feels like in your body, how you feel about the thought and how you feel about yourself.

4. Last round. This time you are going to reframe your statement to 'I am noticing that I am having the thought that . . . ' For the next minute, repeat the phrase about noticing that you are having

the thought about [. . .]. At the end, check in with how this version of the practice felt in your body, how you feel about the thought now and how you feel about yourself. Is anything different to how you felt in steps 1 and 2?

I hope this process shows you how to create some space around your thoughts, helping you feel less fused with them. You can't outrun your thoughts, you can't stop them, but with gentle acceptance and compassion, you can learn to dial down their power over you. With repetition, this practice will help you remember that your thoughts are just a passing experience. They come and they go and we can notice them and carry on with what matters to us regardless.

Dealing with persistent thoughts – try 'dropping the rope'

Come back to your phrase – maybe it's 'I'm not worthy. I can't rock the boat. I can't be selfish.' Whatever your phrase is, please know we all have one! You know it's futile trying to get rid of this thought – you can't just silence it – but you also don't have to let it define you, keep you stuck, deplete your energy or distract you from what's important to you. Think of how you engage with this thought as a game of tug-of-war. As long as you're battling with it, it is taking your energy away from wherever you want to place it. Instead of pulling with both hands in an attempt to win this impossible battle, we can simply *drop the rope*.

Just acknowledge you've had the thought – there it is again, that old chestnut – and rather than refuting it, or giving yourself grief for having had it, or mulling it over ad nauseum, just drop the rope. Let it go and bring your attention back to what matters to you. This is a constant process of noticing, letting go and choosing. With practice you might notice sooner, you might let go with less self-flagellation. Just keep dropping the rope and coming back to what you value, moving towards your heart's desires.

Humour definitely helps. Here are a few phrases I use to greet my own self-limiting statements: 'Hello you! There you are again! Wow, that was a doozy!' Or I imagine I have Teflon shoulders and I can let it slide off – it's not my stuff, it doesn't belong to me. I use the toolkit to feel safe to bring me back to a feeling of calm. With time, you'll notice your thoughts won't have the same hold over you.

How to cultivate constructive self-talk

That inner critic can be so vicious, but at the same time can be hard to give up. Are you attached to yours in some way? Sometimes we think it is necessary for us to atone for our errors, or even for having needs, and we use our self-talk to punish ourselves. Some people think punitive self-talk is part of the process to fire ourselves up and perform better. Let's take a closer look at the steps to changing our self-talk.

1. Get clear on why you want to develop the skill of kinder self-talk. What's in it for you and those you love? Recognise that you have a choice here. You can either trash talk yourself or use more encouraging words. Think of this as crossroads. To the left is the path of shitty self-talk. Where is it taking you? What are the short-term benefits? It feels familiar. It requires no effort. It's easy. What are the long-term costs? Negative self-talk is a form of self-harm. Can you see the impact it has on your stress levels, performance, self-esteem and confidence? Does it make it more likely that you will be critical of others? What impact is your sharp tongue having on them – what are you modelling for them? To the right lies the path of kind self-talk. What are the immediate costs? Yes, it can take effort to cultivate this approach. Maybe it feels uncomfortable or insincere. Do you worry that being softer with yourself will lead you to

being less disciplined? Will it make you lazy or self-indulgent? In fact research shows that kind self-talk helps us delay gratification and make healthier choices![1] What are the long-term benefits – will you be more peaceful and more energised? Can you see yourself sleeping better? Will your work performance improve? Will you find it easier to cope with errors? Will it give you confidence to stand your ground and honour your boundaries? And what impact would self-kindness have on your ability to be compassionate with others, how will your loved ones benefit? You are standing at this crossroads, which path will you choose? If you're not ready to work on your self-talk, come back to this page when you are. It is entirely your choice. If you are ready, write down why. What do you stand to gain? Let's go!

2. Become aware of your self-talk without judgement. We can't change something we're not aware of, so start by noticing how you interact with your thoughts. Do you habitually tell yourself off, call yourself derogatory names or swear at yourself? Just notice first.

3. Whatever your inner experience is, whether it is a thought, feeling, sensation or memory, acknowledge it, allow it to be there. Our self-talk is not just in response to thoughts, we also berate ourselves for emotions and mood states. Without judgement, extend the noticing to what's happening for you.

4. What can you say to yourself to help you weather this experience? If in doubt, respond to yourself as you would talk to a close friend going through the same thing. If you wouldn't say it to them, don't say it to yourself, sweetheart. I like to think of it as passing the mic from my inner critic to my inner elder. She is just waiting for me to listen to her soothing voice. Trust me, you have one too. If she's hard to hear at first, feel free to consider what I'd say to you. Let me take you through a few examples.

- If you've made an error and launched into 'you idiot', here's what to say instead: 'Darling, no one gets it right all the time. It's OK to make mistakes. Permission to learn and grow.'
- If you're feeling guilty about something, no character assassination is needed; instead check in with your moral compass: 'Am I actually doing something wrong? If so, how can I repair or course correct?'
- If you're feeling guilty for taking care of yourself, you know that's not a transgression of your values. You can say: 'Guilt, you can just come along for the ride. I'm not doing anything wrong. I am deserving of nurturing too. I am resourcing myself.'
- If you're feeling embarrassed, coax yourself with these words: 'No one is immune from embarrassment. What will I do differently next time? I can be gentle with myself.'
- If you're anxious, greet the feelings with these words: 'I just want to feel safe. It's totally normal and natural to need comfort and reassurance.'
- If worry is getting in the way, say: 'I acknowledge my giant heart. It's beautiful that I care so much.'
- If your feelings are hurt, rather than berating yourself, ask: 'How would any human being feel? I give myself permission to feel.'
- If you're feeling bored, greet that experience by saying: 'What do I need? It's OK to have human needs.'
- If confusion or uncertainty descends, say to yourself: 'It's OK to want clarity but it's also OK to not have all the answers right now.'
- If doubt looms large, ask yourself: 'Is there some preparation that I need to do?' Remind yourself, 'I am capable.'
- And hello again 'I'm not good enough' thoughts, you are so tenacious. Please get these swaps on loop: 'I don't have to be

perfect. I am learning and growing. I can give myself grace. I am deserving of tenderness.'

5. When you notice your self-talk is turning shitty, don't let this be another thing you beat yourself up for. Just notice it and reframe it to something supportive – pass the mic! Also check in with yourself and make sure you're not hangry, dehydrated, over stimulated, or sleep-, nature- or movement-deprived. Address any of these needs with nourishing action and see how your self-talk naturally becomes more buoyant. Turn to the toolkit below for some other ideas that are especially useful in times of stress. We don't have to greet thought just with more thought, we can use the body and the breath to help us get tender with ourselves.

Your toolkit to cultivate kind self-talk

If you're still winding up trash talking yourself, try these three practices to bring greater tenderness to your inner dialogue. Remember that you don't choose the first thought, but you do have power to influence how you respond to it – and that shitty self-talk really doesn't serve anyone.

- Use a pet name

    Research shows that when we refer to ourselves as 'you' or 'I', it tends to create harsher self-talk.[2] Conversely, when we call ourselves a pet name like 'honey', 'poppet' or 'sweetie', it cultivates more encouraging words. Choose a pet name that resonates for you – maybe it's something your grandparents used to call you, or the name of a treasured pet or just a generic term of endearment. Use it often and see how this softens your words. I hope you've clocked that I use them when I'm writing to you. Imagine what I would say to you and how I'd say it. Darling, you are deeply deserving of kindness.

- Try a 'somatic hold'

    Sometimes we need a physical practice to provide a circuit breaker for our thinking. Instead of relying on another cognitive strategy, use your body. Hold your own hand or place your hands on your heart. I find it really hard to be punitive when I do either of these gestures. Couple it with a pet name and you're cooking with gas.

- Imagine your favourite baby animal

    When you're feeling down on yourself, try bringing to mind your favourite animal. Picture it as a baby, and if it is small enough, imagine you are cupping it in your hands. Imagine the words that you would use, the tone of voice, the gentle, caring vibes that you would extend towards this little being. Imagine you are this baby animal, so worthy of tenderness, and speak to yourself as you would to this little creature. Even if you don't feel deserving, try it. And keep trying it.

> ### Love note for times of self-doubt
>
> *Sweetheart, you are the authority of you. When doubt taps you on the shoulder, as it will from time to time, ask yourself if it's helping you to prepare for something or identify some gap in your knowledge. What is it prompting you to do? If it's just an annoying critical voice, you don't need to silence it, you can direct your attention to the voice that's gently coaxing you. To connect with that wise, encouraging part of you, spend a little time thinking about similar challenges or reflecting on previous success. You've done hard things before, and you are resourceful and capable in response to what you are facing right now. Look at what you've already weathered, you can navigate this! Remember, confidence isn't something that happens exclusively in your head, you can use your body and breath to tap into a feeling*

of strength. Hop over to the toolkit to build confidence (page 236) for inspiration. Connect with your values and feel how affirming them in a mantra can help you take aligned action, even in the midst of self-doubt. 'I know my why', 'I am resolute', 'Nothing will blow me off course.'

Or borrow the words of author and activist Glennon Doyle and remind yourself that 'We can do hard things'. While I want you to know in your bones that you can step up and do what your heart is calling, you don't have to do it on your own. Part of this journey to self-advocacy is allowing others to support you. Reach out, let people in. It's OK to lean on others and let them remind you of your worth. You are thoroughly deserving of that nurturing too.

STEP 2

I RECLAIM MY ATTENTION

In learning how to meet our needs, we first need to hone our ability to notice what is happening in our own bodies. Step 2 is all about reclaiming your senses, choosing how to direct your attention and trusting your own inner experiences. In a culture that's full of noise, calls to abandon ourselves, and prods from temptation and the myths of not-enoughness, let's recognise that choosing where we place our attention and turning it inwards is a truly revolutionary act. I applaud you for making this commitment to yourself. You are deserving of your own attention and this is the foundation upon which we build all our other skills of self-advocacy. I hope you relish this process of coming home to yourself.

Dial down the external noise

For you to be able to tune inwards and hear yourself, it's helpful to dial down external noise, so let's begin with an inventory of sources of stimulation and communication. Make a list of all the things currently tugging at your attention. Write down anything you can identify in addition to:

- Communication: emails, texts, WhatsApp, Zoom/Teams meetings, social media post comments and direct messages, mail, newsletters, voice notes, online networking or support groups

- Information: consulting Dr Google, online blogs and forums, courses, lectures, presentations, newspapers, magazines, books, audiobooks, podcasts

- Advertising: posters, billboards, in magazines and newspapers, junk mail, product placement, suggested posts on social media, influencer ads

- Other people in your own physical space: conversation, touch, physical items

- Incidental noise from the environment around you: nature sounds, traffic, appliances, TV, radio, phone notifications, conversations, your music, other people's music

- Technology: phone, computer, AI device, watch, clocks, other beeping gadgets, games console, virtual reality headset

As you look through this list, which forms of stimulation involve some kind of choice? Some are beyond your control, but others can be tweaked to make them more conducive to your well-being. Are there some sources of stress that you can eliminate or reduce? Do you need all your notifications, for example, or can some go? Is it time for a social media cull? Can you unsubscribe from some mailing lists? Are there some unused apps you can delete? Consider addressing your relationship with screens and having a little more silence in your day. It's not just the amount of time on screens, the nature of what you are consuming matters too. What kind of impact is your visual and auditory diet having on your nervous system? Is it serving you to listen to a podcast while you walk or could you benefit from some solo-tasking? Do you need to find some forms of entertainment or means of staying informed that are less agitating? Are there some boundaries around communication that it would help to articulate? See where you can dial down external noise first, and then it is easier to become more skilled in where you direct your attention. Jot down the adjustments you'd like to make.

What to do when you feel selfish for not responding immediately

Darling, it is OK to prioritise life that is happening right in front of you, giving your full attention to what *you* deem important. Remember that often the reward for replying swiftly is not a closed tab, but another response! Grant yourself permission to choose your timeframes of response and let urgency culture slide from your shoulders. What's vital, what's not – you get to define it. If it helps you relax, inform people of your anticipated response time as part of your email signature and have a strategy for making sure messages don't slip through the cracks, such as marking them unread or deleting completed exchanges. You can buy yourself more time by sending an acknowledgement that you will respond when you are able to. Let this take the pressure off and remember, you might answer more effectively with some percolation time.

The volume of communication can be overwhelming so every so often, take an inventory of what comes your way. Be discerning about newsletters or advertising mailouts and allow yourself to delete personal emails without replying where appropriate. Part of defining your boundaries around healthy tech use is giving feedback to others on your preferred methods of communication. For example, if voice notes don't float your boat, let people know. It is not selfish for you to be mindful of how often and when you check in with correspondence, so here's your dispensation to be ruthless with your apps. Switch off notifications, turn off read notifications and use quiet mode. If you need to be contactable, make sure people know which means of communication you are monitoring and turn off notifications for everything else. Gifting yourself this space can take some getting used to, so use the toolkit to feel safe (page 94) and then bring your focus back to the object of your choosing. You have every right to direct where your awareness and energy flow.

Reduce the inner noise

In addition to reducing the number of things that pull at you externally, let's also examine the factors that can create internal noise and what you need to feel relaxed and present. To be able to choose your focus, some basic commitments to self can make all the difference. We will take a deeper dive into your boundaries with yourself in Step 6, I Prioritise Myself, but let us plant some seeds of healthy habits that have a huge impact on your ability to direct your awareness via your senses. If you find it hard to focus, take a gentle but honest look at your relationship with caffeine, sugar and alcohol. Notice how a combination of these can have you feeling like a jittery mess where it is impossible to be present and effective – that's a function of being human, no one is immune. How well are you hydrating yourself? No grand or elaborate change is required at this stage of the journey to knowing yourself better and acting in your own interests. This step is more about connecting the dots and getting clear on what serves you and what hinders you. In these moments where you turn to compensatory behaviours, such as a shot of coffee to wake you up, remember it's OK to need a boost. The practices in this chapter will give you some direct swaps to try out.

Make a note of any tweaks you might like to make. Write down the commitments to yourself that will help you feel more at ease and better able to be present.

With the following practices, I invite you to get out of your head and into your senses. By immersing yourself in your senses you can anchor yourself in the present moment, feeling less tugged by thoughts of the past and less pushed around by fears about the future. Getting present via your own sensory experiences will also help you become a more active participant in your own life. You can use your senses to direct your attention, breaking free from distraction and the things that disconnect you from self. Your senses are the foundation for self-awareness, for knowing yourself and your preferences, and also for self-soothing and healing. It's not about being present every minute of the day, though; that wouldn't be achievable and trying would be pretty exhausting. These practices are about pockets of presence and being able to choose where your attention flows.

There are five basic human senses: touch, sight, hearing, smell and taste. There is also the vestibular sense, involving balance and movement, which helps with skills like riding a bike, as well as proprioception, the body sense, which helps with knowing where a body part is without looking at it. What's to come in this chapter is a practical guide to reclaiming the power of your senses, with meditations for you to explore. Enjoy diving in wherever you feel drawn.

Connecting with your mouth

I invite you to get acquainted with your mouth. This is the place from which you communicate your truth, a part of you that receives nourishment and love. How you hold your mouth has a tangible impact on your nervous system functioning – whether you feel calm or on edge. When you brace with your mouth, it's a signal to the nervous system that it needs to stay on high alert. A soft mouth is a cue that it's safe to relax. So our goal here is initially to gain awareness of what you are doing with your mouth and then we want to create a softening of the mouth, of the lips, tongue, throat and jaw.

Start with becoming aware of your mouth. Identify an activity that you do regularly in your day and set the intention to check in with your mouth consciously at the same time. It could be when you're cooking, commuting, sitting down to open your inbox, watching TV or loo breaks. Become aware of whether you bite, lick or purse your lips, press your teeth together, tie your tongue in knots or breathe through your mouth. Whatever habits you notice, see if you can cultivate a softening. Don't get cross with yourself, just notice and do what you can to let go. We will address mouth breathing together later in this chapter.

A ritual to release your mouth

Start with the tension-releasing movement from your toolkit to feel safe – the tongue stretch (page 97) is the most powerful one. Try the 'fish mouth' from the tender touch-strategies (page 97). Finish this sequence with a jaw massage, taking the heel of your right hand and stroking it from the centre of your chin, up to the right ear ten times, before repeating on the left.

Now that you've relaxed your mouth, sit still and tall and consciously let your lips, cheeks and throat come to rest. Gently press the upper palate with the tip of your tongue, feeling the ease you've created and that lovely sense of loftiness of the roof of your mouth. Imagine that your upper palate is like the dome of a cathedral, there is real space and poise in there. As you press the upper palate, can you feel a sense of lift through the crown of your head too, like your ribcage wants to lift away from your hips?

Let your tongue come to rest, allow it to be wide and relaxed at the floor of your mouth. Hold your mouth like a soft closed smile, letting there be space between the top and bottom rows of your teeth and allowing your eyes to crinkle a little. Notice what the smile does for your nervous system. Feel how it relaxes your jaw, tongue and throat, and broadens the nostrils, making it easier to take a calm breath in. The soft inner smile reminds me of the hammock-like structure of the diaphragm, the muscle in the lower abdomen that supports your breathing. Feel it providing internal support; it might even tap you into a feeling of buoyancy, like the upper palate stroke you practised earlier. Notice too how it feels to breathe through your nose rather than your mouth.

Commit to nasal breathing

Where possible we want to avoid mouth breathing, unless of course you are congested, in which case you breathe however you can. Chronic mouth breathing is another cue to the nervous system that it needs to be on high alert and it has its own health consequences. When we breathe through the nose, nitric oxide is released, which dilates blood vessels and allows greater oxygenation of body tissues. As the nostrils are smaller than the mouth, we have to engage the diaphragm to pull air down into the lungs, helping us breathe more deeply and fully. The stress-busting, relaxation-boosting properties of diaphragmatic breathing are well documented.[1] Nasal breathing also filters and humidifies air as it enters your body, and it engages the parasympathetic nervous system, further promoting a feeling of relaxation. Not only do we miss out on these benefits when we breathe through the mouth, but this also dehydrates the body and can lead to higher incidences of periodontal disease and cavities in your teeth.

Just as you became aware of what you habitually do with your lips and tongue, try to become aware of how you are breathing and where possible opt for nasal breathing. Begin with nasal breathing at rest and as you move through the tasks of your day. You could even incorporate nasal breathing into your exercise, starting with gentle flat walking and building to higher-intensity activity, such as hill walking or jogging, guided by your comfort. Notice how much easier it is to breathe through your nose at rest when you've done some nasal breathing during physical activity, and in time, observe the impact that nasal breathing has on your stress levels.

Welcome to a greater feeling of calm and a very powerful practice to bring your focus back to self.

Get juicy: A 30-second self-soothing exercise

When we are in 'rest and digest' mode, this is when the body gets juicy – releasing all the enzymes and hormones we need for digestion. Production of saliva is part of that natural response. There is a dual-feedback loop at play here: saliva is produced when we feel safe, and the nervous system takes the presence of saliva as a cue that it's safe to relax. So we can encourage the production of saliva to soothe the nervous system. In fact, this is a basic litmus test for all relaxation practices – if after the practice you feel more saliva in your mouth, this is a sign that it is working a treat; if not, maybe that strategy isn't effective for you right now.

Try this simple practice, at first in times of ease and then, once well practised, turn to it in times of anxiety, stress and even panic. Run your tongue around your top row of teeth ten times in one direction, ten times in the other direction. Notice how this stimulates the release of saliva and observe any accompanying sensation of comfort and ease in your bodymind. Couple it with gentle and coaxing inner dialogue and it's a powerful addition to your collection of stressbusting techniques.

Meditative eating and drinking

Other pleasurable ways to develop your awareness of your mouth and enjoy your sense of taste is to eat and drink mindfully. You won't have time to eat every meal and imbibe every drink in this way, but perhaps you can savour the first few mouthfuls or sips, or when you are indulging in your favourite treats, you could give them your full attention, observing the taste, flavour, temperature, texture and consistency. Notice how it feels not only to chew but also to swallow, taking your time with the whole process, taking smaller bites, chewing for longer, pausing to savour the experience.

Harness the power of a yawn

Get intentional about yawning and appreciate the stress relief it offers. Try a daily practice of a minute of yawning, using any stretch that stimulates a yawn; faking a few can lead to some decent genuine ones. Try this whenever you're feeling stuck, fatigued or anxious and notice how a good yawn lubricates your eyes and releases your throat and jaw, and how the deep in-breath and rise in heart rate both help you feel a sense of calm alertness.[2] Noticing authentic yawns can also give you clues to your focus and energy levels. Enjoy using these natural cues to get to know yourself and your needs better. The more you listen, the more skilled you become in taking nurturing action.

Hum for wellbeing

The final practice I'd love you to explore with your mouth is humming. Making sound is a way of deepening the breath, which promotes a feeling of calmness, but vocalising is also developing a foundational skill of self-advocacy. Together we are building our capacity for speaking up so that we can be heard and understood. Nothing fancy required here; hum your favourite song, or whenever you need a moment to recalibrate, place your hands on your heart and make like a bee. 'Bee breath', just a simple hum on the exhalation, feeling the vibration in your chest with your hands, is a lovely way to reset and release tension. If you're up for a laugh, whinny like a horse – let your mouth and lips go completely floppy and shake your head from side to side while making a wuzzying sound on the exhale. These daily practices will prepare you well for honouring your boundaries in Step 6, I Prioritise Myself.

Connecting with your eyes

You have already started being selective with your visual diet (page 122) and the following practices will help you refresh your eyes and can be used as powerful screen breaks. In addition to curating your social media feed and choosing entertainment that uplifts you visually, I'd recommend dotting your home environment and workspace with meditative anchors that you can feast your eyes on. Choose your screensavers well, position photos, art and nature talismans in your line of sight, and let these nourish you effortlessly throughout your day. Train your eyes to seek out these focal points and they can be a useful distraction from the chaos of family life and the delightful mess that comes with it. Treat yourself to some single stems of cut flowers and pop them in places you frequent. I keep one next to the kitchen sink and focus on it while creating order, making it feel much less of a chore. Notice the lift this simple act brings you and how affirming it feels to extend kindness to yourself.

When you are out walking, observe your habitual line of sight. If you are accustomed to looking down, try looking out and up, and seeing what impact this has on your mood and your propensity to notice things that pique your curiosity. While walking, set the intention to seek out anything that you find awe-inspiring, from natural or architectural beauty to people holding hands, and be open to the eye contact that's often a precursor to a cheery greeting. Notice the kinds of stimulation you are allowing in via your eyes and remember that you have every right to choose where you direct your attention.

A ritual to refresh your eyes

1. Begin with a firm massage of the brow area, using the insides of your pointer fingers and stroking from the centre of your forehead out to your temples several times.

2. Squeeze and release the whole eye area with the following sequence: close your eyes tight shut and open your eyes wide while looking right, then repeat while looking left, upwards and downwards. This is particularly good for dry or fatigued eyes.

3. Rub your hands together to create warmth and place your palms over the eye socket, feeling the heat penetrate the eye area, releasing tension. Enjoy the absence of visual stimulation and remind yourself that you are deserving of a break.

4. Finish with one last ritual of touch to close some mental tabs: 'massaging your horns'. Make a fist with both hands and press the base of your thumbs firmly into your forehead, feeling your eyes soften and your rate of breathing slow down. Hold here for five calm breaths and allow this to lead you into your day with greater visual clarity, directed by your choice of focus. Where your attention goes, your energy flows, so enjoy being back in the driver's seat.

Connecting with your ears

We have explored ways to make your auditory diet more supportive to your wellbeing (page 122) and I invite you here to keep noticing what you choose to fill your ears with. I also have a soothing practice to use when you've not been able to protect yourself from unwanted or unpleasant auditory stimulation.

Ask yourself: do you crave silence or is it sound of your choosing that you need? If you need silence, how can you gift that to yourself? We all need it. How else can we hear ourselves? Can you take yourself off for a quiet, solo walk or, if that's not possible immediately, can you schedule one? Even the anticipation of it can be sustaining. If you have a bathtub, make sure all in your care are safe and, if possible, close the bathroom door, fill the tub and enjoy the silence that comes with submerging your ears. Bathe in the silence you've claimed for yourself and see the toolkit to keep safe (page 94), and the love note below on silence and solitude, if guilt interferes with your enjoyment.

If you prefer stimulation of your choosing, have a selection of audiobooks, podcasts, guided meditations, nature sounds and music playlists ready to enrich you. Notice the sounds that bring you a feeling of zest and peace and deliberately seek these out – rainfall and birdsong are two of my personal favourites.

A self-massage ritual for your ears

1. Pinch the top of the ear between the thumb and forefinger, and work your way down the edge of the ear to the fleshy part of the lobe. Rub to stimulate nerve endings and increase blood flow to the area.

2. Starting at the top of the ears, hold the ear cartilage between the thumb and forefinger, and pull it up and outward away from your head, letting the ear slide through your fingers until it is released. Repeat starting halfway down your ear, taking care to reach all the way to the spot behind the ear where the ear attaches to the side of your head before gently pulling outwards. Finish with tugging downwards on the earlobes. The sequence can be repeated several times.

3. Use your index finger to stroke gently down the crease where the ear joins the head several times, being guided by your comfort.

> ### Love note for when you're feeling guilty for needing solitude or silence
>
> *Darling, we live in a noisy world, full of stimulating correspondence and information. It is a lot for our senses to cope with. It is OK if you need time and space to yourself. It is not indulgent or weak to need silence. It is human to feel touched-out. It is not selfish to desire stimulation of your*

> *choosing. Wanting the freedom to express your autonomous interests is not selfish but part of how you resource yourself to be present, patient, available and all the other values you hold dear. Where you can, give yourself permission to savour the absence of stimulation, and relish it. Let yourself turn inwards, allow these sensations of feeling alive to flow through you. Observe how this practice of seeking solitude or silence enables you to hear the whisper rather than waiting for the shout of illness, injury or depletion. That earlier meeting of your needs pays such beautiful dividends.* **Commitment to meeting your needs doesn't mean you don't love your nearest and dearest; it allows you to love them better.**

Connecting with your nose

Of course, the most pleasurable way to focus on your nose is to use scent you enjoy. Just as you made an inventory of sounds you love, list your favourite scents available to you. What are the aromas that you naturally encounter in your day and how can you savour them? The scent of your morning herbal tea, fresh-baked goodies, cut grass, the pavement after it rains, your baby's head. Regularly turn to the mood alchemy of scent with perfume, facial mists, hand balm, body butter, room sprays and candles, and feel the nurturing this provides. Permit yourself to seek out these pleasant experiences and give your full attention to them and to *you*. It is OK for you to receive.

We've already talked about the benefits of nasal breathing (page 127) and another way you can use the nose to support your wellbeing is to work with 'nostril dominance'. It is totally normal for one nostril to be more open, facilitating greater flow of breath, and this dominance changes without our conscious awareness every 30 minutes to six hours, depending on your individual nasal cycle.[3] Breathing through the left nostril stimulates the parasympathetic nervous system while the right nostril activates the sympathetic nervous system. Research shows that breathing through one nostril can have a relaxing effect on the sympathetic nervous system.[4]

A nostril-breathing ritual

This nostril practice can help you feel more alert, energetic and balanced and can relieve headaches and tension. Sit upright and hold either a small mirror, CD or smartphone screen parallel to the floor beneath your nose. After you breathe out through your nose, look at the pattern of condensation to detect which nostril is most open. Use your index finger to close the dominant nostril and, with the first two fingers of your other hand, draw back the flesh of the cheek, opening the less dominant nostril. Take ten breaths through this nostril, making the exhalation longer than the inhalation. If both nostrils are equally open, you could do five breaths through each nostril. Feel the clarity this facilitates.

You can also use nostril dominance to promote sleep: lie on your right-hand side to encourage left nostril dominance, which activates the parasympathetic nervous system, helping you feel drowsy. Enjoy exploring how you can use these subtle practices to support yourself through your day, receiving your own love and care.

Connecting with your hands

Bringing your awareness to your hands can be a beautiful way to help you feel more present in your own life, anchoring you in this moment with compassion. There are a variety of different gestures and actions that you can use to experience a feeling of grounding via your hands. If you enjoy seated meditation, add a hand mudra (gesture) to focus your attention inwards. There are many to choose from but my favourite is chin mudra, where you rest the back of your hands on your thighs and bring the thumb and forefinger to touch lightly, focusing your mind on the sensation of touch between them. This hand gesture facilitates diaphragmatic breathing, which is soothing and quietening. If you want to feel more energetic, try sitting with the palms facing upwards, fingertips relaxed, and notice how this makes the inhalation feel easier. Conversely, placing the palms downwards can enable a deeper exhalation, cultivating a feeling of letting go. Using all three at different times can keep your meditation feeling fresh and responsive to your needs, and remember, this needn't be a huge investment of time, even pausing to sit between emails for a few breaths can be enough to check in and recalibrate.

Rituals for your hands

While you're relaxing in front of the telly or listening to a podcast, try holding your own hand to feel a sense of comfort. It doesn't matter which hand, wrap one hand around the thumb of the other hand and connect with the warmth of your hands and how pleasant it feels to be held. You can be your own safe place. In the process of tending to the skin on your face, whether that be taking off your makeup or applying your moisturiser, add this somatic hold to the ritual: the 'face hug'. Cradle your chin in your hands and give your full attention to the feeling of being held, consciously extending tenderness towards yourself.

For rituals that feel empowering and galvanising, try pressing your hands against a wall at chest height or on a counter top. Spread the fingertips wide like starfish and imagine your palms are like suction cups, the outer ring firmly grounded but the centre of your palms domed and elastic. Apply pressure through your hands while keeping a softness in your elbows and feel the whole of your arms leap into action, supported by the muscles in your abdomen, noticing your own strength. You have your own back, darling.

Enjoy connecting with your inner strength. If you're familiar with yoga, downward dog is a pose that will take this action to the next level, strengthening also your shoulders and back muscles.

For a simple ritual you can weave into daily life with ease, place one hand on your heart when you are drinking a glass of water. As you hydrate yourself, feel the sensation of your hand against the solidity of your chest, helping you feel alive to this moment, reminding you that in this moment you are safe. Be reassured by the sense of containment created by this ritual.

Connecting with your feet

If you want to stand firm and be seen and known, I invite you to get reacquainted with your feet. Please develop a loving relationship with them. They have supported you every step of the way. When was the last time you fondly connected with them? Our feet are an expression of our relationship with the earth and speak to how we feel about our right to be here. Do you claw at the ground with your toes, clinging on for dear life, are your feet collapsed into submission, or do you feel cut off from them, like they're not really part of you? It's time to reclaim them for the incredible structure they are – all 26 bones, a superb feat of natural architecture.

From a firm foundation via connecting with the feet and toes, we have greater access to the muscles of the ankles, shins and calves, lifting upwards like a pair of internal knee-high socks, supporting us. Healthy feet need circulation, and you can support their functioning by working on the flexibility and dexterity of your toes. Barefoot walking, ideally on grass or sand, is a wonderful way to encourage this. If it's not possible right now, perhaps because of the season or where you live, invest in a spiky massage ball or an acupressure mat. When seated, roll the ball with your feet or rest your soles on the mat to encourage blood flow to your feet and help you connect with them. Please massage your feet and use movement that will help you articulate your toes. Imagine that you can spread your toes wide just like you can splay your fingers. Can you move just the little toe on its own? Try doing 'starfish' hands at the same time as attempting to spread your toes – it can help reawaken your feet. This is another thing you can play with while you're watching TV.

A grounding ritual for your feet

Try this simple barefoot walking practice, indoors will do. Step forwards with your right foot, grounding just the heel first, and fan out all your toes. Slowly ground the whole sole of your right foot, keeping the toes wide. Transfer weight onto your right foot, while simultaneously rolling onto the top of your left foot with your left toes under, stretching the top of your left foot. Then ground your left heel and repeat on the other side. Feel how this alternating walking action creates supple toes and feet, helping you feel more in control of them. As you feel more connected with your feet, notice the effect that this has on your posture, allowing you to stand taller and feel more resolute.

How to develop trust in yourself

Self-trust is awareness and belief in your own feelings, opinions and needs. When we trust ourselves, we don't need to rely on the observations and opinions of others so much. This can feel tricky when we haven't been validated or where certain emotions or needs have been unacceptable. You can understand why this is challenging; offer your younger self compassion, and remind yourself that in this moment, you *can* learn to trust yourself again.

Journaling can help with rebuilding connection with yourself. Write down what you are thinking, read it back to yourself and notice what you feel in your body. Try to describe the feelings that are present, using an emotions wheel to broaden your vocabulary. If it is helpful, try writing about how someone else might feel if they had walked in your shoes. There's no right or wrong, just notice what comes up for you. To connect with the younger you, find a picture of you from your early childhood, your teens or your earlier adult life. Hold it in your hands and check in with yourself at this time. Can you connect with how you felt in this chapter of your life? Is there something this younger you wants to share with you? Is there something they need to hear now? Be present to the feelings that emerge, knowing that the feelings won't harm you. They might be painful but the suppression of the feeling is more damaging. If it's hard to use words to make sense of how you feel or to move through your emotions, then consider other creative outlets, such as drawing, painting, scrapbooking, singing, dancing, breathing or just taking it to Mother Nature and letting her support you. Being in or by water, or surrounded by any other natural beauty, can be so healing.

To develop a feeling of self-reliance, work on your ability to keep promises to yourself. Start with really small commitments and build confidence that you can be there for yourself. You have your own back. Take stock of what you've done well and be really gentle in the face of setbacks (see the toolkit on page 239) If you don't know where to begin, let it be with encouraging self-talk (see page 118 for the strategies you need).

Practices for whole-body connection

Now you've had a chance to get back in touch with various parts of you via your senses, let's bring it all together with some whole-body practices. As you explore them, allow these mantras to guide your awareness, repeating them silently to yourself. If you enjoy these affirmations, you can repeat them in everyday life to remind you of the state of calm you cultivate in the following practices:

- 'I am here.'
- 'I am present.'
- 'I am safe.'
- 'I can choose.'
- 'I trust my senses.'
- 'I can cultivate comfort and ease.'

Lying-down practices

By their nature, lying-down rituals are calming and soothing, perfect for when you need to receive energy or when you are preparing for sleep. Try the following practices to feel a grounding of the back or front of your body:

- Lie on your back, knees bent, feet flat on the floor. Place your left hand on your left thigh and place your right arm out by your side at shoulder height, palm facing upwards. Breathe in and relax. Breathe out, press your left hand down on your left thigh and let your head roll to look right. Breathe in, relax your hand and let your head roll back to centre. Repeat ten times before changing hands and letting your head roll to the left. Once you've done both sides, don't be in a hurry to move. Either keep your legs bent or, if it's comfortable, stretch them out long and take ten breaths at rest, feeling each point where your body comes into contact with the floor. Flopping and dropping.

- Bend your knees, ground your feet and this time, place both hands on your thighs. As you breathe in, let your body soften. As you breathe out, press your hands down into your thighs and your feet down into the floor. Repeat ten times, feeling the muscles in your abdomen leap to attention each time you ground your hands and feet. Again, return to a resting position and let your body soften, tuning into the pulses, gurgles and sensations that arise.

- Restorative yoga poses, like savasana, are another glorious way to feel grounded. Lie down on your back with your arms and legs extended, adding a weighted blanket to deepen the feeling of being held.

- To experience an earthing of the front of the body, roll onto your stomach and find a comfortable position for your head. You can either turn your head to the side for a few breaths and then change to the other, or rest your forehead on folded hands. It can also feel nice to roll your heels from side to side, massaging the fronts of your thighs. For a stronger sensation, bend your legs, raise your heels above your buttocks and rock from side to side. Come to stillness with your legs outstretched, toes together, heels dropping outwards, and rest your senses. Enjoy closing your eyes and becoming alive to information from within. You are coming home to yourself.

Standing practices

- Simply stand and rock, feeling your feet on the floor. Babies like to be rocked and we adults are no different. Alternatively, stand still and run your hands over your thighs to help you feel more solid, present, here.

- Go for a walk and let your arms swing. Let yourself take up space, no apologies for being here. Play with the speed of your gait and the length of your stride, and notice how a different pace feels. Sense the grounding of your feet, the length of your spine and the ascent of the crown of your head.

- To connect with the sensation of your breathing, alternate between these two stretches. This frees up tension in the ribcage, chest and upper back, helping your muscles be more elastic and responsive to the expansion and retraction of your breath. As you breathe in, mesh your hands behind your back and look gently upwards, then exhale, round your spine and bring your arms forwards as if you're hugging a tree, letting your chin drop to your chest. Feel how this alternating action helps your inhalation be more spacious and your exhalation feel more complete.

5, 4, 3, 2, 1 practice to integrate all your senses

As you notice your connection with your senses growing, you can bring them all into one practice with the 5, 4, 3, 2, 1 exercise. Identify a salient moment in your schedule to engage in this check-in, or use it whenever you feel off-kilter, letting it guide you back to yourself.

Insert a purposeful pause into your day and get still and quiet. Without judging the experience, just hone your powers of observation and notice the following:

- 5 things you can see
- 4 things you can feel
- 3 things you can hear
- 2 things you can smell
- 1 thing you can taste

Re-enter your day, reminding yourself that you get to choose what you do next. Once this exercise has become a habit, notice the impact it has on your wellbeing.

Follow your impulses

Well done for choosing to claim time and space to come home to your senses, building your skills of being present in your life. When you can hear yourself, you have the power to know yourself. I hope this final practice in the chapter will give you the last clues you need to allow your senses to guide you in your journey to self-advocacy.

As you familiarise yourself with your senses, I hope you are noticing all the ways your body communicates with you about your needs. Are you observing a greater awareness of hunger, thirst, needing the toilet, boredom, loneliness, craving, jitteriness or fatigue? Can you take early action to meet each need and, in doing so, see how that serves you? For example, rather than delaying going to the loo because of other pressing things, notice that when you go sooner, you return to the task making fewer errors and with greater decision-making capacity than if you denied this need and pushed on.

Dig deeper than the want . . . what need lies beneath? I want to reach out for my phone, for comfort food, for coffee, for booze . . . what need is driving this desire? And can we meet that need via a means that supports connection with self, that promotes honouring of self? Look for ways that you can pace yourself with greater compassion. Feed yourself. Move your body. Get some fresh air. Feel some sunlight on your face. Connect with another human being. Let these micro-moments of nourishment fuel you. We're going to take a much deeper look at this in Step 6, I Prioritise Myself, but for now just see if you can build your skills of noticing and responding with care. This is how you take your power and peace back, one tender response at a time.

Your toolkit to seek your own approval

- Know yourself

    This is where we begin. See page 137 on self-trust for useful starting points. Embrace your imperfections as much as you acknowledge your strengths. You are a glorious human being, flaws and all. Write down all the things you appreciate about yourself.

- Accept yourself where you are right now.

    You are where you are. You can take pride in the things that feel aligned and precious to you. You can also grow in areas of your choosing without this involving a character assassination. We are malleable. We can evolve, but let it come first from a place of compassionate acceptance. You are enough, deserving and worthy right now, as you are.

- Understand yourself

    Get to know what drives you. Become aware of those beliefs you hold about yourself and the world. It's OK to challenge what you've outgrown or what never served you. Know your limits in terms of your energy, your pace and your non-negotiables with yourself (see the toolkit to set boundaries with yourself, page 223). Identify your responsibilities. Remember, you are the authority of you. If you find yourself second-guessing yourself, be gentle with yourself. When your reality has been questioned or your feelings invalidated, it can take some time to feel confident in your knowing.

- Identify kindred spirits

    In moments of wobble, allow them to bolster your self-approval. You might like to let them know what you appreciate about them and get brave in asking what they value about you. Hold a loving mirror up to each other, share the journey together, all the twists and turns. With practice, you might find yourself needing to do this less, just remember it's not about doing it all on your own all the time. Let people support you.

- Validate yourself

    Back yourself. This is a skill we build with practice, like developing a muscle. Give yourself permission to acknowledge what is happening for you, within you. Try the following prompts:

    'This is how I feel ...'
    'This is what I like ...'
    'This is what feels congruent to me ...'
    'This is what matters to me ...'

STEP 3

I RECLAIM MY BODY

I am excited to embark on this step with you, helping you reclaim your physical body. You developed your connection with your body via the senses in the last chapter; let's now build upon that awareness to cultivate a healthier relationship with your body, understanding how you can use it to feel safe, confident and courageous in speaking up for yourself. Our goal in this chapter is to come home to the body and reawaken your capacity to be your own safe place, and we'll get 'selfish' by reclaiming the right to experience pleasure. I hope that sounds enticing to you!

Your relationship with your body

Let's start with exploring your current relationship with your body. In Step 1, I Reclaim My Mind, you observed some of the beliefs that get in the way of you extending kindness to yourself. Please revisit any thought loops that came up for you regarding your body. Pause to consider the following: How do you feel about your body? What do you tell yourself about your body?

When I surveyed my 60k plus community on Instagram about the most common themes of negative self-talk, body shaming was top of the list. I'm not surprised by that, but what did stagger me was that people got in touch saying they didn't even realise that critical inner dialogue about their appearance constituted negative self-talk. This script is so familiar, so automatic, so standard that we don't even question it. Watch a few episodes of *Friends* or *Next Top Model* and you'll see why body negativity is the norm. We've been shape shifting for centuries, chasing miniature feet, cellulite-free thighs and everchanging ideal eyebrows, waist measurements and booty size. Until we examine our beliefs about what our bodies are for, we will remain stuck in these self-sabotaging thought and behaviour patterns. It's not enough just to challenge the shitty self-talk, we need to unpick the beliefs that lie beneath them.

Can we allow this exploration to be an ongoing process? The messaging about our physical manifestation runs so deep. The next time you body shame yourself, ask yourself what you've been told your body is for. Is it for sex, for procreation, for other people's titillation, to provide pleasure for others? Or must it be covered to avoid tempting others? What have you been told it should look or be like? What do you see bodies being celebrated or praised for? What is a good body? An acceptable body? A worthy body? *Who* is your body for? Who does your body belong to? It's time you chose the answers to these questions. These enquiries become all the more important if you're in perimenopause, when society has you questioning your relevance, making you feel invisible. Your *own* answers to these questions can set you free.

Let me summarise here:

You don't belong to your parents – they are your protectors, your custodians.

You don't belong to your partner – they are your companion in life.

You belong to yourself.

Your body is not for procreation.

Your body is not for giving pleasure, comfort or nourishment.

You are not a receptacle for someone else's enjoyment or, while we're at it, their wild oats.

Your body is not a trend.

Your body is not a fashion accessory.

The worth of your body is not determined by your appearance, fertility, special feats of physical achievement or any degree of functioning. You may cherish these capacities but the ability to do these things is not the purpose of your body.

The heart of this chapter is reclaiming your body for YOU. What is its purpose? Your body is your home.

Love note for when you notice your body ageing

I thought that ageing was something that happened to old people... I had no idea it started so young! It was in my mid-forties that I began to grapple with changes to capacity and function. At 47 my arthritic toe has recently been joined by a gammy knee that's impeding my ability to move as I desire. As I type it is seven months since my last run. I've noticed age spots on my forearms. I can't seem to grow my hair even to a chin-length bob and those laughter lines, they're deepening, but thankfully not the furrowed brow... I might be feeling old but I'm definitely smiling more now I'm becoming more boundaried – a true gift of ageing. Less tolerance for bullshit.

> One thing I'm learning, having stopped comparing myself with other people, I now need to broaden that skill and stop comparing myself to previous incarnations of me. It doesn't serve me. Look for beauty in this age. It has its own unique charms. I am learning to love my lived-in skin; she tells a beautiful story. Grief and gratitude sit side by side. There are genuine losses but I'm so damn glad to be alive and I won't let anything dim my light – not even me.

How to feel more at ease in your body

To feel more at peace, you need first to pop those bubbles of untruths that you've been told about your body. Keep coming back to the truth that your body is for you. Your body belongs to you. Your body is your vessel, your instrument, your home. How can you actively develop a healthier, more loving relationship with your body? We'll explore in depth your commitments to yourself in Step 6, I Prioritise Myself, but for now, consider these simple everyday ways you can offer up a little more tenderness in how your treat yourself:

- Choose kind, encouraging words (see your toolkit to cultivate kind self-talk on page 118).

- Clothe yourself in garments that feel good against your skin, in colours that make you feel alive. Make sure waistbands, collars, sleeves, cuffs and bras allow you to move and breathe with ease.

- Extend loving touch towards yourself. There are so many ways you can seek opportunities to be gentle in your touch, in how you massage in your face cream, brush your hair, shower or bathe, and remove your makeup. Notice how the quality of your action, the feeling behind it, changes your feeling towards your body.

- Offer your body compassion in how you choose to move. Exercise needn't be unpleasant to be effective, and it certainly doesn't have to be 'huff and puff' stuff. Enjoy moving and stretching for pleasure itself, not only for the physical benefits. Relish engaging in movement that has nothing to do with shrinking yourself – in fact, enjoy filling the room with expansive shapes.
- Can you get curious about sensation? Exploring your relationship with sensation itself can be helpful in cultivating a more peaceful relationship with your body. Rather than leaping to judgement or trying to get rid of challenging sensations, let's set the intention to make space for them. Try this exercise:

Lie down on the floor with your knees bent and your feet flat on the floor. Take your arms out by your sides at shoulder height like a 'T' and start with both palms facing upwards. Make the following stretch with your dominant hand first. If you are right handed, keep your right thumb grounded and rotate the little finger side of your right hand to the floor so that the palm now faces downwards. Keep your left arm relaxed where it is. Gently spread the fingers of your right hand and as best as possible, press your palm towards the floor. Notice the powerful twisting, stretching sensation this creates through your forearm – it is quite intense but see what happens if you can get curious about it. Rather than labelling the experience as negative, see if you can just watch what happens over time, feeling the sensations change when you take a few calm breaths. Can you allow it to be as it is? Can you also notice how the left arm feels at rest, making space for an awareness of other parts of you, rather than allowing only your right arm to feature in your investigation of your body. Aim to be here for at least ten breaths before exploring the non-dominant hand. Hopefully by attending to the dominant hand first, the other one might not feel so intense!

See if you can bring this quality of curious awareness to other physical sensations; this can be particularly necessary amid the aches and pains of perimenopause or when recovering from injury. With this practice we acknowledge that there is this area of tension or pain, although we don't have to get rid of it, and there are other parts of us that feel at ease. In making space for the discomfort, breathing into it, we can create a softening, helping us weather the experience.

My failsafe: The 'face hug'

This is my favourite way to come home to the body with tenderness. When my inner dialogue defaults to body shaming, I get out of my head and into tender touch. Try this loving gesture: rub your hands together to create warmth. Gently cup your chin in your hands, allowing your head to bow and your eyes to close. Notice how reassuring it feels to be held, how comforting this gesture is, reminding you that you can be your own safe place. Affirm to yourself that you are deserving of that same kindness that you so generously extend to others. Melt into the softness of this gesture, feeling how your body is your home and that its mere existence warrants kindness, regardless of shape, size or physical capability. You exist, therefore you are worthy.

Reflection time: What is your body telling you?

Your body is more than your home, it has an inbuilt security system letting you know what it needs. Let's build on the awareness that we tapped into via the senses in Step 2 and broaden it out to the body, looking for ways your body communicates your needs to you. How does your body let you know about hunger, dehydration, or the need for rest, sleep or connection with others, nature or yourself? Read through this list and consider how you can tune into your body to help you identify when things feel off-kilter. Your body can guide you back to alignment. Below are some of the signals to look out for – which ones speak to you?

- Whole-body fatigue or feeling bone tired
- Heaviness in your arms or legs
- Feeling wobbly
- Restless legs
- Shaking or jittery hands
- Sensation of tightness in your chest or shoulders
- Clenching in the jaw or holding in the throat
- Tension in your neck, shoulders or back
- Headaches
- Dry mouth
- Dry eyes or diminished clarity of vision
- Sweating
- Shivering
- Racing pulse
- Rapid changes in your body temperature
- Short or shallow breathing
- Feeling dizzy or spaced out
- Changes to your appetite and libido

- Disruption to your digestion, heartburn, bloating, constipation, excessive need for the loo
- Difficulty getting to sleep or getting back to sleep, early morning waking
- Feeling easily startled or irritated
- Skin issues – rashes, redness, itchiness or other signs of inflammation
- Changes to your menstrual cycle
- Recurring or lingering ailments

Love note for when you're feeling full up

Use this meditation to help you speak your needs more effectively without doing harm.

Dear heart, it's OK to be full up. We all need a little pressure release, a moment to recalibrate. It doesn't mean you're not enough. It doesn't mean you should be stronger. It doesn't mean you're too sensitive. It doesn't mean you're broken. It doesn't mean you've failed. It doesn't mean you should be more resilient. It doesn't mean you aren't capable. It just means that you are human, and that right now, you are at capacity. You are just full up. There is an underlying need crying out to be met.

So let's meet ourselves where we are. No judgement. No criticism. No shoulds. No character assassination. No punishment. Just a tender enquiry. What's happening for you? There's nothing wrong with you, there's just a human need, a feeling.

In a world that distracts us, disconnects us, demands that we subjugate our needs and feelings, it's OK if this feels selfish; let it. Let yourself feel the discomfort of it while knowing you're not transgressing your moral code and still focus on yourself. Let yourself turn inwards. Let yourself be seen. Let yourself be heard. Give yourself a chance to understand and validate yourself, and from that place of knowing you can better express yourself with others.

What can you hear?

If you feel anxious, turn to the toolkit to feel safe (page 94).

If you've reached sensory overload, seek out the love note on needing silence (page 132).

If there is irritation bubbling up, look up the love note for when you feel angry (page 196).

If disappointment is present, turn to the toolkit to sit with this (page 188).

If you are aware of a tricky conversation that needs to be had, head over to the toolkit on page 236.

Maybe you just need to drink a glass of water, get up and out of your chair or look out the window.

If you just needed a moment to gather yourself, close this practice with a few calming breaths, hands on heart. The job is done. Well done for tending to your needs.

How to use your body to feel safe: soothing your nervous system

Just as your body communicates to you, you can also use your body to communicate to your nervous system, promoting a feeling of safety. I introduced the idea of soothing your nervous system in your toolkit to feel safe (page 94), and many of the practices in the previous step on the senses were designed to move you out of the stress response and into 'rest and digest' mode. I hope you have experienced this shift for yourself. I want to take you a little deeper now into the mechanisms at play here. When you grasp how the nervous system works, you will better understand why you feel as you do in your body, and why your body might respond in certain ways to triggers of stress or danger.

Learning how to regulate your nervous system is all about managing stress and finding your way back to calm. Notice I say 'back' to calm. It is not about remaining calm all the time! When we encounter a threat, we want our nervous system to galvanise us into action. Understanding how the nervous system works, and working with it, will help you to better empathise with other people, delay gratification, make sound decisions and act in service of your values. Whether you are preparing yourself to be present and available when you collect your kids from school, returning home to reconnect with your partner, getting ready for that big pitch or conversation, or just in any situation when opinions differ, the ability to manage your stress response is a vital skill. The skill of self-regulation gives you the power to choose more purposefully what you say and do, it makes you feel alive and aligned, and it also helps you sleep at night!

Nervous system 101

The nervous system is the command centre for your entire body, controlling your movement, bodily processes such as digestion, hormone secretion and breathing, as well as memory, thoughts and mood, and interpreting what you see, hear, smell, touch, taste and feel in the world around you.

It has two main parts – the central nervous system (CNS), made up of the brain and spinal cord, and the peripheral nervous system (PNS), made up of the nerves that branch out from the CNS, extending to your organs, arms, legs, fingers and toes. The PNS includes the 12 cranial nerves, one of which is the vagus nerve, central to our work in soothing ourselves. The PNS is comprised of the somatic nervous system, which controls our voluntary movement, and the autonomic nervous system, which guides involuntary processes, the things we do without thinking, such as blinking, blushing, shivering, keeping a regular heartbeat or the pupils opening in response to light. The autonomic nervous system has evolved to keep us alive and safe; it is our very own self-defence system.

The nervous system transmits signals between the brain and the rest of the body including the internal organs. This is not a top-down process; the organs and this neural superhighway communicate *to* the brain just as much as they receive information *from* the brain, shaping what we think, how we feel and what we do. Gone are the days when we thought of mental health as something that just happens in the head. Once you come to appreciate the vast interconnectedness between brain and body, the dual-feedback loop of information between the organs and the brain, any real notion of separateness between mind and body falls away. We all have a 'bodymind' and an understanding of how the nervous system protects us from danger will help us better navigate moments of squeeze in our lives.

Want to feel this feedback loop for yourself? If you witness or even just think about something funny or uplifting, you will naturally smile in response, cultivating a warm feeling of 'positive affect', but let's observe how cultivating a smile by using just the musculature of your body can elicit the same real upsurge in mood. Try this: 'fake' a smile using just your mouth, eyes passive, lifting just the corners of your lips. Hold for a few breaths and just notice how you feel. Don't worry, I don't expect you to feel much in response to this. Let it go. It might even feel good to release that imposter facial expression. Now allow a smile to begin in the crinkles of your outer eye, let it grow to lift the apples of your cheeks and, lastly, let the corners of your mouth lift upwards. Sit with this more genuine smile for a few breaths and observe the warm, spacious feelings it creates. A genuine smile involves the muscles of the eyes – the orbicularis oculi – and research has shown that activation of this muscle influences our emotional state, helps us connect and dials down our stress response.[1] It's not just what we say to ourselves, we can also use our body to help us find our way back to being calm.

What is the stress response?

The stress response is our emergency reaction system, designed to keep us safe when we consciously perceive a potential threat or when the nervous system senses danger subconsciously, via a process known as 'neuroception'. The nervous system is constantly searching our environment for cues, interpreting and responding to it, signalling to the body to relax when it senses we are safe, or sending us into self-defence/survival mode by orchestrating a cascading of physiological responses when it senses danger. To be clear, you don't consciously choose these responses; your nervous system chooses them for you, trying to protect you. If ever you've felt that your body is out to get you, darling, it's not. It is only ever trying to keep you safe. And if you've given yourself a hard time for freezing or not fighting back, darling, it wasn't your choice, your nervous system chose for you, and it is time to forgive yourself.

According to the Polyvagal Theory proposed by Stephen Porges, there are three patterns of nervous system response to our environment:

1. When the autonomic nervous system concludes that we are safe and there is no need to defend ourselves, we are in the state of 'social engagement and connection', also known as 'rest and digest'. In this mode we feel at ease, grounded and settled. The parasympathetic nervous system is engaged, calming the body by lowering heart rate, relaxing our muscles, and the body can devote its resources to digestion, healing and growth. In this state we can be present and connect and empathise with other people; we are more open, curious and able to feel contentment, joy and love. This is a desirable state to be in, not just

because it feels good, but for the health of our relationships, for our ability to respond in mindful, rational, planned and constructive ways to life as it unfolds, and for its promotion of sound, restorative sleep.

2. If the autonomic nervous system detects danger, with a surge of activation, hormones including cortisol, adrenaline and noradrenaline are released, and we then move into the 'mobilisation response', also known as 'fight or flight', characterised by frustration, irritation, anger, worry, fear or panic. Even if we are not yet consciously aware of the danger, we shift into self-defence mode, in preparation for running away or fighting off the threat. There is reduced activation in the prefrontal cortex, the brain's executive command centre, responsible for impulse control, reasoning, problem solving, planning and empathising, and the more primitive amygdala becomes highly active, focusing on threat detection and galvanising the necessary behavioural and physiological responses. These are clearly unfavourable conditions for compassionate conflict resolution. The sympathetic nervous system engages, increasing the heart rate and blood pressure, making us breathe faster. This is no time for digestion or immune response, blood flow is redirected from the skin, stomach and intestines to the brain, heart and muscles, stored energy is released, and we are all geared up for escaping, or failing that, facing the threat head on.

3. If we are unsuccessful in our attempts to flee or fight, the autonomic nervous system has a third survival option available. This is the 'immobilisation response', also known as 'freeze or flop'. If we can't get away, we shut down, we become numb, we disconnect from our bodies, we don't download memories, and our nervous system does all it can to protect us from experiencing pain.

4. Where there is abuse in a relationship, there is another survival response called 'please and appease', which involves all

the polyvagal states.² Appeasement is when your behaviour attempts to pacify or de-escalate a threat. It is a very skillful neurobiological strategy of survival that makes the aggressor or abuser believe that they can trust you, that you are a safe person, that you are not going to fight back, harm them or run away, that you are on board with what they're doing, and it takes a very resilient nervous system to access this social engagement mode voluntarily when under extreme stress. These cues of appeasement can be a valuable attempt to navigate abusive situations where if you don't appease, you are vulnerable to physical and mental injury. Fawning is a type of appeasement that focuses primarily on pleasing others to avoid conflict and promote safety by subjugating one's own needs and boundaries and offering subservience and compliance. It is characterised by befriending or being agreeable, hiding or becoming invisible, numbing and hypervigilance. You can see how relevant the 'please and appease' survival response is in understanding self-abandonment. 'Please and appease' is not your personality or character; it is a state of nervous system functioning. If you are in this state, it is vital to know that you can heal your relationship with your self. You are on that healing journey via these 7 Steps.

After the threat has passed, the parasympathetic nervous system re-engages, bringing us back to 'rest and digest' mode, but it is easier to switch on the stress response than to switch it off, and the frequency of stressors in our modern environment can have us feeling like we are permanently on high alert. Research shows that the neural circuits responsible for conscious self-control are highly vulnerable to triggers of even mild stress, and when they shut down, more primal impulses go unchecked and compassionate reasoning goes out the window.[3] It's not just physical threats that have us responding in this way; the same stress response is elicited when our beliefs are questioned.[4]

It's also the same survival mechanism that's prompted when we turn on the morning news and witness horrific global injustices, during the traffic snarl or sardine commute to work, reading a terse client email, right before that call with your boss, when you receive this quarter's energy bill, as the kids kick off at bedtime, and when you've been lying in bed for 40 minutes, exhausted, tossing and turning, and still sleep won't come. We can see how the body's preparation for fighting, fleeing or freezing doesn't serve us so well in these very natural, frequent and often unavoidable circumstances of modern life.

Meet the vagus nerve

How can we better navigate the volume of stressors and sensory load we encounter in our day? Let me introduce you to the vagus nerve. This is one of the 12 cranial nerves, emerging directly from the brain without travelling through the spinal cord. The cranial nerves are responsible for controlling the smooth muscles of the organs as well as the striated muscles of the head, neck and trunk, and they have the important job of receiving sensation from these areas and sending this sensory information to the brain. In our discussion of the three patterns of nervous system response, we noted that the sympathetic nervous system is in charge of the 'fight or flight' response, firing us up and preparing us for action, and that the parasympathetic nervous system is like applying a brake, calming and slowing us down. *The vagus nerve is the main neural component of the parasympathetic nervous system – and healthy vagal functioning is correlated with our capacity to regulate the stress response.*[5] When the vagus nerve is not working well, research shows an increased risk of conditions including digestive issues such as Crohn's disease and IBS,[6] heart disease,[7] PTSD, depression and anxiety.[8]

The vagus nerve is the information superhighway between the brain, the heart and the gut, and takes its name from the Latin word *vagus* for 'wandering'. It originates in the medulla oblongata in the brainstem and is the longest of all the cranial nerves, reaching from your head, through the neck and all the way down into the abdomen – giving real credence to the notion of 'gut instinct'. The vagus nerve controls the motor functions of the heart, lungs, digestive system, liver, gallbladder, spleen, pancreas and kidneys, playing a vital role in stimulating the 'rest and digest' functions of these organs. It also controls the muscles of the mouth, pharynx (the muscle-lined space that connects the nose and mouth to the voice box and oesophagus) and larynx (the area of the throat containing the vocal cords), facilitating safe swallowing of foods, and speech.

There are two sets of pathways in the vagus nerve – the dorsal vagus complex and the ventral vagus complex. The dorsal side evolved first and is responsible for responding to cues of danger, moving us into the self-protection mode we see in the 'freeze or flop' response. The ventral side is the more recently evolved branch, which responds to cues of safety, supporting our feelings of physical safety and emotional connection with others.

When we feel safe, the ventral vagus is in charge, facilitating social interaction, growth and recovery, inhibiting older defence circuits from being triggered. What we mean by 'regulating the nervous system' is supporting the healthy functioning of the ventral vagal complex, promoting a feeling of calm presence.

It's not all about the vagus nerve though; this is just one of the five cranial nerves involved in the social engagement system. In addition to the vagus, the trigeminal, facial, glossopharyngeal and accessory nerves help us communicate via speech, and non-verbally via eye contact and facial expressions. Together they work to communicate sensation from different parts of the head and neck, and all have a role in helping us feel safe and at ease in our environment.

How is all this relevant to our goal of learning the skill of self-advocacy? Reducing tension or constriction in the face, throat, tongue, jaw, scalp, neck and shoulders, and stimulation of these areas via stretching, movement, massage, oscillation, vibration, deep breathing and posture correction support the healthy functioning of the cranial nerves, helping you stay anchored in calm[9] when you need to. You need to feel safe to be able to represent yourself. I hope you enjoy going back to your toolkit to feel safe (page 94) now you understand why all these facial movements, stretches and massages are so powerful!

In addition to the cranial nerves, the reticular activating system (RAS) is a structure of interest in self-regulation. The RAS, a network of neurons located on the brainstem, governs our feelings of wakefulness, focus and sleepiness, and plays a part in our stress response.[10] Specifically, we want to deactivate the RAS to dial down the stress response. Research has shown that there is a link between forward head posture, where the chin juts forwards, and autonomic nervous system dysfunction.[11] Hello 'turtle neck' (page 99) – now you know why this exercise works.

In addition to your toolkit to feel safe (page 94), I'd like to share with you a fresh practice for soothing your nervous system. This is restorative in nature and can prepare you for sleep by cultivating the ability to relax, and it's perfect for when you can't sleep or in the aftermath of poor sleep.

A body-wrapping ritual

This practice offers a powerful sense of containment, helping you know your outer edges, giving you the reassurance of knowing where you are in space, and the therapeutic feeling of being held. You will need three yoga bricks or foam blocks, a blanket, a pillow, two pairs of socks (the fluffier the better) and, ideally, an eye pillow.

Gather your props and set yourself up so that you can lie on the cushioning of carpet or rug, or use a folded blanket or a yoga mat for comfort. If you have them, place one yoga brick lengthwise at the top edge of your yoga mat, and one either side it to form a box for your head to lie within. If you don't have yoga blocks, you could use three stacks of books to create the same feeling of containment. Lie back with your head nestled within your box, to establish where you need to be in relation to the blocks, and then sit up to arrange the pillow underneath your knees for comfort, and fold the blanket in half and drape it over your hips and legs. Lie down again and tuck the blanket around your hips and thighs to create a feeling of being held. Locate your eye pillow and socks, pop the eye pillow in place and place your arms out by your sides, lightly holding one pair of socks in each hand. Don't skimp on comfort here; add layers for warmth, make sure your head feels cushioned enough, and once you feel completely supported, allow yourself to flop and drop, lovingly enveloped by the props. I hope this feels like a glorious antidote to distraction and a beautiful way to come home to self. Stay here for ten minutes or as long as it feels good to you. You may need to set an alarm.

Rest is a necessity, not an indulgence

Just as we need to eat, hydrate and sleep, we also need rest and relaxation. Rest isn't just a reward for hard work, it fuels you to deliver what is required of you. Don't wait to clear your to-do list (that moment will never come), rest when you need to resource yourself. Far from being selfish, rest makes you more effective in your work, more sound in your decision making, with less faffing, fewer errors. Rest doesn't take your attention away from more important things, it is not a waste of time, it saves time. See the messages you've absorbed about 'doing nothing' for the untruths they are and allow yourself to soften, drop or replenish – whatever you need. Maybe a dose of nature or movement will refresh you. If someone has suggested you're selfish for pacing yourself, see the toolkit to feel safe for how to respond to their judgement (page 94).

If you struggle to allow yourself to rest, take some time to contemplate these prompts and write down your observations as a personal reminder:

- When you are depleted, how does that show up in everyday life, in your behaviour, choices, health and enjoyment of life itself?

- What do you stand to lose if you don't allow yourself time to rejuvenate?
- What does rest and relaxation give you access to that matters to you?
- What are your favourite ways of resting? Include some practices you can turn to when time is tight or energy is low.
- If it doesn't feel safe to rest, which practices from the toolkit to feel safe (page 94) speak to you?
- Complete the mantra: 'I am not doing nothing, I am ...' (Take your pick: resting, healing, replenishing or something else ...)
- Reflect on your favourite self – what does this version of you need?

Now that you're ready to soften, read this love note.

Love note for when you feel selfish for resting or relaxing

Sweetheart, you are human, not a robot. No one has infinite capacity. Don't expect yourself to have laser-sharp focus, to be firing on all cylinders and primed for action all the time. Permission to have a brain fade or just a little moment to yourself. I invite you to allow some spaciousness, some aimlessness. You don't always have to be doing, you can pause and just experience what it's like to be here in this moment. Nothing required of you. Feel this next smooth inhalation, notice the tiny pause and how it turns the corner and becomes the next relaxed exhalation. Feel all the edges to your breathing smooth themselves out.

Recognise how this begins to create a softening in your body. Where do you notice it first? Is it in your shoulders?

Can you feel them drop effortlessly from your ears? Is it in your jaw? Can you feel the space between your top and bottom rows of teeth? Can you feel your tongue broaden and come to rest on the floor of your mouth? Can you feel your eyebrows slide away from each other?

When your mind gets drawn to busyness, can we just acknowledge that it's OK if we don't get everything done today? Can we make space for incompletions, tasks pending, for letting some things wait, for dropping other tasks altogether? Can we allow ourselves the space, the grace?

I know it sounds morbid, but if we died today, the earth would keep turning and the important things on our slate would be taken up by someone else, and so much else would fall by the wayside without cataclysmic effects. Come back to a true perspective of what really matters to you.

We are very much here and present, so let's now cultivate an appreciation for the precious life we have, take it with both hands and ask ourselves, is there something we need to be truly purposeful and effective today? Sometimes it's nourishment, sometimes it's planning time, sometimes it's a hug. Maybe this moment of rest was enough for you to be able to take aligned action, but if something else calls, go do it, darling. You are thoroughly deserving.

Standing-up practices to feel confident and courageous

There's a time for soothing and retreating and there's also a time for standing firm. We can use the body to help us connect with our personal power, stand up for ourselves and take bold, values-led action. Save the lying-down stuff for soothing and replenishing, but for confidence and courage we turn to the standing-up poses. These poses are active and dynamic in nature, connecting you not only with the different parts of your body, but also with how strong and supportive they are. Darling, you have your own back. It's time to feel it for yourself.

'Mountain breath' to ground you

Stand tall with your feet hip width apart and your arms down by your sides. Take ten mountain breaths to get present to the sensation of your body. As you breathe in, stretch your arms out to the side, palms facing upwards, and as you finish breathing in, touch your palms together above your head, looking up. As you exhale, look forwards, turn your palms to face downwards and slowly swim your arms back down by your sides as if you are propelling yourself through water. Aim to grow taller each time you reach your arms above your head, and taller still each time you slide them back down by your sides. There is a simultaneous feeling of sending roots down through your feet and a reaching upwards of shoots through the crown of your head. Notice how much taller you feel after this sequence. Does this feeling of poise give you a little more confidence to speak up?

Greet your upper back

Let's revisit mountain pose, but this time hold it in stillness to connect with the muscles behind your shoulders. We will add a cushion squeeze between the thighs to help you activate the muscles of your thighs too. With a cushion placed between your thighs, raise your arms above your head, cross your right wrist in front of your left and press your palms together. You might need to soften your elbows a little to help you draw your shoulders away from your ears. Press your palms together gently and, reaching up through the crown of your head, lift your kneecaps and squeeze the cushion between your thighs, feeling your body leap into action. Hold here for 5–10 breaths before releasing, shaking out your arms and legs, and repeating with the left wrist in front. While this might feel intense, does it also feel good to you to connect with these muscles of your back? The stronger these are, the less you have to think about good posture – they will hold you effortlessly there.

Meet your side body

Let's explore another variation of mountain pose, this time using 'pistol grip'. Keeping the cushion in place between your thighs, with your arms overhead, interlace your fingertips and then release just the index fingers. Pressing your fingers together, tilt your body up and over to the right, forming a banana shape for the left side of your body, and hold here for 5–10 breaths. Come back to the centre and repeat to the left, stretching the right side of your body. Come back to the centre; you're not done yet! Repeat once more to each side with the opposite interlacing of your fingertips. Feel how this sequence gets you acquainted with the muscles in the sides of your body and reminds you of the strength of your legs.

Connect with your core

Last version of mountain, this time we're adding a twist. This is a very small movement, but it is a powerful way to both strengthen and feel the strength of your abdomen. Keeping the cushion in place between your thighs, raise your arms above your head, interlace your fingers again, but this time press your palms away from your head. Straighten your arms, keep pressing the palms away, drawing your shoulders down away from your ears and, without moving your hips, slowly turn your upper body towards the right. Hold here for 5–10 breaths, before coming back to centre and repeating to the left. Don't let go just yet! Again, change the interlacing of your fingers and repeat once more to each side, keeping the hips still and only turning from your navel upwards. I know this is effortful but recognise how good it feels to connect with this strength in your abdomen.

Fire up your legs

Good news, lose the cushion now and return to feet hip width apart. Having connected with your upper back, side body and abdomen, we're going to bring it together with one last pose. Raise your arms skywards but keep them apart and, looking forwards, bend your knees and sink into a squat as if you are hovering just off the edge of a seat. The lower you go, the greater the challenge, so please adjust according to what feels sustainable. Hover here for 5–10 breaths, reaching out through your fingertips and the crown of your head, feeling the fronts of your thighs, inner thighs and buttock muscles supporting you. Release the pose and notice the liveliness in your legs. Poses like this can help us break free from the feeling of stuckness or numbing of the stress response. It's good to feel alive!

Repeat this entire series several times a week and feel your connection with your body and your strength improve. Notice the impact this has on how you feel about standing up for yourself. Connect with those strong muscles in your legs, your core and your back. Stand tall and remember you have every right to advocate for yourself.

Using posture to help you advocate for yourself

In these exercises, have you felt for yourself how your posture can help you better represent yourself? If you want to stand your ground, use the YES posture – tall like a mountain, open hearted, with an uplifted gaze. It is really hard to speak up for ourselves when we're in the NO posture – rounded spine, downcast gaze. Notice what happens in your body when you move between these two postures. If you look around the room with the stance and attitude of the slumped 'no' posture, what kind of thoughts and feelings does it tend to elicit? If you tell yourself in this stance that you're not worthy, you're not good enough, that you can't do it, that you're selfish, how does it feel? I hope you want to break out of that position and mindset swiftly. Shake it off and now try the 'yes' perspective and posture, and notice how that feels. Couple the stance with phrases like 'I can be OK with this', 'I can try', 'I can be flexible', 'I can speak up for myself' and notice how this makes you feel. You are building the skills to use your body in cultivating the courage and confidence you need in moments where you are called upon to speak up for yourself. More to come on this in Step 7, I Advocate for Myself!

Reclaiming your pleasure

And now for the juicy stuff. I can't wait to explore pleasure with you and encourage you to take your body back for your own enjoyment; to allow yourself to *receive* pleasure. How 'selfish' is that? Historically, women were told to lie back and think of England, not to prioritise their own pleasure, but how much has this changed? So much modern-day messaging about sex comes from porn, where the priority is man's pleasure, often at the expense of women's basic comfort, let alone her enjoyment, and where she is still expected to reach some kind of gratifying theatrical climax! The fact that so many women in heterosexual relationships 'fake it' speaks to the lack of priority commonly placed on female pleasure. I'm here to tell you that *your pleasure matters*.

In this chapter we've explored the science behind the stress response and how your nervous system responds to stressors. Now

I want to introduce you to the concept of glimmers, a concept coined by Deb Dana, complex trauma specialist and author.[12] You can think of glimmers as the opposite to threats – they are cues, internal or external, that help you feel joyful, at ease, peaceful or safe, and they are fundamental to your health. Glimmers shift your nervous system out of the stress response and into the ventral vagal state of 'rest and digest', allowing you to do exactly that – to heal and assimilate the nourishment available to you, resourcing you to cope with life's demands. Far from frivolous, glimmers help you heal, boost your immune function, provide you with pain relief and promote better sleep – in fact, your health depends on them. Pleasure and joy lift your mood, replenish your energy levels, help you recover from stress, alleviate worry and facilitate better creative planning and problem solving. Glimmers give shape and meaning to your life, enhancing motivation and staying power. They can also deepen your bonds, allowing for shared humanity, connection and memory making. Do watch out, however, for short-term pleasure with longer-term costs!

Being open to glimmers in your life

How can you give yourself permission to experience more pleasure? How would you like to receive pleasure? What feels pleasurable to you? I hope that in becoming more alive to your senses in the last chapter, you are already experiencing more warm and fuzzy moments in your day. Enjoy pondering your favourite glimmers, and if you feel stuck, here are a few ideas:

- Feeling the sunlight on your skin
- Listening to birdsong
- Watching a sunset

- Enjoying a hug
- Seeing the reflection of sunlight on water
- Feeling the warmth and comfort of a blanket
- Imbibing the scent and warm glow of a candle
- Sitting with the cat on your lap
- Wrapping your hands around a warm cup of tea

Receiving erotic pleasure via your body

You don't have to wait for the next rainbow to appear to experience pleasure, you can deliberately seek it out. Perhaps the source you're looking for is within fingertips reach ... When was the last time you turned to your body to seek pleasure? Perhaps you're thinking, 'I haven't got the appetite for that ... ' It's not you, it's a function of your energy. Depleted or struggling with the weight of your mental load? It is no surprise that sexual desire is low. Close some mental tabs, maybe reapportion some responsibility, have a rest to replenish and see what blooms. Darling, it is time to get your mojo back.

Now that you are aware of all the beautiful benefits of pleasure, I hope it can get bumped back up your list of priorities. Find some quiet time to explore you again. Start where you feel drawn. There are plenty of resources out there you can turn to but you can't beat listening to your own body. What appeals to you? Do you want to turn out the lights, close your eyes and explore? Do you want to turn *on* all the lights and use a mirror? Maybe the bath or shower might provide some time for you. Get curious here! This is not about anyone else's pleasure, this is all for you. What sensory stimulation calls to you? Is there a scent that seems sensual to you? Do you want to read something stimulating? Do you want to watch or listen to something that piques desire? It's all out there, darling, erotic stimulation created with *you* in mind, and it's vastly different to what you have come to expect from porn made for the male gaze. Give yourself permission to go find what speaks to you.

Half the battle is just getting reacquainted again. Raising kids, perimenopause, you might feel like it's been a long time since you felt alive down there, or like it's not really yours anymore. If sex has felt like an act to please someone else or if the orgasm gap has made sex a chore, give yourself time to shift gears and allow a different purpose to guide you. If this invitation touches on a history of trauma, there may be healing yet to do. I wish you the support you need to reclaim your body for you. You are so deserving of your body to be a source of profound personal pleasure. You can heal, darling.

Develop a passion for Kegels

Touch is obviously one glorious way to reconnect and I invite you to explore what feels good to you, but I also want to suggest another way in: relight your fire by rediscovering your pelvic floor muscles! This might give you an unexpected new passion for Kegels! There is research linking pelvic floor strengthening exercises to sexual self-efficacy – specifically the ability to experience orgasm, improving the duration, intensity and frequency of orgasm.[13] It makes sense that connection with this part of your body will help you feel more sensation, more arousal and create more lubrication during sexual intimacy, and believe it or not, you can climax without any touch, just by Kegels or imagery alone.[14] Don't believe me? Have fun exploring. Remember, you are not just aiming for a little lift, it also involves a release. Think less of the 'switch on for ten seconds' kind of pelvic floor exercises you may have encountered postnatally, and more of a little pulse to sense the muscles and encourage blood flow to the area.

Add your pelvic floor pulses to sensual touch, movements of the hips that feel good to you, and perhaps you might want to make sound. Remember the tongue exercise to get juicy (page 128)? That might benefit you here too, not for anxiety relief but to heighten sensual excitement.

> ### Love note for when you feel guilty for seeking pleasure or joy
>
> *Darling, what tales have you been told about pleasure? Perhaps there are valid sources of pleasure according to your rearing, such as self-sacrifice or service, or was joy in general seen as frivolous or indulgent? Can you gently question whether this ethos serves you and reflect on what it has cost you?*
>
> *What is the purpose of pleasure and joy? They're not just nice to have! If good sleep, a healthy immune system, resilience, access to patience and a buoyant mood matter to you, then here is the invitation to prioritise life-giving pleasure! Let glimmers move you out of the stress response into the healing, empathetic state of 'rest and digest' mode, helping you not only feel safe but to be a calm, safe place for those you love.*
>
> *If you reflect on some peak life moments of awe, joy or contentment, times you felt alive, what cultivated them? Were there some you enjoyed solo? Which did you relish with others? Have they provided rich memories that still feed you now? Who benefitted from this joy (not just in the moment but in the beautiful afterglow)? Can you write down your thoughts now on why it is OK for you to experience joy and pleasure in your life? If there are still barriers, I get it, they can be tenacious ... says who? What does your future self think? Can pleasure help you commit to some healthy habits?*

What kind of pleasure would you like your loved ones to embrace? Why are you any different? Maybe it's just that it doesn't feel comfortable yet. Use the toolkit to feel safe (page 94) to pave the way. Go ahead and make another mind map, this time of life-giving joy bringers, thinking along the lines of your senses, movement, meaning, nature, learning and connection.

Choose a glimmer now, darling, and savour it. You are worthy and even if you don't feel worthy yet, I invite you to feel it anyway. Notice how you feel after you have enjoyed just one of life's pleasures, and the benefits it brings to all you love.

STEP 4

I RECLAIM MY RIGHT TO FEEL

Welcome to the next step in the journey of coming home to yourself: granting yourself permission to feel and express all your emotions. We've explored already how our conditioning has made some emotions acceptable and others off-limits. In this step you will learn just how foundational your emotions are in your journey to self-advocacy. As you've been deepening your connection with your senses and your body, perhaps you might have noticed a growing awareness of your emotions? While this is healthy, it comes with its own challenges! In this chapter, using the skill of self-compassion, we are going to develop your capacity to recognise and move through all your feelings in safe and healthy ways. We'll have a look at the evolutionary purpose of all emotions, why we need them all, and recall the potential harm that can come from stifling or ignoring them. You will learn practical tools to address specific emotional states, such as anger, disappointment, grief and shame. Think of this as the step-by-step guide to how to feel your feelings. It's time to get 'selfish' and take back your right to feel.

In this process of reclaiming your feelings, we need to be clear on what we're aiming for. I've had the privilege of working with many women who have come to me for therapeutic support in nurturing their emotional health, specifically to connect with their feelings and harness the power of them. In this journey, sometimes we conflate 'feel better' with 'feel happier'. From the outset, we need to clarify that feeling better is not necessarily going to mean feeling only pleasant emotions more frequently. Feeling better is about being aware of all your feelings, and this is likely to dial up the intensity of all of them! The more progress you make in building your skills of emotional awareness, the more perceptive you become, and this may feel like heightened sensitivity. In this journey to taking back your right to feel, don't interpret it as failure if you are noticing more sadness, more grief or more anger. It is a good thing, but it can be intense and overwhelming. These are in fact triumphs, vital clues that you are reconnecting with yourself; we just need to give ourselves permission to experience them and learn what to do with them.

If you are early on in your feeling journey, or healing in the aftermath of trauma or loss, you might be afraid of opening the floodgates to your emotions. Just the thought of feeling more might be scary. You might be fearful of losing control, feeling like you must try really hard to regulate your emotions or stay calm all the time to avoid overwhelm. Remember, that's not your job. The intention here is to move through your emotions and consider the messages they offer you. Despite the discomfort of some of them, it's not the experience of emotions itself that causes problems, but the resistance to and suppression of them. Emotions are not the problem, in other words, it's how we respond to them. While they might not always be pleasant, let me reassure you, they can't harm you. They are temporary, passing experiences. Given a little time, space and compassion, they will dissipate on their own. I will share a practice that will help you sit with the tricky feelings later in this chapter (page 184), making space for emotions by experiencing them drop by drop, rather than all at once. We'll do it together, darling.

What to do when you feel selfish for having emotions

I want to acknowledge how hard it can be to give yourself permission to feel when you have been shamed for feeling. I'm aware you might be fearful of being seen as selfish, oversensitive, weak or needy, so let's make space for these feelings with this next exercise, learning to meet yourself with compassion.

Find a comfortable and safe place where you can be with your thoughts and feelings undisturbed. Get in touch with the discomfort you feel when emotions bubble up, this feeling of not wanting to be selfish. Let yourself recognise how much of a struggle it is to notice what you feel but to also deny yourself the right to feel, to have needs. Feel the tension between you noticing what you desire and you not wanting to be seen as selfish. Take some time to connect with your body, noticing the sensations. Just let them be there. Allow any thoughts to come up and let any memories float to the surface, helping you make sense of why you feel as you do. You are just connecting with this desire to be selfless, this aversion to selfishness, the discomfort of having emotional needs. Don't try to fix it or change it, just connect with it. As you do, notice the part of you that is struggling as a result. With tenderness, witness the part of you that suffers because of what you've been told and how you've been treated.

As you do this, observe the part of you that is noticing that suffering. Take this observing part of you, imagine it leaving your body so that you can look back on yourself, sitting here, struggling with your thoughts and feelings about emotions, selfishness and your right to feel. Acknowledge what this looks like on the outside, and recognise that inside you, you are hurting. Don't answer yet, but ask yourself: Can I be tender with this person who is hurting? Is this a whole person who deserves a right to choose themselves, to advocate for themselves? Is this person worthy of the right to feel, the right to express themselves, the right to autonomy?

Now allow your observing self to move even further away, all the way to the other side of the room, looking back on yourself sitting here, with these painful thoughts and feelings. Again, ask yourself now from this vantage point, but do not answer yet, what do I think of this person sitting over there. Are they worthy of self-expression, is it OK for them to feel their feelings, honour their boundaries? Are they worthy of the hopes, desires and dreams they have for their life?

Now as you look back on yourself from across the room, imagine that ten years have passed, and your future self is now looking back at you. From this wiser version of you, how do you want to be in relationship with yourself? What would your elder self say to you right now? Can your elder, more compassionate self see someone worth caring for? Someone worth standing up for, even fighting for? Are you worth caring for? Are you worth advocating for? Are you enough as you are right now? What would your future self whisper to you right now? Take note of the advice, darling, let it gently land. Repeat these words: 'You are safe. You are loved. You are held. You have every right to feel.'

Emotional health 101

In Step 1, I Reclaim My Mind, we learned that thinking well doesn't mean that we have only positive or constructive thoughts. We clarified that mental health is the ability to cope with all our thoughts; similarly, emotional health is not the absence of difficult emotions, it is the ability to feel all your emotions and move through them in ways that don't cause harm to you and those around you. There are no positive emotions and there are no negative ones, we need them all. For sure, some feel more comfortable than others, but this binary approach to judging emotions gets in our way. Make space for them all, my friend, and listen to what they have to share with you.

The senses deliver information to the body about the world, and emotions provide information about the self and its relationship to what's happening in the world. Emotions are real-time raw data, sparked by sensation in the body, and they are essential to navigating the landscape around us and within us, keeping us safe. Emotional cues arise before the conscious brain registers our needs. Joy, sadness, anger, fear, disgust, trust, surprise and anticipation are the primary emotions. They move us to fulfil our physical and mental needs, so you can see why they are so important in our journey to self-advocacy. They help us learn from our experiences, shaping our expectations and giving us clues as to how we should act.

Joy encourages us to approach or seek means of repeating something that worked out advantageously. Sadness moves us to find comfort or a replacement for our loss. Fear moves us away to seek protection, it prompts us to correct an imbalance or find a solution to a potential problem. Anger galvanises us into self-defence or self-preservation. Disgust moves us to avoid, steering us away from danger and preventing something unpleasant from occurring again. Surprise ignites us into paying attention. Trust helps us to broaden our focus and be open and vulnerable to deepen our connection with people we deem safe. Anticipation gives us zest and increases the likelihood that we will keep making decisions that affirm this path.

The uncomfortable emotions can be seen as protective signals, physically moving us away from danger back to safety, or motivating us to make course corrections to repair ruptures in our relationships. They help us escape where it's needed, deal with the problem at hand, and accelerate learning how to avoid threats to our health and safety being repeated. The more pleasant emotions can be seen as signals of growth; they are deeply validating, helping us feel confident that we are on the right track. Their purpose is more about self-preservation and self-development.

Emotional feedback is the flow of sensory information back and forward between the world and the body, creating our sense of self and helping us take action that brings safety, alignment and meaning to our lives. When we are ignorant or deliberately dismissive of our emotions, we are at odds with the body, we give out mixed messages and there is a cascading of conflicting hormonal releases, which is harmful for our health and our relationships. Cravings, compulsive habits and short-term pleasure seeking can be signs of a neglected self. We know that suppression of emotion is harmful to our health, being linked with a whole host of debilitating issues including autoimmune diseases, chronic pain conditions and even the risk of earlier death.[1]

Culturally we tend to talk about emotions and feelings interchangeably, but there is a distinction. Emotions are the root response to stimuli anchored in the body; they can be experienced consciously or subconsciously, and they are always present even if we are not aware of them. Feelings are more specific than emotions and you can think of them as conscious expressions of the emotion, mediated by thought and shaped by our learnings. They're the story we create around the sensations, helping us make sense of them. Feelings can be learned responses to certain emotions; for example, we might learn to feel shame or guilt in the presence of anger. Feelings shape our identity, teaching us what we need to develop in ourselves to be able to better represent ourselves and interact effectively with the world. Emotions and feelings have important clues for us and we need to attend to both, digging deeper to find what lies beneath if we want to find congruence and peace in our lives. We are robbed of vital information, crucial feedback from the bodymind, when we are told our emotions are not welcome and are denied the right to feel freely.

A 3-step plan for healthy emotional expression

All your feelings are OK and while they don't require fixing, they do require acknowledgement, understanding and validation. We need all our emotions to keep us safe, but that doesn't mean we can express them however and whenever we want. It is also OK to choose when you attend to your emotions, as long as they are getting a look in. For example, quite often people voice concern that they're delaying the grieving process by not making space in the moment, but modern life doesn't always allow us that kind of freedom of expression. You don't choose how you feel but you do have choice in how you voice your feelings and the actions you take or decide not to take in response to them. There is a difference, too, between validating an emotion and validating the source. For example, we can tenderly acknowledge the presence of anxiety but at the same time be discerning as to whether the threat is real. Emotions need some gentle conscious interrogation – the sensation is just a messenger; it doesn't mean it's the gospel truth. We need a step-by-step plan to connect us with our feelings and to determine what we might need to do in response to them. Our feelings don't tell us what to do; that requires critical thinking to decode what we feel is the appropriate action, guided by our values. Let's work through that plan now.

1. Give yourself permission to feel
   When you notice the sensation of emotion arising – maybe it is fear that shows up as butterflies or tension in your belly; the warmth of joy swelling and radiating in your heart; the heaviness or sinking sensation of sadness; the heat or pinpricks to the cheeks of shame; the pang in your chest of guilt; the dry mouth or racing pulse of anxiety; the drooping shoulders or downcast gaze of grief; the furrowed brow or clenched fists of anger – whatever it is, just notice and if you can, pause to

give it your attention. It might not always be possible to do this but recognise what's emerging and be with it as much as you can. If you're not able to attend to it, in the middle of a work meeting for example, make a mental or physical note and come back to it later. This means you reduce the likelihood of emotional suppression. If you're able to, get *curious* about the sensation, and scan your body for other signs such as your rate of breathing, where in your body you can feel it move, muscle tension or ease, numbness, shaking, nausea, shivering, heat, clarity of vision or lightness. Is it an emotion that is geared towards self-protection or one that's more geared to growth and self-development? Without judging the experience, or giving yourself a tough time for having it, gently notice. Pay attention to the narratives or self-talk loops that pop up too and, if you have a chance, jot down any that get in your way of you feeling as you do.

2. Reflect on what this experience means for you
Having connected with the physical sensation, can you describe the feeling attached? Can you name it? A rich vocabulary to describe your feelings can be very helpful; emotional granularity can give you more nuanced clues to the action you might feel inspired to take. For example, rather than just feeling bad, being able to tease apart boredom from irritation from frustration can help. Can you decode the message in this for you? And remember, while the feeling is real, is the source valid? Have we got the wrong end of the stick or are we imagining a threat that in reality might not be the truth of the matter? At this point you might also like to reflect on whether this feeling is appropriate to the situation, whether its intensity is justified and whether it is helping or harming the situation. Taking the time to check in with *compassion* can bring a little perspective. In the heat of the moment, this might be challenging, and we might need to use our toolkit to feel safe (page 94) to dial down the stress

response and get our empathetic, problem-solving brain back in action.

3. Choose what you do next . . .
   Sometimes we just need to surrender and make space for our feelings, allow them to move through us, like having a good cry to release disappointment or sadness. Sometimes we need to harness them so we can use their energetic charge in standing up for ourselves, like channelling anger to find the courage for a difficult conversation. Sometimes we need to intervene, to soothe and release feelings such as bedtime worries. Sometimes we need to give them our full attention, savouring the ones that have the potential to light us up, such as awe and appreciation. Sometimes we need to listen to their wisdom, guiding us not just in a practical sense to our human needs (such as hunger, dehydration and sleep) but also from the perspective of alignment with our values. Sometimes our feelings will let us know that action is required: a little more preparation if self-doubt pops up; checking in with others or reconnecting with self in the presence of loneliness; a different future course if embarrassment taps you on the shoulder; and repair or course correction if guilt looms large. Let this be a learning opportunity. What might you do differently next time this feeling arises or is there some kind of inner or outer change calling to you? Sometimes there is nothing to be done but feel and be tender with yourself during the process, and other times it can help you to do something physical to discharge the energy of the feeling. You'll find separate toolkits for anxiety (page 95), disappointment (page 188) and how to vent without being toxic (page 193), as well as a love note for anger (page 196). Whatever the feeling, whatever the message, compassion is key. Remember, this too shall pass. No feeling is terminal. Sometimes we need to borrow the calm, abiding centre of a friend or therapist. For those more charged emotional experiences, you don't have to do it on your own.

Your toolkit to sit with difficult emotions

You might be thinking that it's all well and good to be with joyful feelings, but what about grief, anxiety, anger, shame . . . how can we cope with those? Anger we will deal with separately, but here is a practice you can use to help you sit with your emotions. The purpose of this practice is not to avoid or get rid of any emotion or distract you from it in any way. The aim is to develop your capacity for bearing witness with tenderness to what you're feeling, to help you be safe to feel, anchored in this moment not in the trauma of past experiences, and to broaden your perception of other sensory experiences so that feeling your emotions is less overwhelming. You can use the following practice to make space for feelings, and it's equally useful for challenging thoughts, sensations or memories.

1. 'I am noticing the presence of . . . '
   Begin by noticing whatever feeling is present and see if you can name it. Use an emotions wheel to get more expressive. Get curious about where you feel it in your body and see if you can describe it, allowing the sensations to be exactly as they are. Rather than identifying with the feeling by saying 'I am sad', use the phrase 'I am noticing the presence of a feeling of sadness', or anxiety, or whatever is relevant. Notice your reaction to the feeling and counter any self-limiting beliefs or judgements that come up. You have every right to feel as you do. How would any human feel? All your feelings are welcome. Using the phrase 'I am noticing the presence of' reminds you that this is a transient experience; it won't be like this forever. You are accepting that this is how it is right now, and the following steps will help you weather the experience of it.

2. 'I am in this body.'
   You are still noticing the presence of this feeling, and you are also in this body. Run your hands across your thighs to connect with the present moment. Feel your feet against the floor or the support of the chair beneath your sit bones. Feel the chair holding you and the floor rising to meet you. Notice the length of your spine and remember the 'yes' and 'no' posture we explored in the previous chapter. See if sitting taller helps you feel a little more resourced to witness this emotion. Sense the crown of your head lifting and press the tip of your tongue to the roof of your mouth for that inner lift. You are capable. Are there any movements that might feel good to you, helping you digest your feelings? Be guided by your body: try a little shake of the hands to flick off uncertainty, a spacious stretch of the arms to release worry, a twist to see things from a fresh perspective, or maybe put your hands on your heart to offer yourself some comfort. There is the presence of this feeling and you have this body, providing you with support and movement to help you soften into this experience. Seek out parts of your body that feel relaxed and let your awareness span not only the emotion and its related bodily sensation but also other parts of you that are at peace. Yes, there is this heaviness in your chest, but your arms feel at ease or your face feels calm. You are making space for an awareness of it all and perhaps this helps you cope with the emotion.

3. 'I have this breath . . .'
   The emotion is still present, but let's check in and see whether it is changing at all. It doesn't matter if it isn't, we're just reminding ourselves that feelings come and feelings go. You are noticing the presence of this emotion and you are also experiencing this breath. Nothing fancy is required here, just allow your breath to be calm and relaxed. Sometimes it feels better to move with the breath, making it easier to breathe expansively. Place your fingers on your shoulders and move

your elbows with your breath: inhale to lift them up; exhale to take them back and down. Notice if moving with the breath has any impact on the sensation of the emotion, or on your ability to be with it. I hope you experience that a calm breath gives you courage to feel. Perhaps if you welcome a more spacious breath, it might help you release a few tears and that can be such a powerful wordless release. There's no right or wrong though, darling.

4. 'I am in this place . . .'

    You are still noticing the presence of this feeling, observing how it might be changing, and you acknowledge that you are in this place. Look around you, just the act of looking up and left and right can soothe the nervous system. Allow your eyes to soften and take in the peripheries. We spend so much time in close vision, narrow focus, which is very activating for your nervous system. Encourage ventral vagal activation by looking out the window at the canopy of moving trees in the distance or the changing cloudscape and feel this calm you. Look around the interior space and seek out anything that piques your curiosity or uplifts you, such as photos or art on the wall. Yes, there is this feeling, and you are in this environment with the sounds, scents and sights available to you. Some are providing you with the comfort that you need to be able to sit with this feeling.

5. 'I am in relationship with . . .'

    You make space for the presence of this feeling and you connect with other beings around you. If you can see someone dear to you, you can remind yourself that you are having the experience of this emotion and that you are also connected with this other person. You can reach out to the other person for love and support. Even if you don't know the people around you, you can remember that no one is immune from these feelings, and that feeling less alone in it can help. Maybe you have a pet you can snuggle with for comfort. Even in the absence of people, you can connect with Mother Nature and feel a sense of belonging. Gaze at a photo of someone you care about and feel wrapped up in their love. Yes, there is the presence of this emotion, and you are also embedded in this very real web of support. Does that awareness help you manage the experience of this emotion?

Once you've gone through the five steps, notice if the experience of the emotion has changed at all. Perhaps it has dissipated a little or maybe you feel differently about having it. If you began with sadness, maybe at the end of this process you are noticing that what lies beneath it is love. If there is something you need, reach out for it. You are deeply deserving.

> ### Love note for healing shame
>
> *Sweetheart, shame is healed by your own compassion and the tender witnessing of people you trust. Lightly explore the root of your shame and ask yourself if it was something you instigated or if it was something that happened to you, not of your choosing, completely beyond your control? If the responsibility lies with you, observe gently, darling. You are human and it's OK to make mistakes. You can do a bad thing and it doesn't mean you are a bad person. Forgive yourself and forgive yourself again, every time you pick up this shame. If it was the result of the actions of someone else, or just one of life's blows, darling, the shame does not belong to you. It never did. Either way, it is time to allow yourself to heal. If you've heard the words, 'What's wrong with you?', if you've been shamed for feeling, needing or just existing, the deficit was never yours. If you froze or didn't fight back, that was not your conscious choice. Your nervous system was just trying to protect you.*
>
> *Shame thrives when it is kept secret. Reach out to a safe, empathetic person and share your shame with them. Allow them to comfort and reassure you. Repeat as needed and*

feel the shame dissipate. Consider seeking therapeutic support first for wounds that feel too big to share with your close circle; the healing support can come in waves. Please don't give up on yourself, even if others in your life have. That is more about them than it could ever be about you. We can heal and in time what will bloom from your shame is a deep pride in your survival. Plot out your timeline of grit, what you've weathered and overcome, and feel the warmth in your heart. Place your hands on your heart or cradle your chin in your hands and let yourself receive tenderness. You are healing. You are already worthy. You are already whole.

What would your life look like if shame wasn't present? What would it look like if you allowed gentle pride to take its place? What would you do or say to yourself? Can you do one of these things now anyway? Try, darling, and see what blooms.

Your toolkit to sit with disappointment – in yourself and in others

Disappointment – in others and ourselves – is a natural part of being in relationship with other humans. It's unavoidable despite our collective diligence and thoughtfulness, and we just need a practical toolkit to help us work through it. Use this toolkit when you're feeling let down by others, when you feel misunderstood, when others haven't been able to validate your emotions or meet your need in the moment, but equally use it when you feel disappointed with yourself for failing people you care about. This is likely to happen in our journey to self-advocacy, as we become more skilled in voicing requests or shifting the nature of our boundaries.

1. Let's begin by digging a little deeper beneath the feeling of disappointment. Disappointment is sadness or displeasure caused by the nonfulfillment of our hopes or expectations. There can be many threads to it, so don't pause at sadness, go beneath it and you might also find anger, frustration, irritation, melancholy, even grief. What is it that you're feeling? Name as many feelings as you can and give yourself tender space to feel them. It will help to have this chance to vent or release before trying to make sense of your experiences or seek the growth opportunities.

2. Next, consider why you are feeling as you do. Take a thorough appraisal of the situation, mapping out what happened, noting what went awry and identify the source of your disappointment – was it you, was it the actions of someone else, or was it just life in general? Have circumstances made some treasured plan untenable? I'm so sorry for your disappointment, darling. I hope there will be a fresh opportunity or a new alternative that can bring you joy. It's not selfish to mourn your losses and grieving doesn't negate your gratitude for other blessings. You have every right to feel as you do but it will also serve you to stay anchored in healthy perspective. Give yourself time to move through your feelings and then turn your attention to making plan B or rebuilding in the aftermath.

3. Did someone let you down? Did they fall short of something they promised or were they unable to meet your needs when you came to them for help? In your review of what happened, are you being fair to the other person? What other factors beyond their control were at play? What did you contribute to the situation? Were your expectations reasonable? Did you clearly articulate your hopes or your needs? Did you ask whether they had the capacity at that moment? Were they the appropriate person to lean on – did they have the capability to meet your needs? Can you make some kinder attributions as to why they may have failed to rise to the occasion? Can you depersonalise

it? What was going on for them? Can you also zoom out and look at what they are doing well in your relationship? If there is feedback required, how can you give that in a way that facilitates understanding and growth, rather than it coming across as a complaint? Polite, clear requests serve us all better. What have you learned about yourself, the other person or your relationship from this experience and what might you do differently next time? Who else can you turn to for the understanding, validation and care you need and deserve?

4. If you are disappointed with yourself, ask yourself similar questions to those above. Were your expectations of yourself realistic and was it clear and reasonable what was being asked of you? Other than interpreting it as personal deficit, what other reasons contributed to you not being able to rise to the request or challenge in that moment? Drill down into what your true responsibility was in this situation. Sometimes we come away from exchanges feeling guilty for not being able to take someone's suffering away – but that's not our job, there is no failing there. In fact, it is a great gift to be allowed the permission to feel, to let it all hang out without being rushed back to 'being OK'. A sign of your growth is knowing that your value as a human being doesn't depend on everyone else around you being OK. That doesn't mean that we are uncaring. It means that we allow people to have their own emotions, that we are there for our loved ones without taking it all on, that we can be authentic in our connection with each other.

5. Identify and take any action required. It's important that we take time to listen to our disappointment, because disappointment unacknowledged and unspoken often hardens into resentment, which can be toxic. When you tease apart the different threads of your feelings, what are they calling you to do? Is there something that needs to be addressed with yourself or other people? Is there grieving to be done? Is there an injustice that you have every right to feel angry about and something that needs to

be set straight? Do boundaries need adjusting with yourself or others? Do you need to speak up and give feedback so the pattern can be shifted? If we don't give voice, people won't know the harm they are causing and it's not fair on them to expect any change in behaviour. We have to own our part in patterns continuing and if you're feeling unappreciated, take a look at that. It is not selfish to compassionately let people know how you feel. It is selfish to *not* voice your feelings, expect people to do things differently and then be scornful when they repeat the action. We are not always on the same page as the people we are close to and where there is a mismatch in values, until we bring that to light, we will keep coming into conflict over unmet expectations. Don't just let them simmer away, discuss and seek commonalities and compromises.

Forgiveness is so powerful too. Can you forgive others who've fallen short, can you forgive yourself, knowing that it's not humanly possible to get it right all the time, nor can others be all you need in any given moment? Maybe you need to make amends, repair or just communicate regret that you couldn't assist as they needed, but you do care. Permission to shed people who continually disappoint you after gentle requests have been made, who give apologies, but whose assurances of change never come to fruition. You have every right to choose the relationships you invest in. Please prioritise those characterised by warmth, care, reciprocity and respect.

Disappointment is a valid feeling and, as with all feelings, part of our healing journey is to develop our tolerance for it. Journaling can help to process disappointment – use the toolkit to navigate setbacks (page 239) and take your pick from the practices in the toolkit to feel safe (page 94). Be gentle with yourself, sweetheart. You are doing beautifully. In time some genuine silver linings may just emerge too.

Reclaiming your right to feel anger

We've been told so many stories about anger and perhaps your own experiences of toxic anger have led you to believe that it's a dangerous or unhealthy emotion. My darling, anger has a crucial place in our lives and whether we consciously allow ourselves to feel it and express it or not, there is a cascading of physiological responses in the body when the emotion of anger is present. It is unhealthy not to allow ourselves to feel it and the messages it holds are essential for us in knowing our needs, our limits and clarifying what matters most to us in life. If you find it hard to accept anger, let's look at what often lies beneath it.

There are many valid threads at play here: worry, fear, irritation, annoyance, frustration, feeling hurt, insecure, attacked, violation of our values or personal freedom, feeling overloaded, overwhelmed, overstimulated, stressed, a lack of clarity or control, feeling let down, disrespected, unfairly treated or burdened, invalidated or gaslit, humiliated, shamed or embarrassed. We might also feel anger when present-moment triggers take us back to previous painful experiences, such as the raising of voices. Loss and bereavement can bring waves of rage. We feel anger when we're unseen, unheard, our will is thwarted, and when we're trapped and feel helpless. Anger is also a function of depletion: we feel it when we're mentally fatigued, physically exhausted, sleep deprived, nature deprived, hungry, dehydrated, when we've consumed too much sugar, caffeine or alcohol, or spent too much time on screens. Pain and inflammation are a common source of anger, and you'll probably have noticed a pattern with the hormonal shitstorm of your cycle and even more so in the chaos of perimenopause.

Can you see how anger is a normal part of life? We just need to get better acquainted with it and listen to what it's alerting us to. Now clearly, not any expression of anger is OK; we know how harmful toxic anger can be: explosive outbursts, personal attacks, verbal abuse, blaming, shaming, shouting, gesticulating, physical aggression or violence all leave emotional scars, but please don't demonise anger itself.

There is a place for all emotion, regardless of what you've been led to believe growing up. Anger moves us to stand up for ourselves and those in our care. It physically galvanises us to protect ourselves or defend our beliefs, and sensing it gives us an opportunity to clarify our values and recalibrate boundaries. It gives us not only essential clues to what we need to feel safe but also the energy required to protect ourselves. You need anger in your emotional toolkit to determine where incongruence lies and be able to take action to address it. Where there is injustice, let's not be too quick to soothe anger away. Use it as fuel to fire you up and take courageous action. Channel it, my love. You have every right to feel it and use it purposefully. Consider whether the charge of it is helpful or a hinderance in speaking up for yourself.

Your toolkit to vent without being toxic

We have every right to be angry, but this doesn't give us a dispensation to take it out on people around us. We need tools that keep our expression of anger healthy, helping us let off steam so we can more skilfully represent ourselves with a cool head.

- Shake it off with a deliberate flick of the hands, letting the excess charge of your anger leave the building.

- A 'shrug and sigh' can help you move through the pent-up feelings: breathe in and make a fist, bend your elbow and squeeze your shoulders up to your ears, and exhale with a sigh to let it all go. This feels so good you're likely to want to repeat it at least three times.

- Making sound can help (you can try 'bee breath' for this – see page 129), or humming or singing a song you like.

- Some cathartic swearing (away from other ears) can feel good.

- 'Lion breath' can help you roar it out with a wordless release: breathe in through the nose and exhale through the mouth with the tongue extended as far out as possible. Repeat three times for some deep catharsis.

- Write it down and then toss it away so you don't read it back and swallow all the angry feelings again.

- Once you've dissipated the excess charge of your anger, you might still need some validation. Ask a friend if they have the capacity to be there for you and when the time is right, voice it so you can be witnessed and validated – of course you feel as you do.

After you've shaken off the jangly energy with some of the above strategies to vent without doing harm, use these next practices to connect you with your personal power so you can advocate for yourself from a place of contained, controlled, values-led energy. You are channelling the fuel of anger to be deliberate in standing up for what you believe in, keeping the empathetic functioning of the pre-frontal cortex so you can commit to peaceful but powerful word choice. Nonviolent communication is vital – what we say and how we voice it matters. But we must voice it – if we don't speak up, how will we ever be understood? How do we get ready for these conversations? This is where your 'yes' posture is essential (page 167), allowing yourself to take up space and command the room with your physical presence without being threatening. Try your 'mountain breaths' (page 165) to fill the room, use 'monkey grip' (page 237) to feel the strength of your core, and practise 'moving warrior' (page 237) to feel confident and resolute.

Your toolkit to stop losing your shit

Let's reframe this gently to 'stop losing your shit so often'. It's not feasible to 'never lose your shit'. Sometimes anger will bubble up and we won't handle it ideally; this is human. Perhaps we can aim for 'not completely losing your shit'.

- If you want to learn how to better manage your emotions, especially anger, don't start in the heat of the moment. Start with moments of relative peace and in those pockets of time, connect with your body, your breath and your senses. Just notice what's happening and see if you can come to a sense of acceptance of what's unfolding inside you. Our mission here is to be in 'rest and digest' mode, where the breath is spacious and our muscles are relaxed. Go back to your 'candle breath' (see page 96) to cultivate a feeling of calm: breathe in through your nose and exhale through pursed lips as if you are cooling a cup of hot tea. Try five breaths and feel how this soothes you. Consciously relax your body and extend a quality of softness towards yourself. Once you've built your capacity for doing this in peaceful times, you can start practising this skill in more charged moments, helping you express anger and advocate for yourself in constructive ways. It's a muscle you build with practice.

- Managing your emotions begins with self-awareness. Develop self-insight with the habit of regularly checking in – noticing your energy levels, mood, hunger, the impact of caffeine, tension, pain, discomfort. We're going to take a much deeper dive into this in Step 6, I Prioritise Myself, but why not plant the seed here? Make a list of things that often lie beneath your anger and proactively nourish yourself to stop it from building and turning you into Mount Vesuvius. Regular self-care is non-negotiable if you want to manage your emotions and your stress.

- Dialling down anger is a function of your ability to relax and how often you give yourself an opportunity to replenish. If anger is an issue for you, develop a daily savasana practice. Savasana is that gorgeous lying-down practice you do at the end of a yoga class (see page 140 for a description; it can be done with or without the body wrapping). Do this daily for ten minutes and see how this builds the skill of relaxation and how, when you find your way back to calm, you can better communicate and empathise when life squeezes you. I hope this is the happiest homework anyone has ever given you.

- Emotional regulation isn't just down to what's happening on the inside; you also need to give yourself permission to pace yourself and tweak self-expectations. This is where boundary management is so important and we're going to explore that in Step 7, I Advocate for Myself (page 241).

- Self-forgiveness is an essential part of learning to manage your anger. No one gets it right all the time and when you fall short of your intentions, your job is to learn the lesson. What will you do differently next time? Identify an option that's aligned with your values, and then forgive yourself. The forgiveness allows you to learn the lesson, grow and move on rather than just hitting yourself over the head with it. Place your hands on your heart and forgive yourself and forgive yourself again. You might find that your journey to healthy expression of anger is expedited by developing the skill of self-forgiveness. The next time you drop the toast, the milk bottle lid or forget something, tell yourself: 'It's OK, sweetie, I learn the lesson [most often it's "slow down"!]. I forgive myself and I can move on.'

Love note for when you're feeling angry

Sweetheart, it's not wrong to experience anger. All humans feel anger from time to time, just like they do hunger or thirst. What stories have you been told about anger or your right to express it? What narrative have you created in response to your own lived experiences of anger? I know when you've witnessed the toxic effects of anger it can feel incongruent, even unsafe, but feeling anger doesn't make you a bad person. Anger galvanises us to stand up for ourselves, for our beliefs, and for those in our care. There are so many different threads to anger, so we need to dig a little deeper and see what lies beneath it. Use the toolkit to feel safe (page 94) if the presence of anger itself feels threatening. When you are ready, read through the following prompts to see what might be happening for you:

Is there fear, worry or insecurity? Is it irritation, frustration or are you about to hit overwhelm? Do you feel unappreciated, disrespected, misunderstood, maligned or humiliated? What value has been violated? What boundary has been transgressed? Are you feeling trapped, triggered, manipulated or gaslit? Is there a sense of grief, guilt or powerlessness? Or is it exhaustion, rubbish sleep, feeling touched out, hunger, dehydration, a lack of movement, excess screen time or simply too much coffee?

What are the messages for you in your anger? What aligned action is required for your self-protection or health, or the safety of those in your care? We know the right to feel anger does not give us the right to behave in ways that cause harm. Let's observe where guilt prods us if we've expressed anger in hurtful ways. What repair is needed? How might we move through it and advocate for ourselves in a more compassionate way next time? Remember, we are learning and growing every day.

STEP 5

I TAKE BACK MY MORAL COMPASS

Welcome to Step 5. I invite you to pause and see just how far you've come already. You're working towards getting your self-talk on side and redefining your relationship with your thoughts (it's OK if this is a lifelong process!). You've observed where you are placing your energy and by directing your attention to your senses, you are becoming more awake to what's happening within you, more connected with your needs. You're reclaiming your body for you, developing your capacity for self-acceptance, and are making beautiful progress in allowing yourself to feel the full gamut of human emotions. Having dialled down the external noise and dropped some baggage that no longer serves you, it's now time to choose what you want your life, your unique expression of self, to be about. You need to get clear on your own personal compass, the strengths and values that give your life purpose, meaning and direction. You know what you've been told; now you get to choose what you hold onto and affirm, what you tweak and what you toss! You get to choose what a well-lived life looks like. From this moment forward, what matters to you? What's important to you? What direction do you want to move in? What makes you feel alive? Knowing yourself is the next step that's fundamental to your ability to prioritise yourself. Let's find that clarity together now.

Knowing your strengths and your values

If you don't know yourself, how can you trust yourself or advocate for yourself? Let's get clear on what knowing yourself allows you to do. When you know your strengths and your values, you have the key to creating alignment, zest and peace in your life. It helps you feel good about yourself in the moment, simplifies your decision making and provides you with a road map for moving forwards. This self-insight helps you understand how conflict arises from values that conflict with your own, or in moments of friction with other people. When you use your strengths, you feel like you are doing what you have been put on this earth to do, which is empowering, affirming and energising. When you move in the direction of your values, that's when you feel congruence in your life and this too is galvanising, helping you dig deep and muster that resolve from within. This step is all about helping you gain an understanding of what makes you *you* – your strengths (those skills that come easily to you, which perhaps you have also spent a lifetime cultivating) and the values that you hold dear (which perhaps don't always come effortlessly but nonetheless speak to you deeply).

Your timeline of grit

We've taken a look already at some of the messaging that you have received throughout your life (see your timeline of selfishness, page 40). You could use those notes as a foundation for this next exercise or start afresh, as you feel inspired to. Create a timeline of your life, reflecting on milestones, chapters, turning points or challenges – think of this as your timeline of grit or your timeline of pride, whichever resonates most for you. I hope you feel ready to reclaim the right to feel pride in yourself! Use this practice to acknowledge what you have weathered as a human being, not just seeing the achievements but digging deeper to identify the strengths and values that you drew upon to see you through. If you find it difficult casting your eye back over your whole lifetime, please be guided by what feels comfortable for you. You could focus just on the last year of your life if you prefer. As you journey through these reflections, write down those skills, qualities and values that are emerging for you, helping you see in greater clarity how you have grown in response to these life events, and what they have revealed about what matters to you as an individual. Start exploring what makes you, you.

> ### Love note for when you're feeling lost or invisible
>
> *Sweetheart, you can never lose yourself, the connection just gets a little obscured. There are so many ways that we hide ourselves in our attempt to be good corporate citizens. We hide our parenthood, our menopause, our sexuality, our grief, our mental health challenges, our family secrets, our disabilities and health conditions, our emotions, our opinions, our hopes and our dreams. In all of this keeping up appearances, are you feeling a bit untethered? This doesn't mean you are lost; it means you've lost connection with your grounding or your purpose. Make space for that feeling, grieve what's come to pass, and give yourself time to seek fresh purpose. Look at the noise, all the outside influences, the experiences you've had. Gently recognise what you have weathered and reframe any thoughts of 'What's wrong with*

me?' to 'What happened to me?' You did your best to cope and this tendency to shrink yourself, silence yourself, hide yourself, hide from yourself is a coping mechanism. You can always come home to yourself. You are always learning and growing. Perhaps there are parts of you that you want to reclaim? They are yours, just waiting to be found again. That curious younger self. The part of you that seeks pleasure. That version of you full of hope. Are there new parts of you, fresh shoots, that want to be expressed?

You are more than your roles. You are more than your responsibilities, parental or otherwise. You are more than your occupation. You are more than your circumstances. Do not let society decide your relevance. 'Tetherlessness' is a passing feeling, it doesn't mean you are unimportant. It is something many people feel, as we age, as our children fly the nest, when we retire, as relationships change or the family unit or friends disperse. Come back to the you that remains unchanged across different settings, connecting with what matters to you. Let your mind's eye settle on what you are proud of, the tiny acts of kindness, the willingness to keep trying, the courage to evolve. What brings you joy, darling? Who do you feel safe with? Where do you feel alive? It's time to plug in and seek new ways of belonging (see the toolkit to find your flock, page 272).

Reflection time: What will you celebrate about yourself?

I'd like to offer some other reflective prompts to help you flesh out this celebration of you, and while you're at it, why not let this be a date with yourself? When was the last time you romanced yourself? You get to choose everything:

where, when, what ... and please enjoy! Savour your own company, your preferences, your delights. (And if you're wondering, staying curled up at home is more than OK too. You don't need anyone else's approval.)

Consider the following:

- What were you good at doing as a kid?

- What did you enjoy doing growing up?

- What holds your attention now? What absorbs you? What do you get lost in? What piques your curiosity?

- Is there something that you used to enjoy that you've given up in the last decade?

- What do you find easy that other people admire or struggle with?

- What kind of support, advice or help do people come to you for?

- What qualities are important to you in relationships? If you are a parent, what do you want to model for your kids or what qualities would you love for them to possess? What do you value in your friendships, family or career life?

- What brings you satisfaction in life?

- What makes you laugh?

- What makes you feel angry and what does this tell you about what you value?

- What's your favourite thing about you?

- What are your favourite things in life: your favourite colour, song, film, food, flower, season or place, and have you let other people know these joys unique to you?

- When do you feel alive or when do you feel like your favourite version of you?
- What are your hopes or what would be a glorious plot twist in your life?
- Who inspires you and why?
- What would you give yourself permission to do if no one knew about it?
- What is a good human being?
- What is a worthy human being?
- How are you currently spending your time, energy and money, and what does this say about your values?
- What does your future self have to say to you now? What are they proud of?

Moving towards a flexible expression of your values

Identifying your values and strengths is just one part of our task here. The next part is looking for new ways of bringing these qualities to your life while also meeting your own human needs and expressing your inner life. This calls on you to be honest with yourself and get creative. We need to take a look even when it comes to things you think you've got nailed, like kindness, self-discipline, diligence, forgiveness. How might this fresh expression of your values and strengths look when you also make space for emotional expression and the honouring of your needs?

Pick a value that's important to you. Jot down why you care about this. When in your life has this value been important to you? What has unfolded when you pursued it? What have you seen when other people pursued it, or not? When have you violated this value and what have been the consequences? What current actions reflect your commitment to this value? What are some different ways you can express this value?

You might need some examples to get you thinking of fresh expressions . . .

- Kindness – can you expand your kindness to also include yourself? Can you make space for the values of honesty and integrity and give negative feedback, knowing that while it doesn't feel pleasant, the real kindness lies not in withholding the truth but in providing a gentle opportunity for growth? There is a useful distinction to be made between being nice and being kind.

- Forgiveness – in your ability to forgive, don't be so swift that the other person doesn't even know that they've made an error. Allow them to learn the lessons. Sitting with the discomfort is part of that learning journey.

- Peace – must your commitment to harmony always come at the expense of your own peace?

- Commitment to excellence – if you value excellence, can you make a distinction between quality and perfection?

- Diligence – if you value dedication, can you also be conscientious in your rest?

- Creativity – by all means value your creativity but please watch if it manifests in shape shifting to please others or a plethora of excuses for other people's bad behaviour.

- Self-discipline – maybe you take pride in being tough on yourself because that worked up until a point in your life, but perhaps there will come a time when tenderness is more helpful. What other shapes might self-discipline take? (See the section on developing a compassionate inner voice, page 208.)

- Responsibility – your compassion might open your eyes to the struggle of those around you, but can you be skilled in identifying where your responsibilities truly lie? What really belongs to you and can you allow others to take responsibility for their learning, their growth?

- Resilience – please celebrate your ability to cope but can you question when you equate resilience with bypassing emotion, subjugating human needs and hyper-independence? Can resilience look different? Can you allow it to be messy and can you let others in?

- Grit – yes to celebrating your staying power but it's OK to allow some softness and breathing space too. Sometimes you will need time and space to heal, and it doesn't serve you to relentlessly push on. This is not failure, it's growth. No human has infinite capacity. No human is immune from painful experiences and the toll these curveballs take on your bodymind.

Reflection time: Your willingness contracts

It is not easy to shift the expression of our strengths and values. I want to be honest about that. I think it helps to be transparent about it and make some contracts with ourselves about the difficult thoughts and feelings we are willing to experience in order to move in our desired direction of authenticity, integrity and personal power.
It is OK to find these things challenging. These questions will help you articulate your purpose, so you are galvanised to take this aligned action in the face of that difficulty.

- What are you willing to do or stop doing in order to feel whole, healthy, enough?

- Are you willing to feel selfish in order to take nourishing action?

- Are you willing to feel bossy in order to voice your opinion?
- Are you willing to feel lazy or judged in order to rest?
- Are you willing to feel selfish in order to prioritise your health?
- Are you willing to feel uncomfortable in order to express your feelings or give feedback?
- Are you willing to risk disapproval in order to honour your boundaries or say no?
- Are you willing to sit with the discomfort of nourishing yourself if you don't yet believe you're worthy?
- Are you willing to champion yourself?
- Are you willing to feel a fear of disappointing others in order to be honest about your current capacity?
- Are you willing to let other people's judgements slide from your Teflon shoulders when you honour your sensitivity?
- Are you willing to allow yourself to be OK when others around you are not OK, letting them take responsibility for their own stuff?
- Are you willing to feel guilty in order to be truthful in relationship with other people?
- Are you willing to feel vulnerable so you can lean on other people and let them in?
- Are you willing to make mistakes as you learn how to share your inner life and your needs?
- Are you willing to forgive yourself for the errors you'll make in your journey to self-advocacy?
- Are you willing to renegotiate your definition of success, allowing softness to feature rather than toughness,

> interdependence rather than how little you need other people, and peace and harmony over perfectionism, relentless striving and productivity?
>
> - What are you willing to do to bring healing to your life?
>
> You have the toolkit to sit with difficult emotions on page 184 and this will build your capacity for following through on your willingness contracts.

Developing your compassionate inner voice

Allowing self-discipline to have a different shape might feel challenging, but you can move away from a punitive, self-critical voice to a more coaxing, encouraging one and stay just as conscientious!

Let's take a closer look at your inner critic and your relationship with this voice. Perhaps you feel like being gentle with yourself just lets you off the hook or paves the way for weakness? Let's see whether self-criticism really serves you as you think it does. Are you prepared to try something different and see if that works better for you?

I'd like you to let your imagination run wild with me here. What if I told you I could wave a magic wand and instantly you would be cured of self-critical, punitive, judgemental thinking? You would never be tough on yourself again. Think for a minute what this could look and feel like. What would it allow you to do? Are there some niggling worries that creep in? What are you afraid of? Do you fear that in the absence of self-criticism you'd be selfish, lazy, unkind or uncaring to others?

But let's delve a little deeper. Let's interrogate this idea that being critical of yourself helps you perform better or look after other people better. Is this belief true? If you listen to what you say to yourself and observe how you treat yourself when you are being self-critical, how does your inner critic feel about you? What does it want to do to you? Does it want to motivate or encourage you? Does it want you to step up and shine brighter or does it want to push you down, attack you, even obliterate you? I know it's painful to take an honest look, so go gently. How does this attack on you as a person make you feel? Does it help you stand taller, does it resource you to keep giving and keep going? Does this inner critic genuinely help you at all? I'd suggest not! The fact is you are already deeply committed to being a good person. Just look at how worried you were about falling into the trap of being selfish, lazy and uncaring; you don't need your inner critic to remind you too. Do you want to be selfish? Do you want to be self-absorbed or unkind? No! You do not need your harsh inner voice to motivate your behaviour, that's already woven into who you are as a person.

Your inner critic is not trying to help you, it is attacking you and you don't have to validate its job by honouring or upholding it. Your inner critic is coming from a place of fear, so what is it so afraid of? We can understand this – we know the rejection, judgement and loneliness we've felt for voicing our thoughts, feelings and needs. We can greet that fear with tenderness and understanding. We don't have to silence, fight or eradicate our inner critic, but neither do we need to hold onto it as some kind of safety blanket preventing us from sliding into selfishness. We can make peace with it and with ourselves in the process.

Even when we can see that the inner critic doesn't serve us, punitive self-talk can be a hard habit to break. Let's try the following exercise to cultivate a more tender way of relating to ourselves. Allow this to take some practice, some getting used to; it's a skill we build with repetition. Take a moment to get comfy and let yourself settle into your surroundings. Make any adjustments you need until you feel completely at ease.

Now bring to mind an image of someone you know but don't know very well – a casual acquaintance that you see on a regular basis, perhaps someone you meet at the school gate, a colleague from another team, someone who lives down the road or a person who serves you on the checkout. Imagine this person as vividly as possible and, as you hold on to this image, repeat the following phrases: 'May you be kind to yourself. May you be healthy. May you feel safe and at peace. May you know it's OK to voice your thoughts and feelings. May you know that you are welcome, you are needed and that you matter.' Notice how nice it feels to extend warmth, care and kindness to this person that you don't know very well.

Take a few relaxed breaths and come back to your surroundings, back to your body. Make any further movements to maximise your comfort and enjoy the sensation of the breath as it moves through your body. For the next couple of minutes you are going to conjure the image of someone you care about deeply, someone with whom you enjoy a simple, healthy, safe relationship. Bring to mind this person that matters to you and let their image become as vivid as possible. Repeat similar phrases of warm well wishes: 'May you be healthy. May you feel protected and at peace. May you be joyful. May you express your feelings and needs freely. May you be kind and gentle with yourself. May you know that you are valued, you are worthy, and you are whole.' Let yourself connect with the loving intention these words express, noticing how it feels to extend these wishes of warmth and care to this person who means so much to you. Allow the image of this person dear to you to gradually fade away.

Come back to the environment around you, to how your body feels and how it feels to be breathing. Take another couple of calm breaths. I invite you now to think of a time when you felt a sense of connection, a recognition or understanding with another being. This might have been in the form of a shared moment with another human, someone you know or even a stranger – it could be as simple as a friendly nod when your paths crossed, a smile from someone across the room, a wave from a neighbour or a moment of care from someone you love. You are not limited to human connection, you could also select a moment of deep unconditional acceptance you experienced with a pet. Choose one moment of kind validation of you from a person or animal and really picture this other being in this moment, when they made you feel so cared for, so worthy of affection, so loved and lovable. Remember how they looked, remember what they said, how they said it, and savour how you felt in that moment.

Now I invite you to come back to the room again, bringing your attention back to your body or your breathing. Stay with your breath for a couple of moments. Lastly, I invite you to recall a time when you felt guilty for speaking up, embarrassed for being vulnerable and showing a tender side to yourself, ashamed for prioritising yourself, for making a request or sharing an opinion that wasn't met with respect. Or think of a time when your mind had a thought that you weren't worthy, when your old story of not being enough came up, or a time when you kept silent or made yourself small. Pick just one, and gently bring this salient moment into focus. Picture it in your mind's eye, the time of day, where you were, the environment around you, using all of your senses recall that memory as vividly as possible.

As you bring this image to mind, repeat the words: 'May you be kind to yourself. May you be free from shame and guilt. May you be met with acceptance and understanding. May you forgive yourself for any errors. May you give yourself grace. May you learn and grow. May you be healthy, safe and at peace. May you know your worth. May you speak your truth. May you advocate for yourself with power and freedom. May you be loved and accepted for who you truly are. May you have the courage to love and accept yourself for who you truly are.'

Feel the warmth and kindness these words cultivate and let them envelop you. Let every cell and fibre of your body drink in that love and care. Take a moment to acknowledge what this self-compassion feels like in your body. Notice how different this feels in your body compared to the effects of being tough on yourself. Sweetheart, you've been punished enough, and you don't need to keep punishing yourself. You can treat yourself with dignity and respect and this self-compassion will allow you to grow in the most beautiful ways.

As you re-enter your day, take this feeling of self-compassion with you. Use it to weather moments of self-doubt and criticism. Recall it when your mind tells you stories about being selfish for advocating for yourself. Use this practice to help you move in the direction of kindness, encouragement and gently coaxing yourself. This is not weakness, it's a superpower.

How to make choices – are you moving away or towards what matters to you?

Your list of strengths and values gives you beautiful clues as to what you would like to cultivate in your life. Perhaps it might feel good to you to set some kind of overarching intention for this current chapter of your life – is it healing, a feeling of being whole, feeling worthy, knowing in your bones that you are a good human being? Is it acting with integrity and authenticity, speaking up for yourself, learning how to express your feelings and needs, or modelling skills of self-advocacy for your kids?

I want you to think of this overarching intention for this part of your life as a destination – something that you are, with each action, each habit you build, either moving towards or away from. Face this destination, visualising what life would look like when you get there and how it would feel from the inside, and bask in its beautiful glow. Notice how good it feels to take action that brings you closer to this vision; try actually taking a step closer to it. Now turn your back on it; this is what happens when we are miserly with ourselves, deny our feelings, push our truth down deep inside us. Feel how painful it is to turn your back on a future so precious to you, how horrendous it feels to step further away physically from what matters to you. Every day we are faced with a plethora of choices. Please keep giving yourself permission to take steps that take you towards, not away from, what your heart desires. This is how we take our power back, one choice at a time. You choose, according to your moral compass.

You are moving away from	You are moving towards
Dishonesty	Healthy boundaries
Silence	Authentic connection
Repression	Energy management
Anger	Emotional health
Frustration	Peace
Resentment	A compassionate pace
Martyrdom	Self-trust
People pleasing	Nervous system health
Hyper-independence	Personal power to live a purposeful life
Relentless striving	
Inauthentic relationships	Making a valuable contribution of your choosing
Energetic bankruptcy	
Loneliness	Flourishing relationships
Unvoiced disappointment	Flourishing communities
Self-criticism	Being a resourced person who can rally to support those in need, creating social change
Isolation	
Invisibility	
Emptiness	

Recalibrating your relationship with failure

In your journey to self-advocacy, you are going to make errors and experience setbacks. I'm sure you will have come across the practice of journaling about gratitude, but I have a different suggestion for you: try keeping a log of disappointments and setbacks. Start a journal just for recording these low moments – sounds heavy, right? But you might be surprised by what blooms from this practice!

When you encounter a bump in the road, write down the failure, disappointment or setback. Note what happened, how you feel about it right now, and explore your concerns about how this might play out or affect your future: how other people might react, the costs or the potential consequences. Leave several lines for two additional future entries. Put a couple of notes in your diary to come back to this journal entry in 30 days and again in six months.

Return to this page after 30 days and write down what you learned about this setback. What has happened since? Were your fears confirmed and how did you cope with what unfolded? When you are six months down the track, return to this entry and record your observations again, specifically considering whether anything constructive came as a result of the setback. What did this experience teach you? What have you learned about yourself? How have you grown? How does this shape your feeling about disappointments? In time, I hope you will begin to see that failures aren't necessarily good or bad, they provide you with valuable information. You don't need to avoid them or fear them, you can accept them and learn from them with less struggle. I hope this helps you greet curveballs with a greater sense of curiosity, anchored in an awareness of your capability to cope with tricky situations.

How to cope with the disappointment or disapproval of others when you've advocated for yourself

In your journey to advocating for yourself, sometimes you will disappoint people you care about. Sometimes people you love will not understand or approve of your choices. Darling, please make a distinction between disapproval or disappointment in an action or choice, as opposed to disappointment in you as a human being. Sometimes people disapprove of something that feels integral to you as an individual; this is where you need to come back to your own moral code and remember what motivated you to embark on this action or expression of self. Seek internal validation rather than relying on external validation to feel good about yourself. You can use the toolkit to seek your own approval to guide you (page 143). I know this can be hard because when you were growing up, your safety and comfort depended on keeping other people happy. Observe this desire to please others as a coping mechanism that you no longer need, or be aware of the relationships where some degree of this is still required of you. Sometimes we just can't extricate ourselves completely. Ask yourself what the cost would be of you not taking this action, of you not behaving in a way that was true to yourself? Evaluate the costs in this moment, but also down the track. Comfort yourself with the knowledge of why you made this choice. There was purpose in it.

Sometimes people aren't disappointed with us due to conflicting values, but because we let them down in some way that feels incongruent to us too. Sometimes there have been competing demands on us and despite our best intentions we weren't able to act as we would have liked and people feel neglected. Is there some information they aren't privy to that might help them better understand our actions or choices? Even when we have valid reasons, we might have to sit with the acknowledgement that we've hurt their feelings. Perhaps they've communicated that displeasure and there is a wound to recognise. This can be painful to witness. Can we make space for that discomfort without being in a rush to get rid of it? Can we also recognise that we might be leaping to conclusions that other people are upset with us when in fact they're just busy! It can be exhausting for people around us to provide constant reassurance, so be mindful if this assumption comes up frequently for you. Is their upset with us real or imagined?

5-step process to sit with the disappointment of others

1. Just notice
   'I am noticing the presence of a thought about disappointing someone dear to me. I am noticing a sadness that it's not possible to keep all the people happy all the time. I'm recognising that sometimes there will be conflicting needs, that sometimes even my own needs and values might compete and I will have to prioritise one over another. I am remembering this feeling is temporary and I can repair as I need to.' Let these thoughts and feelings be present and use the toolkit to feel safe (page 94) to bear witness to them.

2. Own your part
   Recognise the part you played and consider too the part played by other people, or other factors. Take responsibility for just your own part. Communicate regret for hurt caused and apologise for what you could have handled better. Let people know what you will do differently next time. If they felt hurt by how you articulated your boundaries, consider whether you caused harm by not being direct or clear, or perhaps your means of communication could have been improved (for example, having an in-person conversation

rather than attempting to communicate via text). If you were giving someone negative feedback, had you been stockpiling frustrations and did they all come tumbling out at once in what felt like an overreaction to a single incident? These are important considerations because it is easy to think that our boundaries are the problem when really we just need to give ourselves time to develop our skills in communicating them. It's messy business, so give yourself permission to learn and grow. Remember, if you didn't set this boundary or give this feedback, what would the consequence be? Once you've made your attempts at repair, if necessary, forgive yourself. You did the best you could at the time with the knowledge and resources you had. You have now done what you can to mend it. Be tender with yourself when your mind is drawn back to the situation and don't poke the wound. That doesn't reduce pain for the person you hurt, it only hurts you, and this achieves nothing constructive. Just notice the presence of the bruise with compassion and forgive yourself again.

3. Give voice to shame
   Reach out to someone who understands you and has your back. Talk through the scenario and let them reassure you. In sharing it we can release it. It can help to know that other people might have made the same difficult choice or had a similar experience of their own.

4. What have you learned?
   What information have you gleaned about yourself, your limits, your values, other people, boundaries or communication? If you found yourself saying yes when you wanted to say no, what were the consequences? If you embarked on doing a friend a favour, could you do the whole favour? Or did resentment leak out or maybe you overestimated your capacity and ended up flaking out partway through? Are you taking responsibility for something that wasn't yours – can you make the distinction between a

'me' problem and a 'them' problem? Take note of anything valuable.

5. What is going well?
   Make space to acknowledge other areas of your life that are flourishing, beyond this painful experience. What relationships are functioning well? Yes there is this disappointment, yes there is this disapproval, there might even be rejection, but there are also these other sources of validation, understanding, acceptance, love or championing. If this episode feels like a turning point in your relationship with someone, turn to the toolkit to navigate grief (page 246).

How to stop apologising all the time

You've seen all the ways we've been silenced and rewarded for keeping ourselves quiet and small, so it's no wonder that you find yourself apologising for speaking up and taking up space. Please, give yourself permission to stop this incessant and needless practice of saying sorry for entering a room, taking a seat or opening your mouth. Here's how we break this knee-jerk habit:

1. Notice when you are apologising. Keep a log to begin with to bring this behaviour to light. Jot down the scenarios and frequency, and notice the patterns. Write down the impact apologising had on you and others. How did it make you feel? How did the other person respond? Any clues in these observations as to why it's time to create change? Stick with this practice of noticing for a week and record your insights. The first step, as ever, is awareness and the second step is identifying purpose.

2. Once you're more aware of your tendency to offer apologies, before you do, ask yourself what you are apologising for. Check in with your moral code and ask whether you are in fact deviating from what feels aligned to you. Clearly, there is a time for heartfelt sorries. We apologise for hurt caused, for

misunderstandings and even for being late, but you don't need to apologise for being here, for having human needs and feelings. Feel the power that comes from choosing when to use the word sorry.

3. In those moments where you feel uncomfortable, instead of a 'sorry', soothe yourself with one of the practices from the toolkit to feel safe (page 94). A beautiful alternative could be to communicate appreciation. 'Thank you for your patience' might be the perfect greeting if you are one of the last to enter a team meeting. Choose your sorries well and feel how this provides collective relief.

What to do when someone calls you selfish

It is going to happen from time to time, especially when your family and friends aren't used to your self-advocacy. When someone calls you selfish, check your moral compass. Are you actually doing anything wrong? Why did you embark on this course of action? What values does it honour? Sometimes our values conflict or our relationships are in competition. Remember, we can't be all things to all people! Do we need to redefine what it means to be a good daughter, a good wife, a good mother, a good sister, a good friend? Sometimes one role will have to take precedence over another. When our actions are being questioned, are there different beliefs at play? Is that worth exploring?

Was this person benefiting from your previous lack of boundaries or self-sacrifice? Do you really need their approval here? Seek your own validation. If this person matters to you, why might they not understand your choices? Are they privy to your motivation, your purpose or the real circumstances? Whose interests are they protecting?

Once you have explained yourself, if that is indeed necessary, and you are sure you're both on the same page in terms of information, you don't need to defend yourself or convince the other person. You've taken values-directed action and you can relax into that knowing, even if they don't approve. If things become barbed with this person, you may wish to evaluate your boundaries further or even your relationship with them. The toolkit to navigate grief (page 246) can help you if you feel this is a turning point. Remember that there is a difference between being liked and being loved and even if some disappointment occurs, your loved ones should respect your basic needs. Make repairs as needed and communicate regret for any hurt caused.

Acknowledge the upset but stand firm that you won't be made to feel guilty for prioritising your own health. Use the toolkit to feel safe (page 94) if you feel shaken. Come back to what matters to you and stay on that aligned path of action. You get to choose, darling. Your own permission is plenty. You know yourself. Don't let anyone else tell you who you are. Use this mantra: 'I am a kind person with healthy boundaries, and I have every right to protect my peace.' If there's still a residue, call a friend and talk it through. It's OK to lean on others too.

STEP 6
I PRIORITISE MYSELF

You cultivated some beautiful clarity in the last step on what feels important to you. This next step is about the nourishment you need to support the life directions you've selected. This is all about how to prioritise you. You'll have heard about the necessity of boundaries with others (and see Step 7, I Advocate for Myself, for more on these), but this step is going to help you clarify your boundaries with yourself: what you need to feel safe and healthy in relationship with yourself, and the life-giving habits that will enable you to flourish. Think of this as the scaffolding that you need in your life to be able to meet the demands of each day *and* honour yourself as a human being.

I hope that having journeyed thus far in the book, you are coming to appreciate the importance of your needs and feelings and are beginning to feel comfortable ranking your own self high in the order of what you consider worthy of your own attention and energy. This is what it means to prioritise yourself – recognising your worth, treating yourself as if you matter and actively asserting yourself by advocating for your needs and feelings. I am so thrilled we have finally arrived at learning *how* to actively prioritise yourself, but before we move on to the nuts and bolts of how to make it happen, you need to clarify what prioritising yourself is in service of. It's not enough on its own to say we are going to focus on ourselves; we need to attach a deeper meaning to this to feel galvanised to take action. (If you want a reminder of why intrinsic motivation is vital, hop back to page 34.)

In Step 5, you made a mind map of your strengths and values, and you considered what you might like this next chapter of your life to be about (see page 212 on making choices and whether you are moving away or towards what matters to you). Your next step in self-advocacy is to think about what's calling to you right *now*. Maybe you want to understand yourself and your behaviour patterns better, maybe you want to be a bit kinder to yourself, perhaps you'd like to develop your capacity for speaking up, maybe it's time to find greater balance or reciprocity in your relationships or perhaps you'd like to set yourself a more compassionate pace . . . get specific in your aims and they will motivate you better. Then ask yourself, in the context of what matters most to you, what does prioritising yourself facilitate in your life? What do you stand to gain by bumping yourself up your list of priorities? What do you access when you let your needs feature in your own planning and decision making? When you give yourself permission to honour your feelings, what does this allow you to do or be? Think about how coming home to yourself impacts your opportunity for honest communication, true intimacy and connection, and how you can make a difference by being aligned in your action. Conversely, if you deny yourself the right to take up time and space in your own planning and execution, what are the consequences? If you keep negating your needs and your feelings, what do you stand to lose? At what cost do you not prioritise yourself? Flesh this out, write it down, keep it somewhere prominent and read it every time guilt taps you on the shoulder, to remind yourself that others also win when you prioritise yourself.

Perspective shift . . . To be this incarnation of yourself and to move in the direction that calls to you, what nourishment do you need? Can you see how this is a fundamental perspective shift? You are moving away from a constant focus on 'What do *I need to do*?' (i.e. your to-do list) to 'What do *I need* to deliver what's required of me?' (i.e. your human needs). Welcome to your boundaries with yourself.

Your toolkit to set boundaries with yourself – your energy bank basics

Setting self-boundaries is all about knowing what works for you – the conditions necessary for you to feel good, to function well, to make sound decisions – and sticking to those commitments. What do you need to feel safe and healthy in relationship with yourself? What is acceptable behaviour? How do you agree to treat yourself? Alternatively, you could ask yourself: what does self-respect look like?

The concept that you might find helpful in establishing boundaries with yourself is thinking of your 'energy bank basics'. Just like a car needs fuel to go, you need energy to navigate your day. Energy bank basics are the scaffolding required in your life for you to pitch up as you aspire to. These are the things that help you cope in the moment and they also make tomorrow easier. They are distinct from those things we rely on to distract or numb ourselves, helping us cope in the moment but sabotaging our future self. Let's get granular with these self-commitments.

Consider the questions below to choose supportive and healthy habits that help you stay present and poised (or any other quality that is important to you as a human being).

- What kind of **self-talk** is OK? What would it sound like to speak to yourself with dignity and respect?

- What kind of **nutrition and hydration** do you need to make sound decisions? Take a close look at your relationship with caffeine, sugar and alcohol. Get specific here, for example: how many coffees a day work for you (if any) and do you have a cut-off point in your day? Do you need similar structure around cola drinks? In terms of booze, when is it healthy for you to drink alcohol and how much? Does it serve you to make the commitment to only drink in the company of others, or on special occasions, and do you want to establish how many units per week it feels healthy for you to drink, or a maximum number of units for one sitting? What are the thresholds that feel healthy for you?

- What regular **movement** habits help you feel alive or allow you to meet other goals important to you?

- What are the daily **hygiene** commitments that help you feel clear headed and put together? I know it sounds obvious but don't discount the power of brushing your teeth, showering, brushing your hair and getting dressed in an outfit that helps you feel good. If these are commitments you have already nailed, then you can broaden them to include other new rituals – and if you can do these, you can apply the same diligence to other new habits.

- How much **sleep** do you need to function well (most adults need 7–9 hours of sleep daily)? What's your ideal bedtime and rise time? What are the lifestyle choices that support good sleep and the pre-bedtime activities that prepare your mind and body for sleep?

- What kind of time in **nature** do you need in your life?

- What kind of **fun and self-expression** do you need to make space for?

- What kind of **social connection** do you need to feel a sense of understanding and belonging? Who's in your circle and how do you like to stay current and communicate care?

- What are the **restorative practices** that help you manage your stress and emotions?

- What are the **reflective rituals** that help you feel clarity and alignment?

- What does **healthy spending** look like to you?

- What are your **digital health** boundaries around communication, screen time and your hours of availability? What guidelines to your online life help you function well?

When making these agreements with yourself, it helps to focus only on what you have control over. While you might know you need eight hours of sleep, you can't make yourself sleep, so aim to have at least eight hours in bed as often as possible, that is more within our sphere of influence (although even then life might choose otherwise for us). It might help to have some contingency plans, too, for when life throws a curveball. If you want to create some order around movement, for example, make sure you have options for low-energy days or exercise alternatives that take little time.

Looking at this list of healthy habits, you might feel a bit overwhelmed at first. Remember, you have the rest of your life to fine-tune this stuff! If you are integrating new behaviour, don't try to make too much change at once. Choose one area, such as sleep or screen time, and start by making one small commitment that you can keep. Once this is just a normal part of life, look at the next issue. Sustainable change is made best in small increments. Use your journal regularly to track your progress and record your insights about what's serving you and what's not. This will help you determine patterns and know yourself better. Seeing how far you've come will also stoke your motivation. Getting present is the first step, take your time setting ideas in motion and use the toolkit to navigate setbacks (page 239) to help you stay committed. If there is some letting go required, the language we use in these self-commitments is important. Rather than 'I can't', choose 'I don't' to feel more empowered in that decision.

You might also look at your plans and feel paralysed by selfishness. Allow yourself to act on what's important to you, even if you feel selfish in doing so. Don't wait to feel worthy before keeping these promises to yourself. The feeling of worth comes from the nourishing action. Your boundaries are a reflection of your values in life. If kindness, nurturing, forgiveness and compassion are important to you, they are incomplete if they don't also include yourself. Look for self-limiting beliefs here too. What stories do you tell yourself about your strengths and weaknesses? Maybe you think you're bad at self-control? Look for evidence to the contrary. For example, maybe you find it tricky to stick to your healthy food choices, but you've been able to make a regular exercise habit. Maybe you find it hard to get to bed on time but you're never late for an appointment – look at how you've been able to keep other promises to yourself and see how you can find more meaning to encourage you to move in your desired direction. Can you bring greater presence to that habit, connecting with why that habit is important to you? Watch how your beliefs support or sabotage you. Look at what you invest your identity in. You choose. You can create change. 'I am the kind of person who . . .' – you fill in the blank!

What to do when you feel guilty for taking time to look after yourself

1. Identify one role that's precious to you in your life right now and ask yourself how you want to be experienced in that role. What qualities do you want to model?

2. Ask yourself what you need in your day to be able to be this version of you.

3. Ask yourself what happens in this role when you are overstretched, overstimulated, undernourished.

4. Ask yourself how your loved ones, your team, other people you care about benefit from this self-expression. Would you want this for your daughter, your son or your best friend? You are no different. Does this action allow you to model important skills? Does it also give your loved ones a dispensation to prioritise or pace themselves? Are you allowing your children to develop bonds with other caregivers or to grow in their autonomy or independence? Will this replenishment help you to be more present, connect more authentically or manage your levels of stress so you don't take it out on the people you love? If you do this thing for you, will it allow you to better support the people who matter most to you? If you can't yet do it for you, please do it for them.

5. Soothe yourself, using the toolkit to feel safe (page 94), and then let guilt go along for the ride. It's OK to do what you need to do to sustain yourself. Any external objections, see the section on what to do when you're called selfish (page 219).

Remember, these self-agreements are not about being perfect but treating yourself with respect, and understanding what kind of nourishment is necessary for you to feel healthy and resourced to meet your responsibilities. This is the loving action that ensures you don't deny your needs and feelings and abandon yourself again. It's a lifelong *practice*, not something you have to perfect. When you fall short of your aims, please meet yourself with compassion, not condemnation. Are you setting your sights too high? How can you meet yourself where you are and gently encourage your growth?

Bear in mind that as your life variables evolve, your boundaries might also need some tweaking. To allow your boundaries to be responsive, ask yourself: 'What do I need more of right now? What do I need less of? What do I need to allow more flexibility? What requires a little firming up? What do I need to say no to? What do I need to say yes to? What will allow me to pace myself more compassionately during this chapter of life?' In terms of pacing yourself, you can ask yourself if something is reasonable today, and if it is *sustainable* moving forward, bearing in mind all the other demands on you. This is how we cultivate a healthy relationship with ourselves.

Prioritising yourself – the barriers and how to overcome them

It's all well and good to have an idea of what we'd like our boundaries with ourselves to be, but how do we execute this? How do we actually live it? Let's acknowledge how difficult it is to prioritise ourselves in our busy lives, with all the time pressures and so much resting on our shoulders. What are the barriers to taking action and what can we do about them?

- Distraction and decision-making fatigue
  Can you free up some head space for the important decisions by reducing the number of less important ones or limiting the options? Alternate between three different breakfasts, for example. Change your sheets on a Saturday. Do your grocery shop on a Sunday. Pick just one healthy habit, one small commitment to self, and get that under your belt before you even think about attempting more. If you're finding it hard to follow through, sleep might be the best place to start. Commit to doing what you can to improve your sleep and notice the impact this has on your decision making and quality in life in general. Make sure you are well fed and well watered too – we can't think straight when we're hungry or dehydrated. To avoid mental fatigue, identify where

solo-tasking helps, and where it's useful to multitask. It might feel pleasant to listen to a podcast while folding washing but if you are drafting an email or working on your finances, do it without distraction. Notice when you are habitually scattering your attention, like scrolling while also watching TV, and build your ability to be present with just one thing at a time. Let other people know when you are focusing on something and be direct with requests for fewer interruptions where possible. It's OK to speak up.

- Procrastination
  Remember, your boundaries with yourself are not something you wake up and just ace one day. Choose one place to take action and find the smallest step you can do today. Connect with the purpose and plan your reward or try body doubling – just having someone in the same room can make a difference. Who can help? It's OK to ask.

- Delaying gratification
  Sometimes it is really hard to stick to your guns and temptation looms large. What can you do to reduce temptation so you can save your willpower for the more important challenges? What temptation can you remove from your home? Can you let others know about your goals so they don't unwittingly sabotage you? Come back to what this commitment is in service of and let your purpose shore up motivation.

- Overwhelm
  Attempting to do too much at once is a recipe for overwhelm, as are unrealistic, unreasonable or inflexible goals. Keep tweaking your boundaries with yourself and your goals to integrate new healthy habits according to your available resources, anchored in what you can control or influence. Flexibility and responsiveness are key, as is compassionate self-talk.

- Lack of motivation
  If motivation is low, then perhaps what you've set out to achieve isn't that important to you. Change your plan or look for ways to energise yourself. Sometimes a lack of mojo is due to fatigue. Get some decent rest, fresh air, an early night, eat something nourishing and motivation often bounces back. Be honest with self-limiting beliefs and commit to some unpicking. Be gentle with yourself.

- Lack of time
  If you are too rushed to achieve what you want, ask yourself how you are apportioning time. Is your time allocated to what is most important to you? Sometimes we genuinely don't have enough time for everything we want to do and all that's required of us. If this is the case, can you find a new means of self-expression that is do-able with your current time constraints? Make sure it's not *you* and your health that are constantly losing out. Without our health, what do we have? If your own priorities can never take centre stage, is it time to look at other life choices? What wiggle room is there in this chapter of your life? This is just one chapter, so if there isn't the possibility of more freedom right now, feel the grief and nourish yourself as you can. Your time will come. If there is potential for change, seize it with both hands. Make the difficult choices (see page 212). Have the tricky conversations (see page 236).

- Lack of energy
  If you never have the energy to do the thing you want to do, consider the time of day you get around to attempting it. Can you rejig your schedule so that it features in your day when your energy is running high? If you just can't muster the energy for that habit, change the practice to something that requires less pep.

- Lack of knowledge or not knowing where to start
  Fill in the gaps by drawing on the knowledge of friends or enlisting an expert. No one knows it all so there is no failure in admitting where you need some help. Find out and crack on. If you have to wait for information to come to light, acknowledge that, and find another area to action sooner.

- Guilt
  Go back to your purpose. At what cost do you not prioritise yourself? What do you stand to gain by doing this thing? Don't let guilt stop you, do it and let guilt go along for the ride. Once you've done it, write a love note to self for the next time guilt attempts to derail you.

- Low self-worth
  Don't wait to feel deserving to take care of yourself; the feeling of worth *comes* from the nourishment. What's the smallest action you can take, even if you don't feel worthy? Do it and see what blooms.

- Perfectionism or all-or-nothing thinking
  This is just a habit. Recognise what perfectionism and all-or-nothing thinking cost you. Notice the tendency and remind yourself that you can do things differently. Find the smallest action you can take and go do it. Repeat, repeat, repeat. It doesn't matter if you 'fall off the wagon' or it doesn't look exactly like you wanted it to, choose progress over perfection every time. Keep your journal to track your progress and look for long-term trends. Keep moving in the direction of your choosing, knowing that it is often two steps forwards, one step back. That's just life!

- Not enough funds
  I hear you. Look at how you are budgeting and make sure your funds are diverted to what's necessary and important

to you. Sometimes we don't have the resources to do the things we want. This can be a painful realisation. Please extend tenderness towards yourself if this is your current reality. Things can change so don't lose sight of this desire. It's just parked until conditions are more favourable. In the meantime, turn to what is available. Keep coming back to Mother Nature and look for moments of awe – they are abundant, they are free and they are life changing. Become an awe hunter with me and you'll find the sustenance you need right before your eyes. The sunlight through bare branches, a single flower, a purring cat and lots of hugs. Not a penny required.

- Having too many things to remember
  You're not alone if memory is an issue or brain fog is getting in the way; the simple fact is, it is hard to remember everything! Leave some love notes for self to remind you. Pop objects that can act as cues for healthy habits around the house – walking boots by the front door, resistance bands by the sofa, a list of stretches by your computer, your journal by your bed. Piggyback new habits on existing ones to help you build a new routine. Tack something onto brushing your teeth, for example, or make use of that golden time of waiting for the kettle to boil, or use any other waiting time for reflection, nurturing and planning. If you keep forgetting, make an appointment with yourself and diarise your nourishing activities.

- Starting something with excitement but not seeing it through to completion
  Again, this is a habit and you can do things differently. Break your new project down into tasks and perhaps each stage can feel like something new. Observe when having too many open mental tabs is dissipating your energy. What can you see through to completion and savour the deep sense of achievement this brings? Ditch what's no longer important to

you (I know that can be painful and might feel like a waste but at what cost do you not?) and simplify the path ahead, committing to just one new thing where possible. Make space for the awareness that perhaps we have different chapters for different activities. Maybe it's not possible to sustain everything we embark on and that's OK. There might be a season where we meditate daily, another where we have a journaling habit. This isn't failure, it's just an acknowledgement that time and resources are finite, and some choices have to be made. Know the difference between vital and nice to do. Cut yourself some slack but do try to keep up the habits that feel fundamental to you feeling good.

- Self-criticism
  Head straight to the section on developing a compassionate inner voice (page 208) and finish up with the toolkit to cultivate kind self-talk (page 118). We are done with this form of self-harm.

Your toolkit to break free from self-sacrifice

- Open up your diary and schedule time for yourself. If you can keep appointments with other people, you can keep an appointment with yourself. Fill this time with something that nourishes you or helps you connect with yourself. As little as five minutes can make a tangible difference to your day.

- When deliberating a request or invitation, give yourself permission to say no, remembering that your downtime is not your free time, your capacity is distinct from your capability, and it's not your job to please all the people all the time.

- When guilt pokes you, ask yourself whether you are equating 'selfless' with 'good' and 'selfish' with 'bad'. Remember that self-advocacy is necessary to be a healthy human being. Question these beliefs and reclaim not only time for you but energy and compassion for you too.

How do you know what you need?

You can identify what you need by checking in with yourself at regular intervals and asking exactly that – 'What do I need right now?' Couple this enquiry with the hands-on-heart gesture to tap into a feeling of self-compassion, freeing you up to meet that need. The energy bank basics of nutrition, hydration, movement, nature, social connection, rest, sleep and self-expression will guide you to the nourishment you need in your life, but there are also many other things that we need to feel healthy. When trying to work out what you require, it can help to make the distinction between a want and a need. Beneath the want lies a need. Your journey to self-advocacy requires some enquiry into the needs that drive your wants; for example, 'I want to eat chocolate' might speak to the need for comfort . . . the question then becomes how you can meet that need in a more aligned way. Use the pick-and-mix word map on the next pages to help you recognise your need.

Right now I need to feel...

- worthy
- understood
- validated
- accepted
- cared for
- safe
- comforted
- protected
- respected
- valued
- appreciated
- trusted
- nurtured
- held
- valued
- loved
- forgiven
- championed
- supported

- belonging
- connected with others
- connected with myself
- physical affection
- autonomy and freedom
- fun
- creativity
- personal meaning
- peace
- calm
- warmth
- an energy boost
- a mood boost
- a dissipation of jangly, nervous energy
- emotional digestion, letting go
- physical relaxation
- switched off

Sitting with cravings

Sometimes a craving requires action, but just make sure it's aligned with what's important to you. Identify the need that lies beneath and nurture yourself. Watch for where you sabotage yourself, and find fresh, life-giving ways of meeting that desire. Can you swap coffee for herbal tea or a dose of natural light? Sometimes we can bear witness to a craving with compassion and it will dissipate. We need tender options to help us in these moments. Rituals of touch can help, such as cradling your face (page 150), or movement such as your 'mountain breaths' (page 165). Breathing practices can be an anchor too – try 'candle breath' (see page 96). If you're feeling agitated, try 'straw breathing' where you roll your tongue to form a straw and breathe in through your tongue. Close your mouth and exhale through your nose. Feel how this is cooling and calming. Use your posture to feel more resolute too – 'yes' posture versus 'no' posture (pages 167–8) will help you stand firm. If you're feeling really tested, practise 'moving warrior' (page 237) to connect you with your personal power to choose.

Your toolkit to build confidence in preparation for a tricky conversation or task

In our journey to self-advocacy, we need to become skilled in letting people know about our plans and making requests for what we need. It takes real confidence to have these conversations. Confidence isn't something that just happens in our heads, it's a function of our whole being: head, heart and body. Use this toolkit to ready and steady yourself.

- Head
  When your brain is beating you up for being selfish or you are doubting your ability to speak up, recall why it's

important to honour your needs and feelings. It is normal to feel worried about this, but you are capable of doing difficult things. Go back to your timeline of grit (page 200) to be reminded of moments in your life that you can take pride in, other challenges you've weathered, and the skills and strengths you relied on to see you through – they will sustain you through this too. If there are skills you're still developing, then make peace with that. You can learn and you can grow and it's OK to make mistakes along the way. Encouraging self-talk is a basic commitment and takes top priority when you are preparing for something tough.

- Heart
  What is at stake here? What do you stand to lose if you don't speak up? How could your situation improve if you get brave and address this issue? Connect with purpose and let it spur you on. What values are you honouring? Can you feel how this galvanises you even in the face of anxiety?

- Body
  Get your body involved, using posture that cultivates confidence. Stand tall, allowing yourself to take up space. Use movement to give yourself a surge of energy and use breathing to keep yourself anchored in calm. In addition to your toolkit to feel safe, in particular your 'mountain breath' (page 165), try these two practices:

For a simple practice to connect with your inner strength, try 'monkey grip'. Place one hand on top of the other, palms facing each other, forearms parallel to the floor. Interlock your fingers and try to pull your hands apart. Feel how this works not only your hands but your biceps, chest, shoulders and back muscles too. Notice that your tummy muscles also leap into action! Relax and then repeat with the other hand on top.

For a whole-body activity, use 'moving warrior' to feel resolute. Start standing with your arms outstretched at shoulder height and your feet beneath your wrists. Turn your right toes to point away from you and angle your left heel out a little. Breathe in and raise your arms above your head, look up to your hands touching, legs straight. As you breathe out, bend your right knee deeply, bring your arms back to shoulder height and look over your right hand. Repeat this dynamic action ten times before releasing, shaking out your legs and setting up on the other side. Left toes angled out, right heel pressed away from you, bending and straightening your left leg and looking over your left hand. Mantra: 'I have every right to be here. Nothing will blow me off course.'

Your toolkit to give voice

Next up, fine-tune your preparation for self-advocacy with the following toolkit for giving voice. An essential part of your journey is learning how to speak up and represent yourself – stating your preferences, suggesting alternatives, giving feedback and voicing your opinions, desires and requests. You are developing a verbal expression of self, allowing yourself to be not only seen, but heard. That might instantly feel uncomfortable to you, and I invite you to recall stories you've been told about silence, who has the right to speak up and what you've been told it's OK to express. Please question these messages, evaluate them according to your moral compass, and affirm that you have every right to communicate what's on your mind and in your heart. Ask yourself, how does communicating your opinions, ideas, requests, thoughts and feelings benefit you and the people you care about?

The human voice is like a muscle that you strengthen with practice. Use this toolkit to find confidence in speaking up:

- Open up your jaw and use movement to release tension. Try the tongue stretch (page 97) and 'fish mouth' (page 97).

- Develop your lung capacity so you feel you have more puff when it counts. When you are uncongested, practise nasal breathing rather than mouth breathing, and once this is comfortable, you can incorporate nasal breathing into light exercise. 'Ujjayi breath' can also help you feel more in control, breathing in and out through the nose while partially closing off the back of your throat, like you are saying a soft 'ha' sound with your mouth closed. It has a gently warming and galvanising effect.

- Practise vocalising words or making sounds. Start with humming, singing your favourite songs, rehearsing what you want to say. If there is a difficult conversation to be had, plan what you want to communicate, write it down if you like, rehearse it, record it as you slowly read it out loud and listen back to it. You could also rehearse it with safe people to build your confidence.

- To protect your voice, hydration and avoiding excess caffeine and alcohol are important.

- Where you feel heightened emotion might interfere with your ability to express yourself, try repeating the word 'voo', which you might find soothing, feeling the vibration in the chest and a softening for your throat. If anger threatens to erupt, take a few 'lion breaths' (page 194) to help you communicate without doing harm, roaring out the spleen/resentment.

Your toolkit to navigate setbacks

This may be a rocky ride, darling, so give yourself all the grace as you get to know yourself, connect with your feelings, needs, values and desires, and learn to act and speak up on your behalf. When things go skewwhiff, follow this plan for getting back on track:

1. Remember, everyone makes mistakes, and life has a habit of life-ing on us too, so setbacks will be inevitable. First thing is to acknowledge with tenderness the setback and your humanness.

2. Take a compassionate inventory of what happened. Write down a timeline with all the facts and your observations.

3. Notice the feelings that come up and give yourself time and space to move through them.

4. Dig a little deeper once the dust has settled. Ask yourself these questions to help you find perspective: Will the impact of this setback last forever, or will it be short-lived? Is the setback a result of everything you did, or are there just one or two things that could have been tweaked? Are you the only one responsible for the setback or were there things beyond your control at play?

5. Step out of the vortex of 'why' and get into the power of 'what'. Choose your next steps. This could be soothing your nervous system if you're still feeling rattled – use the toolkit to feel safe (page 94), or for setbacks that feel permanent, the toolkit to navigate grief (page 246) might help. Maybe you'd like to jot down what you've learned, the clarity you've gained on what's important to you and what you can do something about. If you feel ready to make fresh plans, get into a creative mindset with something that brings you joy. Reach out to a friend and let them share the journey with you – remember, it helps them feel trusted, needed and valued.

STEP 7

I ADVOCATE FOR MYSELF

Welcome to the final step in your journey to self-advocacy: learning how to speak up for yourself and honour your boundaries with other people (and yes, boundaries apply even with your parents and children). In this process of coming home to yourself, are you beginning to see the glimmers of opportunity for far deeper, more honest and authentic connection with other human beings? In this step we will explore how to stand firm and feel healthy in relationship with other people and we are going to drill down into the antidotes to our old coping mechanisms of people pleasing, peace keeping and hyper-independence. In the previous step you reclaimed your right to care for yourself; now it's time to give yourself permission to *receive* the respect and care you deserve from others.

Clarifying your boundaries with other people

In the last step you got clear on the kind of behaviour that you deem appropriate in how you treat yourself, so now it's time to find clarity on what's OK and not OK in your relationships. Boundaries involve an articulation of what feels safe and healthy in our interactions with others, and we co-create them with each person we are in relationship with. The boundaries you have with your mum might feel very different to the boundaries you have with your close friends. Conversation about boundaries provides you both with an opportunity to express what feels supportive and sustainable for you. Embark on these conversations when you are both receptive and in the right headspace, share what the ideal shape would be for you and then find the common ground. This is not about ultimatums; however, there will be some non-negotiables.

You can think of these conversations as gentle bids or requests to establish the rules of engagement that allow everyone to feel on the same page, knowing what's acceptable and what's not. There is no point just thinking about what you want, it has to be clearly communicated and agreed. How can you communicate it best? It might be face to face or via a phone call, text or letter – however you feel your request will best be heard to begin the dialogue about what you can both agree to. Boundaries to canvass include how you speak to each other, the tone, the language, the topics of conversation, the modes of communication, the frequency of connection, the kind of activities you are happy to engage in and how you'd like to go about making those plans together.

Some concrete examples include:

- You are not available for gossip.

- Comments about food, eating habits or weight are not welcome.

- You are happy to come when there is no alcohol involved.

- Your children can choose if they give other people a hug or kiss.
- It is necessary to call first rather than just dropping in.
- People need to take their shoes off before entering your home.
- Ask whether you have capacity before launching into charged conversation.
- You prefer texts rather than voice notes.
- You only respond to correspondence during your working hours (and what these are).

For clarity, we make requests of others but our boundaries are what we will do if those requests are not honoured. You can make it clear that you'd rather people call before coming over – your boundary is not answering the door to unscheduled visitors. If your requests to avoid certain topics are not respected, your boundary is asserted by leaving the conversation. Your boundaries are the actions that you take to protect yourself.

~~Good things come to those who wait~~
Great things come to those who ask

If you find this hard, that's OK! Everyone can fine-tune their communication skills and grow their confidence to speak up. Go back to the toolkits on getting prepared for tricky conversations (page 236) and giving voice (page 238) in Step 6. A really simple rule of thumb for you here in terms of boundaries: get practised in making requests. First, identify the support or the action you're looking for; and second, be direct in the request. Don't beat around the bush, get bold and ask for what you want – please can you do X, Y or Z? Find yourself complaining rather than making a request? Turn what could be constituted as a moan about what you don't want into a polite request for what you do. Try it, and in the process, invite others to be more direct with you. Compassion is key here, so cut everyone a little slack as you all get accustomed to this new, more honest way of relating to each other.

Your toolkit to deliver negative feedback

Part of boundary management is providing feedback and there will be times when you need to let others know they've made an error or that some aspect of their behaviour requires attention. It might not be pleasant but it's necessary, and if it feels like it is transgressing your morals in some way, let's make a clear distinction between being 'nice' and being 'kind'. Being nice allows us to override our boundaries, shirk our duty to be honest and skirt around the issue so we don't cause upset or make a fuss, but this leaves you and the other person vulnerable to future hurt and also allows the aftermath of that lack of insight to leak out and potentially wound countless others. It provides a semblance of kindness in the short term whereas the true act of kindness is to be honest and allow that person an opportunity for learning. Of course, the way we give that feedback can make all the difference but withholding it in order to honour our value of kindness is a misstep, and the ramifications of that can be far reaching. Perhaps the next person to be on the receiving end will be far less compassionate in their feedback, so get brave and save them the potential embarrassment. Try these steps:

1. What's your role or responsibility here?
   Who do you need to protect? You can include yourself in that assessment. To feel safe in this relationship, to do your job well or to be a consumer or contributing member of the community in this situation, what do you feel called to do in terms of shaping other people's performance or behaviour? It is not

selfish to share honest feedback; it could be more selfish and harmful to keep it to yourself.

2. Connect with your values
How does giving feedback fit with your values, such as kindness, honesty, integrity, authenticity, fairness, ethical business, protecting others or a commitment to learning and excellence? If kindness feels like a sticking point... yes, hearing this negative feedback might sting, but what possible benefit might this bring to the party in question? What's in it for them? Who else might benefit?

3. Deliver feedback with compassion – both for the recipient and for yourself
Focus on specific outcomes, behaviours or actions, not character traits, and stick to the facts. If there is some positive feedback that feels appropriate, you can always add that so it feels more balanced. In leadership or management roles (be it in the workplace or in family life), get the other person's involvement in the co-creation of a path of action rather than just dictating what needs to be done next. Sometimes your feedback will be well received, sometimes it won't be welcomed, and you might be judged or criticised for it. Consider how you might word it more delicately next time or just let it slide off your shoulders if it doesn't belong to you. Give yourself a pat on the back for doing the right thing, regardless of how it was received, and head over to the toolkit to feel safe (page 94) to tenderly smooth down your own ruffled feathers. I am applauding you for advocating for yourself and others. It takes guts and heart.

Navigating boundary transgressions

If boundaries are accidentally or deliberately transgressed, you need to rearticulate them and confirm that there is fresh understanding and agreement. It can also be an opportunity to redraw lines in the sand and make sure there's common ground, because circumstances and needs evolve. Once you're on the same page, provide an opportunity for growth. Where boundaries are repeatedly transgressed and there is no recognition of the harm caused or communication of regret, apology, willingness to adjust behaviour or assurance that it won't happen again, you may need to evaluate the viability of this relationship, creating distance or other means of self-protection. This can be a deeply painful experience and one that can leave you feeling selfish and guilty, but your boundaries are what you need to feel safe and healthy. Ask yourself, what is sustainable here? It's not selfish to protect or preserve yourself, and at what cost do you not?

You might be surprised about the resistance you experience when you share these decisions with other people, but darling, screw social pressure. You get to decide what a good human being looks like and if being a 'good daughter' or a 'good mother' mean that you are ravaged as a human being, then something has to give. Don't let it be your sanity. You can be a good human being and cut ties with someone who is toxic for you regardless of relationship. And their opinion of you needn't needle you either. In the words of one of my dearest and bravest clients: 'I would rather be the villain in someone else's story than have their presence in my life. My peace is precious.'

Your toolkit to navigate grief when people can't adjust to your new boundaried self and you need to protect yourself

The people that benefitted most from your self-abandonment may not appreciate the change in you thanks to your blossoming skills of self-advocacy ... they are unlikely to welcome your growth or celebrate it. Permission to cull, darling. If you want to feel healthy, boundaries are not optional.

We don't talk enough about the grief that comes with growth. It's not selfish to shed people who can't respect your boundaries or embrace your newfound confidence in advocating for self. Your safety and wellbeing matter. You've acknowledged that your self-silencing and abandoning behaviours were coping mechanisms when it was not OK to be yourself. If you are still not welcome to be honest about your feelings or needs, you have every right to extricate yourself from the relationship, even if it is with family.

If we have made the very difficult decision to go no contact, or have had to alter expectations and come to accept that it might never be a functional relationship, perhaps we're still in touch but there is no emotional intimacy or honest sharing; we grieve what we've lost, and we grieve for what we hoped the relationship could be. Sometimes, despite what's best for us, we can't remove ourselves completely, as when we are co-parenting, for example. This living grief can be so painful, especially when your mind is drawn to 'what ifs' – remember, if you have tried, and there hasn't been reciprocation of interest, willingness to repair or respect, then you've done all you can and it's OK to protect yourself and your family from further hurt. People will question you, they will remind you of your duty, and their lack of understanding is another wound that needs tender witnessing.

Here are some techniques for grieving lost or changed relationships:

1. Decide on the boundaries or expectations of the relationship. Are you deciding to go non-contact or are you maintaining a presence in each other's lives but with limits to how you interact? Be clear and communicate this where necessary, with compassion, for example by agreeing that you will correspond via email only. Write a letter to yourself to remind yourself why

this is needed, what you have tried already to heal the situation and how it was met. Revisit these reminders when you are tempted to try again.

2. Take time to process, digest and release your experiences and feelings. It helps to be witnessed and validated by another human being. See the toolkits to sit with your own disappointment and to feel safe (pages 188 and 94).

3. Proactively develop strategies for coping with triggers, such as birthdays, holidays, calendar dates, events or places of significance, circumstances where you might see each other or just when memories float to the surface. If other people asking about them causes you pain, even when this is well intentioned, it is OK to request that they refrain if that would help you cope. Being honest with people about how they can best support you is not selfish.

4. Extend to yourself all the tenderness and nourishment to help you in your healing journey. This is hard. It hurts, darling. There is no expiry date on healing, especially where this is a living grief and it still feels like there is the possibility of things being different, if only they would meet you halfway.

5. Invest time and energy in healthy reciprocal relationships. Deepen those bonds, express gratitude for the joy and care these people bring to your life and plan some fun together!

What to do when you feel selfish for saying no or for changing plans

Managing your time and your diary also fall under boundary management. Remember, you have every right to choose how you spend your time and energy and as your resources or life demands change, sometimes you'll need to alter your commitments or you might need to decline a request or invitation from the outset.

1. If guilt needles you, ask yourself what story you're telling yourself here. Where does that old groove take you? How are you 'shoulding' on yourself? Remember that it's OK to prioritise your health, your energy, your sleep or your peace.

2. Why do you need to turn this request or invite down, or extricate yourself from agreed plans? What are the immediate benefits to you and how might the other person also benefit? For example, are you giving them greater dispensation to honour their own needs and letting them know they can be truthful with you?

3. What's really at stake here? What is life requesting of you right now that has to take precedence for you to sustain yourself? Let this be the priority without beating yourself up. That's just the way things are right now. It won't be like this forever, but while it is, it's not selfish to let this be the deciding factor in your planning.

4. Come back to a feeling of safety; disappointing someone you care about might feel really difficult. Draw on a trusted friend for support. Share the shame for it to dissipate and let your friend cheer you on as you grow in your skills of self-advocacy.

5. Get brave and let them know. Sometimes a simple 'no thanks' is all that is required, no apologies needed. Notice if you have a tendency to overexplain and try to keep it simple. Sometimes we do need to give more information for others to understand us and we need to communicate regret for disappointment caused. Sometimes even with that information they will still feel let down and we need to build our capacity for sitting with that. Remember, you have every right to manage your diary, your energy and your commitments. What have you learned in this process? Take it and grow, darling.

Love note for when you feel selfish for not playing with your kids

Part of boundary management involves being clear with others on our availability. Let's address now what it means when you feel selfish for not playing with your kids – or for not wanting to play with them. That's part of the human experience too and doesn't mean you don't love your kids enough, it just means you also love other forms of self-expression. Remember that parenting involves a whole lot more than just playing with your kids. Raising children also includes earning money to provide for them, investing time in home/school/life admin to keep things running smoothly, food prep, cooking, cleaning, tidying, washing and sorting for a harmonious home environment. Tending to our own human needs is also part of the picture, resourcing us so that we can keep showing up as we aspire to. Those values of kindness and patience take energy!

When that feeling of selfishness hits, pause and ask yourself, are you truly being selfish or are you just tending to other responsibilities? If you can't play right now, can you schedule time to play later? If your kids are enjoying themselves without your involvement, can you share in their joy without having to be a direct part of the game? It's OK for our kids to have fun and make memories of their own. Perhaps we don't enjoy the activity they're asking us to get involved with (permission to not enjoy making Barbies talk!), can you suck it up for a short time and then change to something you both enjoy? It's important for our kids to learn to take turns.

Even if you're not playing with your kids, you can still share time and space together, enjoying solo pursuits. What else can they engage in while you're doing what's required of you? Yes, there is a time for screens and there are plenty of online activities that are enriching and pleasurable, we just need to choose mindfully. When your kids are engaged in independent play, what skills are they developing? Time without parental steers can encourage self-insight, creativity and resourcefulness.

And a little note on boredom. Boredom is a valid feeling and our kids might need support with it just as they do with other feelings such as anger or sadness. Navigating boredom is a vital skill because it connects us with what we need. It's not something requiring fixing, but we can still sit with our kids through the experience and provide comfort. It can be hard feeling stuck or not knowing what we would like to do with our time, especially if spare time is in short supply. We can acknowledge the feeling and help them find something that calls to them – it might be a desire for movement, fun or rest. Perhaps it's not just boredom but loneliness too. When you're juggling competing demands, depending on the age of your kids, you could fill out a planner to show them the windows you can spend together and the times where they need to find something to keep themselves busy. Kids like to feel in control too and this information can be reassuring. Sometimes it takes a little organisation and encouragement to turn boredom into creativity. Work on it together with your kids, as time allows.

How to protect yourself from emotional dumping

Boundaries are required to protect your energy and just because you might be skilled in bearing witness to the emotions of others, or someone needs to vent, it doesn't mean that you have to make yourself available. Don't let yourself fall into the trap of 'toxic empathy' – taking on the emotional load of people around you to the detriment of your own human needs.

If you identify with being an HSP, your giant heart is a beautiful thing that doesn't need changing, but it does require management. You are not too sensitive, you just need the tools to be able to bear witness to the emotions of others, without taking it all on. Remember that people can express themselves without it being your job to fix it or move them through to resolution, peace or calm. You are not responsible for their happiness, and you can be OK, even if they are experiencing difficult emotions. Be clear on what is yours and what doesn't belong to you. You can be there for them, while letting this be their predicament. You don't need to save them or solve it.

Even though you care, it is still necessary to have boundaries when bearing witness to the struggles of other people. You can ask them what kind of support they'd like – do they want a sounding board, a brainstorming partner, understanding, validation or just listening? But equally, it is not your job to be an emotional sponge, or be on the receiving end of a tirade. You can choose whether it is a good time or whether you are able to provide the kind of support they are requesting. If expectations stray, remind them of how you can be there for them.

During exchanges you can imagine that you are surrounded in a bubble or a ball of light, protecting you from what doesn't belong to you. Imagine yourself encased, allowing only healthy energy to penetrate your space, anything else just bounces off. You are present but you are not touched by it. Nonviolent communication will help all parties, avoiding blaming, personalising and character assassinations, and it is OK to ask someone who is venting to do so with less venom. If it helps, you can ask clarifying questions, reflecting back what you are hearing, or you can just be the compassionate listener. Be aware of your own emotions and know your early warning signs of stress. Notice where it shows up for you: it might be tension in your hands, throat, jaw, chest or stomach, changes to the rhythm of your breathing, increased heart rate or feeling panicky or irritated, even nausea. If you start to feel flooded, request a break or call time. It is not selfish to protect your own energy and peace. Soothe yourself during these conversations to avoid overwhelm, get to know the toolkit to feel safe (page 94) and have a few practices you can alternate between, such as holding your own hand, taking long smooth exhalations or grounding yourself with your feet, sit bones or hands.

After the exchange, imagine you are cutting energetic cords between you. You have been there for them and now it's time to let go. This is their problem to own. It doesn't mean you don't care, but it does free you up to focus on other things that are important to you. It is not selfish to detach and refocus on yourself, your responsibilities and your energetic health. Prioritise spending time with people who reciprocate for you, who can be a place where you celebrate life and share blessings. You deserve people who bring you peace, not just their problems. You can also process this experience with someone else if it has been heavy. Time in nature also helps you cleanse and release. It is OK to pace yourself, to give yourself space or take a break, bearing in mind what kind of support it is sustainable to provide. Every time thoughts about this person come to you, remember that their issue doesn't belong to you. Turn your worry into a prayer of well wishes and let it go again. Repeat as needed, darling.

What to do when you feel selfish for not keeping the peace – learning to cope with conflict

There will be times when you need to prioritise your peace over keeping 'the peace' and this can be painful to acknowledge, especially for those who have historically taken on the role of the peacekeeper; smoothing down ruffled feathers, shape shifting to grease the wheels, bending so the family unit or social circle doesn't break. Perhaps you've been lumbered with a secret, or maybe you're just expected to subjugate your needs for the common good, regardless of the personal toll it incurs. But we know the depletion and angst this brings. Pause for a moment and recognise the direct costs to you right now; and the next question is, how sustainable is it? If you keep sacrificing yourself for the greater good, what lies ahead?

When you are weighing up potential courses of action, ask yourself what your true responsibility is here. There is a collective, shared responsibility to maintaining true harmony, not just you keeping a semblance of it at your own expense. Who else can you turn to for support here? How can you share the load?

What might you lose by honouring yourself? Is this really true and, if so, how likely is that outcome? Can you minimise the damage by being direct and transparent, and by setting expectations or facilitating understanding to avoid leaving people in the dark? Sometimes you have to act even though you risk losing something precious to you. Can you look at the breadth of your values beyond selflessness and duty – what other qualities important to you can you honour in this course of action, such as honesty, integrity, fairness?

There's no doubt, sometimes the truth hurts and we will need all the soothing in the midst of that disapproval, disappointment and even rejection; we will need comforting as we nurse our own disappointment and the grief that can come from us taking a stand and upholding healthy boundaries. See the toolkits on disappointment and grief for support (pages 215 and 246).

Remember, too, that there is every chance that things can improve when we stop self-silencing and enabling, and get courageous enough to bring to light unhealthy patterns. You know that sweeping things under the carpet, downplaying tension or outright avoidance just lay the foundation for future discord on a larger scale. Short-term discomfort might just lead the way to long-term healthy interactions – you will never know what's possible unless you voice it.

If conflict feels frightening for you, please go gently and slowly. Draw on the support of someone who has your best interests front of mind and let them walk this path with you. Remember that it is OK for you to stand up for yourself and protect your peace; this doesn't make you a selfish person, even if it's your own family you need to communicate these ground rules to. It is not selfish for you to speak up about things that are upsetting you. All relationships will encounter conflict from time to time and it's how you navigate it that counts. Use the toolkits to feel safe, build confidence and give voice (pages 94, 236 and 238) in preparation for these tricky conversations. See where there is room for discussion and know that in providing people with honest feedback, you are giving them an opportunity to do things differently. Observe how the feedback is received and what attempts at repair are made. If people do not put effort into restoring the relationship, it is also OK for you to reassess how much of yourself you invest in it. I know it's painful, but it's OK to move away from people who do not appreciate or respect you. It frees you up to prioritise relationships where there is reciprocity and genuine care. You don't need an apology to start healing; the healing begins the moment we give ourselves closure.

How to cultivate trust in others

It's not always about firming up boundaries, sometimes it's about allowing more flexibility or permeability. Boundaries are not there to shut other people out; we all need the love and support of others. If you find yourself pushing people away and avoiding relying to others, there may be a core issue of trust involved. Your job here is to recognise the costs of hyper-independence and think about where it might be appropriate to allow other people in a bit more. You have learned for good reason that *some* people are not to be trusted, but darling, this doesn't mean that all people can't be trusted. Let's look at how to begin healing this core wound. Healing is possible.

In building trust with people, it will help to acknowledge past hurts and to try, as much as humanly possible, not to bring *that* baggage with you to *this* relationship – that was then, and this is now.

Make that distinction. Knowing your past triggers will help you navigate the future. There might be some core beliefs around trust that need to be challenged. Mistrust is a form of self-protection, but what does it cost you? When you think of the word 'trust', what comes up? Are there some new phrases that might help you move in a different direction? If you constantly tell yourself that people can't be trusted, or you can't rely on anyone, you know where that leads you – to isolation, hyper-independence, burnout and loneliness. See where this mantra leads you instead: 'I am open to developing trust.' Let it pave the way for authentic connection, deeper bonds, loyalty and the sense of shared humanity that gives life meaning.

Before we can lean on others and feel safe, we need to look for evidence that it is wise to trust them. Trust is a firm belief in the reliability, truth or ability of someone. Not sure who to trust? Look for people who are true to their word, people who keep their promises and honour their commitments. Who are the people that are respectful of your boundaries and direct in articulating theirs? Notice the people who communicate clearly and are transparent in their requests. Look for consistency and reciprocity of values.

Take small steps and give yourself time. Don't leap in and expect too much too soon – of yourself or other people. Start with minor risks of vulnerability first, small disclosures or requests, and invite them to do the same. Be honest about your feelings and preferences, and encourage honesty in return. Let people know if you find it hard; chances are, they do too! If you are sharing something in confidence, be explicit that this is something not to be shared. You won't always agree and you won't always be able to meet each other's needs in the moment, but be on the lookout for people who can admit their mistakes, who are swift in making attempts at repair and also open to receiving your apologies. These are the people we want to invest our trust in.

Notice when people undermine your self-trust and gently let them know how their behaviour leads you to question yourself. Request that they be more open to validating how you think and feel. If people repeatedly violate your self-trust, what kind of boundary tweak might be needed? Perhaps there is someone else in your circle who you might share this part of your life with. What does it feel safe to bring to this relationship?

Be honest if you feel your trust in a relationship has been betrayed and give the other person an opportunity to repair. If your trust was broken, ask why. Seek to understand as well as to be understood. Was the burden too great? Did they share your information out of concern for you? Give people a chance to change. Part of learning to trust is also learning to forgive. Trust isn't just blind faith, it is teamwork, cooperation, compromise and a willingness to grow together. Communication is key and we need to get brave and have those difficult conversations. (See the toolkits on confidence and giving voice on pages 236 and 238, and the one on coping with disappointment on page 215.)

What to do when you feel selfish for leaning on others

Regardless of what you've been told about needing people or your past experiences of relying on others, people need people. All humans need validation, understanding, acceptance, comfort, companionship, belonging, care and hands-on support. These are basic human needs. There is nothing selfish about it; it is human. Talking helps us process our experiences. Sharing our struggles helps us feel less alone and stops us from bottling things up, and it also makes other people feel less alone in their own turmoil. It is so important to be heard and held and I am sorry if you've been denied this historically or have been made to feel 'less than' for expressing these needs. It can feel scary to let people in or to be vulnerable in making requests. If that fear of being seen as selfish crops up, let it. The more you do that, the less that fear will stop you from reaching out. Feel it and reach out anyway. Recall a time when someone you care about turned to you for support – did you think they were being needy or weak? How did it make you feel about yourself or the relationship? Quite often it is affirming to be needed, it feels good to be trusted, it is calming to know how you can best support someone rather than hazarding a guess and feeling rebuffed. *How* you make requests can make all the difference too.

How to ask for help

Before you ask for help, think about who might be the appropriate person to reach out to. Choose the right person in your circle with the current resources or strengths to support you. If you're not sure, check. Ask them whether this is a good time and, if not, when might be convenient? Get skilled in being direct and if you are asking something of someone, be clear as to what would be most helpful – do they have the capacity to do 'X'? You can let them know that it is OK to say no, and if it is a no, don't take it personally. If they can't meet your exact request, is there some other way they can support you that feels doable for them right now? If they can't do it now, is there another time when they can? Allow it to be a co-creation but be honest if what they propose is not genuinely helpful. You can thank them for their kind offer and move on. Who else in your circle can you turn to?

Sometimes we have to be patient in waiting for the support that we need, sometimes we need to draft in a professional and sometimes we must grieve the disappointment of not having the support that we deserve and desire. Just because that's how it is right now doesn't mean that it's going to be this way forever. Keep being courageous and keep reaching out. Keep nurturing relationships where there is warmth and reciprocity, even with those people who perhaps you don't know very well. Who knows what might grow from them. Nothing ventured, nothing gained. You will find your kindred spirits. Be gentle with your giant heart in the process.

NEXT STEPS

My darling, we have reached the closing chapter together, but you are just getting started. Well done for getting brave and embarking on this journey to self-advocacy with me. You are casting off the shackles of societal norms and choosing what feels aligned and healthy for you. I hope you are discovering new things about yourself daily – from that self-insight comes power. Use that power to build a life that feels authentic and true to you, in ways that help you feel both alive and at peace. It is yours for the making. Let this be a beautiful work in progress that you have your whole life to cultivate, but don't delay it. Don't put it on hold any longer. What action can you take today? This final chapter will help you decide and once you've taken that action, come back and read it again for fresh direction.

Can you now answer this prompt?

If I was 'selfish' I would . . .

Can you answer this question knowing the distinction between what the world would have you believe is selfish, and self-advocacy? You know I am not suggesting you be a callous, uncaring person, I am asking you what you need to honour in your life – hell, what you do want, what do you desire?! From your joy comes the energy to grow and become the most glorious incarnation of yourself. Resource yourself; the world needs resourced people. How can you have your own back? How can you care for yourself? How can you allow yourself to receive? Let yourself entertain all these invitations, seeing for yourself what it's like to live life centre stage. If this idea of being 'selfish' still rankles, let it, but remember what you stand to lose if you don't, darling, and what you stand to gain if you do!

Signs of self-advocacy

Self-advocacy is not a destination that you reach one fine day. It is a collection of skills, a mindset, a way of living your life. I hope you are beginning to see some of the following gifts unfold in your life already. These are just a few signs that you are making progress in your journey to self-advocacy – please add your own observations to this list:

- You know that your self-talk is the soundtrack to your life and you are deliberately choosing words that lift you up more often than those that tear you down. You also know that you don't choose your first thought and are feeling less provoked by those humdingers that the brain generates. In response, you are learning how to address yourself with tenderness. You are becoming your own safe place.

- You are more connected with your body, feeling sensations and the stirring of emotions with greater sensitivity, and you are learning how to meet yourself with greater acceptance and kindness.

- You are becoming more skilled in directing where your energy and attention flow, giving yourself permission to choose what feels nourishing and supportive for you.

- You're allowing yourself to rest and relax with more abandon and feeling the benefits of those commitments to self.

- You are determining the rhythm and pulse of your own life, your response time, your daily patterns, rather than being directed by the hustle or urgency culture we're embedded in.

- You're more interested in following your own moral compass than being guided by other people's opinions.

- You can focus on yourself, identify your own needs and act in your own interests without feeling ashamed. You can see that your nourishment is essential and while you might still feel guilt, you don't allow it to stop you from meeting your own needs, or from receiving.

- You're honouring your energy and pacing yourself with more skill and ease. It is becoming easier to say no.

- You are less needled by disappointing others, and less rocked by the disappointment you feel when you can't be all things to all people.

- You're seeking your own approval and less bothered by the lack of external approval.

- You're 'shoulding' on yourself less and you are experiencing more peace.

- You feel more comfortable voicing your preferences, values and ideas.

- You are more direct in your requests of others and clear in what you are OK or not OK with.

- You are more confident in your inner knowing, trusting your emotions.

- You are noticing the courage to get messy and to let your guard down. You are becoming more honest and authentic in relationship, growing in your capacity to be vulnerable, to share your inner life, your feelings, your fears, your hopes, your regrets and your dreams, and you are becoming more skilled in knowing who it is safe to do this with.

- You can allow others the freedom to express themselves, knowing that you can be OK even when others around you are not OK. You are experiencing that it's a gift to be someone else's safe place, too, without trying to fix them or rush them back to happiness.

- You are growing in your ability to have difficult conversations, bringing things to light and dealing with conflict and ruptures.

- You feel more in touch with your desires and open to receiving. You know that you are deserving of abundance.

- You are allowing other people to support you, leaning on others, letting other people in with less guilt and shame.

- You are experiencing more pleasure!

- You are finding it easier to accept compliments.

- You are cultivating a fresh definition of success that is distinct from pleasing others, self-reliance, striving, productivity and efficiency, and more concerned with alignment, integrity and peace. You are less fixated on what is still to be done or your deficits, and you can celebrate what you've accomplished, how far you've come and how you've grown.

- You are growing in your capacity to just be, basking in the glow of who you are. Enough. Whole. Worthy.

- You can hear yourself saying, 'Finally, it feels good to be me.'

How to get out of old grooves of thinking and behaving

While you can see the beautiful growth you are achieving, there might still be some sticking points. Let's acknowledge what might still remain to work through, the old patterns that can take a while to rewrite. Throughout this book I have been modelling how to speak to yourself with dignity and respect. I want to make space in this closing chapter for your voice, for the words you need to hear from yourself and the commitments you are ready to make to yourself.

I invite you to complete the following 'fork in the road' exercises in your own words, anchored in what will motivate you, knowing that you have a choice and that each day we wake, we need to renew our commitment to self-advocacy and self-honouring. These three exercises each explore a common trigger, such as feeling selfish for resting or feeling guilty for not keeping the peace. Each time one of these triggers comes up, remind yourself that you have a choice. You can use one of the familiar coping strategies that take you away from the life you want to lead, or you can create a fresh habit, even if at first it is difficult and uncomfortable, that takes you towards the life you want to live. To help you choose which path to take, flesh out the diagram below with details of what this old 'away' coping habit looks like now and what a more healthy 'towards' action could look like, followed by a description of the short-term benefits and costs and the long-term benefits and costs. Get as granular as you can, helping yourself really feel what it would be like to take each path. If there are some barriers to the 'towards' choices, do some brainstorming to overcome them. One path might feel really well trodden and the other might feel uncertain, but you know where they both lead you. Let's do a few together, then please write down your own triggers and use this approach to help guide you through future choices.

'Fork in the road' exercise

Away choice: taking you away from the life you want to live	Towards choice: taking you towards the life you want to live
What does this look like?	What does this look like?
Short-term benefits/costs	Short-term costs/benefits
Long-term costs	Long-term benefits

Trigger: 'I feel selfish for resting or pacing myself'

Away choice: pushing on	Towards choice: pausing and replenishing
It looks like I must keep going regardless of how I feel or the quality of what I'm producing. It looks like ploughing on irrespective of my energy levels or needs.	It looks like refreshing myself by looking out the window and seeing what natural beauty takes my eye, or going to the bathroom and taking a few relaxed breaths. It looks like making an appointment for a treatment I've been putting off, such as seeing the osteo, or booking the whole day off. It can be scheduling an early night instead of meeting friends, or simply 'massaging my horns' for 30 seconds (page 97).
In the short term it can feel comfortable because I'm pleased with myself for being hard working and productive, and I'm distracted from the anxiety I'd feel if I stopped and rested. I get a bit more done of what's required of me, but the work is taking me longer and I am making more mistakes. I am not enjoying what I'm doing, even the things I usually love. I don't even get satisfaction when I finish something; it's just straight on to the next job and it feels endless.	In the short term, I might feel worried about how resting could appear to other people. I might feel stressed that I am not checking something off my to-do list. I might be aware of the volume of things accumulating, but I also know that I can take a breather and it's OK.

The long-term costs are poor-quality performance, potential stress at work when I fall short of expectations, and not reaching my potential which makes me feel down on myself. It leads to fatigue, overwhelm, difficulty switching off and sleep disruption, and that has the knock-on effect of increasing conflict in my relationships.	In the long term, pausing and replenishing myself allows me to focus better, make good-quality decisions and keep my energy and stress levels more manageable. Taking this moment to rest builds my skills of relaxation, which serve me well when I am trying to get to sleep later. This rest I am allowing myself now will also fuel me so that I can be present and available for my loved ones, rather than a distracted human Mount Vesuvius, waiting to blow.
This path leads me to frustration, depletion and potential burnout.	This path leads me to an aligned life, to peace, to calm.

Trigger: 'I feel selfish for leaning on other people'

Away choice: being self-reliant, never accepting help or reaching out to others for support	Towards choice: letting other people in, accepting and reaching out for support
It looks like keeping my worries to myself, withholding requests for support even when I know there are people who have the resources and the desire to help me. It looks like turning down people's offers of support regardless of how much I'd like them.	It looks like being honest with other people when they check in with me. It can be considering who's on my team and who would be the appropriate person to ask for help. It can be accepting the kindness and generosity that is offered, and also asking if there is wiggle room in what's suggested so that it is more genuinely helpful.
In the short term I can feel good about myself and my ability to be strong and self-reliant. I feel less let down by others when I don't give them an opportunity to disappoint me. I feel in control. I also feel unfairly burdened and alone.	In the short term I might feel uncomfortable about burdening others, but I can make it clear that they can say no. I can give them choice in how they support me, depending on their strengths and available resources. My request might be declined and that might result in some disappointment, but this can be tempered by not taking it personally and considering why it wasn't possible this time. I can reach out to someone else.

The long-term costs are that I feel irritated when other people call on me, although I never ask anything of them. I feel annoyed with myself for not accepting kind offers and let down by others for not being able to read my mind. I feel burdened by inequity in my relationships – I'm doing all the work and they don't even know the sacrifices I am making. I am exhausted managing all this on my own all the time. I feel lonely and taken for granted. I don't even feel like my friends know me anymore.	In the long term my friends know that I am honest with them and that they can be honest with me. We collaborate in making our relationship feel balanced and reciprocal. I know they have my back and they know I have theirs. It feels good to share the journey with them.
This path leads me to discord, loneliness and overwhelm.	This path leads me to greater connection and shared humanity. I am better able to face the challenges I encounter in life.

Trigger: 'I feel selfish for not keeping other people happy'

Away choice: people pleasing and hyper-responsibility	Towards choice: letting other people have responsibility for their own emotional wellbeing and challenges, and being honest with other people even if it displeases them
It looks like rushing to fix, save, sort or help other people, an overwhelming need to remove the struggle of others even if it's not my responsibility. It looks like providing support through gritted teeth or saying yes to requests even when I know I lack the current capacity, often to my own detriment. It might be appeasing, pandering or staying quiet when I know that honest feedback might allow insight, ownership or growth, for fear of causing temporary upset. It is also asking questions and indulging someone when I really don't want to engage in a conversation, when the other person is just craving attention, for example. It is swallowing my own hurt so as not to disturb the comfort or peace of others. It can be mollycoddling or over-giving, sacrificing my needs for the benefit of others.	It looks like stepping back from rescuing other people and letting them participate in their own problem solving. It can be providing support where requested but being honest about my available resources and capacity to get involved. It is choosing when to support without taking ownership of the feeling or problem. It can be listening without attempting to intervene, and without taking it on as my own issue and carrying it with me. It can be allowing someone else to be in a bad mood without feeling the need to fix it, and without personalising it. It can be being brave and giving direct feedback even when it makes someone else feel bad or uncomfortable for their actions.

It can feel pleasurable in the short term because I like being selfless, it helps me feel like I am a good human being and I might be praised for my sacrifice or generosity. Often, however, people don't even know that I am making a sacrifice and I feel unappreciated. I worry endlessly about whether other people are OK, but what's harder is that I wind up feeling like I can only be OK if they are, and that's so often out of my control that my anxiety is spiralling. I spend so much time focusing on trying to keep other people happy, at the expense of what matters to me as an individual. This also turns to frustration when I am continually relied on to tend without reciprocity. My shape shifting and self-censoring are beyond tiring.	There are some short-term risks: people might be shocked and interpret my move away from my usual people-pleasing behaviour as being distant or uncaring. There might be accusations or criticism. I might feel guilty for feeling like I'm letting them down, but I can remember that this is not my issue to sort. It might even feel painful and scary when my safety has depended on other people around me feeling appeased, but I can remind myself of ways to feel safe and who I am safe with. I can remind myself that I don't want to enable others, or rob them of their opportunities to learn and grow. I can allow other people to manage their own emotions and if they become volatile, I have every right to remove myself from the situation and reconsider boundaries with this person.

Over time, my own needs get swamped and I feel out of touch with what's important to me. If I do this long enough, I start to feel lost, tetherless, blown about from one person's crisis or bad mood to the next, and only worthy when I am needed or useful.	I get courageous and build my capacity to sit with the discomfort. I notice that people either step up and assume their own responsibilities or I alter boundaries and expectations for the type of intimacy in that relationship. Some relationships I walk away from. There is some grieving but in time, the nature of my relationships changes and I notice my bonds deepen. There's more genuine connection. I feel we come together equally and I can also let go after time together which feels freeing. I have more energy for what matters to me.
I feel unseen and I don't even know myself. I shut down and sink further into invisibility. When I pass, I am celebrated at my funeral for always being supportive, but not honoured for what made me uniquely me. People are sad not because they miss *me* but because they miss what I facilitated.	I feel known, understood and respected. I know and trust myself and it feels good to be in the driver's seat of my own life, choosing what's worthy of my care and attention. People appreciate me for my own unique contribution and this feels like a life well lived.

Your toolkit to find your flock

We all need other people. We also know that some of the ideas in this book go against the cultural grain. There may be some people in your life who will resist this new incarnation of you. See if there's the possibility of recalibrating boundaries and reaching new understanding with them. You have an opportunity for true connection like never before, but there needs to be willingness on both sides. Perhaps you'll need to seek fresh relationships where there can be real reciprocity. You will find your people, we are plentiful! Use your toolkits for having those vulnerable conversations and growing your confidence (pages 236 and 238) to put yourself out there, and let's explore one more toolkit together now. Here are three steps to feel a sense of belonging:

1. **It begins with self-acceptance**
   Hop to the guidance on trusting yourself (page 137) and the toolkit for seeking your own approval (page 143). We need to know and accept ourselves to be able to show up fully in relationship with others.

2. **Connect with other people**
   Find your tribe, the people who have a similar ethos or shared interests. Come together either in person or online via hashtags, support groups, Facebook pages, book clubs, podcasts and so on – there are so many ways to connect with your kindred spirits.

3. **Make a contribution**
   Feel how taking action to honour shared values helps you feel part of something bigger than yourself. Even a few kind words of support can create a meaningful exchange. How can you take part and make a difference? It needn't be financial; you could donate your time or a skill, or just show that you care and appreciate the contributions of others. Get involved

in the change you want to see in the world and you will find your people who are ready to embrace this generous *and* boundaried version of you.

What you hold to be true: Your mantras

This is where I want your voice to ring out loud and true. Take some time reading and saying out loud the following mantras, writing down any additional ones that come to you:

'I have every right to be here.'
'I have every right to take up space.'
'I have every right to be seen and heard.'
'I am whole and worthy as I am right now.'
'It is safe for me to receive.'
'It is safe for me to desire.'
'It is safe for me to trust myself.'
'It is safe for me to rely on my people.'
'It is safe for me to express myself.'
'It is safe for me to prioritise myself.'
'I can live a life of my choosing.'
'I can honour myself.'
'It feels good to be me.'

What you now give yourself permission to do: Your action steps

Your reflective prompts:
You've asserted your right to be here, you've acknowledged that your feelings are valid and your needs are worthy of being met; what do these core beliefs allow you to do in your life? Let's

get crystal clear on the tangible change self-advocacy brings to your life now. Welcome to this powerful new season of your life.

Until now I have . . . From this moment on, I choose to . . .
It is OK for me to . . .
I am open to receiving . . .
I am deserving of . . .
I am ready to release . . .
I feel most alive and at peace when I . . .
I feel most like me when . . .
I give myself permission to . . .

The choice is yours, my friend. Please choose you.

Further Reading and Listening

Some of my favourite books:
Blaskey, Z., *Motherkind* (HQ, 2024)
Boyd, Dr C., *Mindful New Mum* (DK, 2022)
Cox, J., *Women Are Angry* (Lagom, 2024)
Dean, R., *Mindful Drinking* (Trapeze, 2020)
Deiros Collado, Dr M., *How to Be the Grown-up* (Bantam, 2024)
Doyle, G., Wambach, A. and Doyle, A. *We Can Do Hard Things* (Ebury, 2025)
Ford, C., *Fight like a Girl* (Oneworld, 2019)
Foster, J., *Behaviour* (Corwin, 2023)
Haver, Dr M.C., *The New Menopause* (Vermilion, 2024)
Hayes, A. and Andrew, Dr R., *The Supermum Myth* (White Ladder, 2017)
Heale, S., *Now Is Not the Time for Flowers* (Lagom, 2024)
Hepburn, Dr E., *A Toolkit for Your Emotions* (Greenfinch, 2023)
Hobbs, N.J., *The Relaxed Woman* (Rider, 2025)
Lesser, E., *Cassandra Speaks* (HarperWave, 2020)
Lourie, S.C., *The Power of Mess* (Yellow Kite, 2023)
Mathur, A., *The Good Decision Diary* (Penguin Life, 2025)
Mathur, A., *The Uncomfortable Truth* (Penguin Life, 2024)
Pert, Dr C., *Molecules of Emotion* (Simon & Schuster, 2012)
Plumbly, Dr C., *Burnout* (Yellow Kite, 2024)
Ridout, A., *The Freelance Mum* (Fourth Estate, 2019)

Svanberg, Dr E., *Parenting for Humans* (Vermilion, 2023)
Tang, K., *It's not Hysteria* (Flatiron Books, 2025)
Thomas, T., *Women Who Work Too Much* (Hay House, 2024)

My favourite podcasts:
Helen Marie, *I Don't Think We Talk Enough About*
Mandy Lehto, *Enough, the Podcast*
Nicky Denson-Elliott, *Women's Business Podcast*

Notes

Chapter One: Getting to Know Yourself

1 'APA dictionary of psychology', American Psychological Association, apa.org
2 Crocker, J., Canevello, A. and Brown, A.A., 'Social motivation: Costs and benefits of selfishness and otherishness', *Annual Review of Psychology* 68 (2017), pp. 299–325
3 Crocker, J., Canevello, A., Breines, J.G. and Flynn, H., 'Interpersonal goals and change in anxiety and dysphoria in first-semester college students', *Journal of Personality and Social Psychology* 98 (2010), pp. 1009–24
4 Canevello, A. and Crocker, J., 'How self-image and compassionate goals shape intrapsychic experiences', *Social and Personality Psychology Compass* 9 (2015), pp. 620–9
5 Leary, M.R., Tchividijian, L.R. and Kraxberger, B.E., 'Self-presentation can be hazardous to your health: Impression management and health risk', *Health Psychology* 13 (1994), pp. 461–70
6 Dittmar, H., Bond, R., Hurst, M. and Kasser, T., 'The relationship between materialism and personal well-being: A meta-analysis', *Journal of Personality and Social Psychology* 107 (2014), pp. 879–924
7 Krekels, G. and Pandelaere, M., 'Dispositional greed', *Personality and Individual Differences* 74 (2015), pp. 225–30
8 Fritz, H.L. and Helgeson, V.S., 'Distinctions of unmitigated communion from communion: Self-neglect and overinvolvement with others', *Journal of Personality and Social Psychology* 75 (1998), pp. 121–40

9 Martin, K.A. and Leary, M.R., 'Self-presentational determinants of health risk behavior among college freshmen', *Psychology & Health* 16 (2001), pp. 17–27

10 Leary, M.R., Tchividijian, L.R. and Kraxberger, B.E., 'Self-presentation can be hazardous to your health: Impression management and health risk', *Health Psychology* 13 (1994), pp. 461–70

11 Feeney, B.C. and Collins, N.L., 'Motivations for caregiving in adult intimate relationships: Influences on caregiving behavior and relationship functioning', *Psychology and Social Psychology Bulletin* 29 (2003), pp. 950–68

12 Canevello, A. and Crocker, J., 'Creating good relationships: Responsiveness, relationship quality, and interpersonal goals', *Journal of Personality and Social Psychology* 99 (2010), pp. 78–106

13 Crocker, J. and Canevello, A., 'Creating and undermining social support in communal relationships: The role of compassionate and self-image goals', *Journal of Personality and Social Psychology* 95 (2008), pp. 555–75

14 Crocker, J. and Canevello, A., 'Creating and undermining social support in communal relationships: The role of compassionate and self-image goals', *Journal of Personality and Social Psychology* 95 (2008), pp. 555–75

15 Canevello, A., Granillo, M.T. and Crocker, J., 'Predicting change in relationship insecurity: The roles of compassionate and self-image goals', *Personal Relationships* 20 (2013), pp. 587–618

16 Rose, P., 'The happy and unhappy faces of narcissism', *Personality and Individual Differences* 33 (2002), pp. 379–92

17 Bushman, B.J. and Baumeister, R.F., 'Threatened egotism, narcissism, self-esteem, and direct and displaced aggression: Does self-love or self-hate lead to violence?', *Journal of Personality and Social Psychology* 75 (1998), pp. 219–29

18 Brunell, A.B., Davis, M.S., Schley, D.R., Eng, A.L., van Dulmen, M.H.M. et al., 'A new measure of interpersonal exploitativeness', *Frontiers in Psychology* 4 (2013), p. 299

19 Dunn, E.W., Aknin, L.B. and Norton, M.I., 'Spending money on others promotes happiness', *Science* 319 (2008), pp. 1687–8

20 Mogilner, C., 'The pursuit of happiness: Time, money, and social connection', *Psychological Science* 21 (2010), pp. 1348–54
21 Sarid, O., Melzer, I., Kurz, I., Shahar, D. and Ruch, W., 'The effect of helping behavior and physical activity on mood states and depressive symptoms of elderly people', *Clinical Gerontologist* 33 (2010), pp. 270–82
22 Thoits, P.A. and Hewitt, L.N., 'Volunteer work and well-being', *Journal of Health and Social Behavior* 42 (2001), pp. 115–31
23 Piferi, R. and Lawler, K., 'Social support and ambulatory blood pressure: An examination of both receiving and giving', *International Journal of Psychophysiology* 62 (2006), pp. 328–36
24 Heisler, M., Choi, H., Piette, J., Rosland, A., Langa, K. and Brown, S., 'Adults with cardiovascular disease who help others: A prospective study of health outcomes', *Journal of Behavioral Medicine* 36 (2013), pp. 199–211
25 Aknin, L. and Human, L., 'Give a piece of you: Gifts that reflect givers promote closeness', *Journal of Experimental Social Psychology* 60 (2015), pp. 8–16
26 Pasch, L. and Bradbury, T., 'Social support, conflict, and the development of marital dysfunction', *Journal of Consulting and Clinical Psychology* 66 (1998), pp. 219–30
27 Pinquart, M. and Sörensen. S., 'Associations of stressors and uplifts of caregiving with caregiver burden and depressive mood: A meta-analysis', *The Journals of Gerontology Series B, Psychological Science and Social Sciences* 58 (2003), pp. 112–28
28 Pinquart, M. and Sörensen. S., 'Differences between caregivers and noncaregivers in psychological health and physical health: A meta-analysis', *Psychology and Aging* 18 (2003), pp. 250–67
29 Kiecolt-Glaser, J.K., Marucha, P.T., Mercado, A.M., Malarkey, W.B. and Glaser, R., 'Slowing of wound healing by psychological stress', *Lancet* 346 (1995), pp. 1194–6
30 Vitaliano, P., Zhang, J. and Scanlan, J., 'Is caregiving hazardous to one's physical health? A meta-analysis', *Psychological Bulletin*, 129 (2003), pp. 946–72

31 Kiecolt-Glaser, J.K., Preacher, K.J., MacCallum, R.C., Atkinson, A., Malarkey, W.B. and Glaser, R., 'Chronic stress and age-related increases in the proinflammatory cytokine IL-6', *Proceedings of the National Academy of Sciences* 100 (2003), pp. 9090–5

32 Schulz, R. and Beach, S., 'Caregiving as a risk factor for mortality: The Caregiver Health Effects Study', *JAMA* 281 (1999), pp. 2215–19

33 Quinn, C., Clare, L. and Woods, R.T., 'Balancing needs: The role of motivations, meanings and relationship dynamics in the experience of informal caregivers of people with dementia', *Dementia* 14:2 (2013), pp. 220–37

34 Chen, F. and Greenberg, J., 'A positive aspect of caregiving: The influence of social support on caregiving gains for family members of relatives with schizophrenia', *Community Mental Health Journal* 40 (2004), pp. 423–35

35 Hawkley, L.C. and Cacioppo, J.T., 'Loneliness matters: A theoretical and empirical review of consequences and mechanisms', *Annals of Behavioral Medicine* 40 (2010), pp. 218–27

36 Reinhardt, J.P., Boerner, K. and Horowitz, A., 'Good to have but not to use: Differential impact of perceived and received support on well-being', *Journal of Social and Personal Relationships* 23:1 (2006), pp. 117–29

37 Renna, M.E., 'A review and novel theoretical model of how negative emotions influence inflammation: The critical role of emotion regulation', *Brain, Behavior, and Immunity – Health* 18 (2021)

38 Kanbara, K. and Fukunaga, M., 'Links among emotional awareness, somatic awareness and autonomic homeostatic processing', *BioPsychoSocial Medicine* 10:1 (2016), p. 16

39 Brod, S., Rattazzi, L., Piras, G. and D'Acquisto, F., '"As above, so below": Examining the interplay between emotion and the immune system', *Immunology* 143:3 (2014), pp. 311–18

40 Ke, S., Guimond, A.J., Tworoger, S.S., Huang, T., Chan, A.T., Liu, Y.Y. and Kubzansky, L.D., 'Gut feelings: Associations of emotions and emotion regulation with the gut microbiome in women', *Psychological Medicine* 53:15 (2023), pp. 7151–60.

41 Chen, Y., Zhang, L. and Yin, H., 'Different emotion regulation strategies mediate the relations of corresponding connections within the default-mode network to sleep quality', *Brain Imaging and Behavior* 18:2 (2024), pp. 302–14

42 Lopez, R.B., Brown, R.L., Wu, E.L.L., Murdock, K.W., Denny, B.T., Heijnen, C. and Fagundes, C., 'Emotion regulation and immune functioning during grief: Testing the role of expressive suppression and cognitive reappraisal in inflammation among recently bereaved spouses', *Psychosomatic Medicine* 82:1 (2020), pp. 2–9

43 Masedo, A.I. and Esteve, M.R., 'Effects of suppression, acceptance and spontaneous coping on pain tolerance, pain intensity and distress', *Behaviour Research and Therapy* 45:2 (2007), pp. 199–209

44 Koechlin, H., Coakley, R., Schechter, N., Werner, C. and Kossowsky, J., 'The role of emotion regulation in chronic pain: A systematic literature review', *Journal of Psychosomatic Research* 107, pp. 38–45

45 Chapman, B.P., Fiscella, K., Kawachi, I., Duberstein, P. and Muennig, P., 'Emotion suppression and mortality risk over a 12-year follow-up', *Journal of Psychosomatic Research* 75:4 (2013), pp. 381–5

46 Denollet, J., Gidron, Y., Vrints, C.J. and Conraads, V.M., 'Anger, suppressed anger, and risk of adverse events in patients with coronary artery disease', *American Journal of Cardiology* 105:11 (2010), pp. 1555–60

47 Jakubowski, K.P., Barinas-Mitchell, E., Chang, Y.F., Maki, P.M., Matthews, K.A. and Thurston, R.C., 'The cardiovascular cost of silence: Relationships between self-silencing and carotid atherosclerosis in midlife women', *Annals of Behavioral Medicine* 56:3 (2022), pp. 282–90

48 Bowers, H. and Wroe, A. 'Beliefs about emotions mediate the relationship between emotional suppression and quality of life in irritable bowel syndrome', *Journal of Mental Health* 25:2 (2016), pp. 154–8

49 Emran, A., Iqbal, N. and Dar, I.A., '"Silencing the self" and women's mental health problems: A narrative review', *Asian Journal of Psychiatry* 53 (2020), 102197

50 Maji, S. and Dixit, S., 'Self-silencing and women's health: A review', *International Journal of Social Psychiatry* 65:1 (2018), pp. 3–13

51 Srivastava, S., Tamir, M., McGonigal, K.M., John, O.P. and Gross, J.J., 'The social costs of emotional suppression: A prospective study of the transition to college', *Journal of Personality and Social Psychology* 96:4 (2009), pp. 883–97

52 Angum, F., Khan, T., Kaler, J., Siddiqui, L. and Hussain, A., 'The prevalence of autoimmune disorders in women: A narrative review', *Cureus* 12:5 (2020)

53 Drillinger, M., 'Why women are more likely to die after a heart attack', Healthline.com (2023)

54 Tolin, D.F. and Foa, E.B., 'Sex differences in trauma and posttraumatic stress disorder: A quantitative review of 25 years of research', *Psychological Bulletin* 132:6 (2006), pp. 959–92

55 Albert, P.R., 'Why is depression more prevalent in women?', *Journal of Psychiatry and Neuroscience* 40:4 (2015), pp. 219-21

56 McLean, C.P., Asnaani, A., Litz, B.T. and Hofmann, S.G., 'Gender differences in anxiety disorders: Prevalence, course of illness, comorbidity and burden of illness', Journal of Psychiatric Research 45:8 (2011), pp. 1027–35

57 Hübel, C. et al., 'Genomics of body fat percentage may contribute to sex bias in anorexia nervosa', *American Journal of Medical Genetics* (2018)

58 Arout, C.A., Sofuoglu, M., Bastian, L.A. and Rosenheck, R.A., 'Gender differences in the prevalence of fibromyalgia and in concomitant medical and psychiatric disorders: A National Veterans Health Administration Study', *Journal of Women's Health* 27:8 (2018), pp. 1035–44

59 Zhang, B. and Wing, Y.K., 'Sex differences in insomnia: A meta-analysis', *Sleep* 29:1 (2006), pp. 85–93

60 Kim, Y.S. and Kim, N., 'Sex-gender differences in irritable bowel syndrome', *Journal of Neurogastroenterology and Motility* 24:4 (2018), pp. 544–58

61 Allais, G., Chiarle, G., Sinigaglia, S., Airola, G., Schiapparelli P. and Benedetto, C., 'Gender-related differences in migraine', *Neurological Sciences* 41:2 (2020), pp. 429–36

62 'Nearly one in five American adults who have had COVID-19 still have "Long COVID"', National Centre for Health Statistics, CDC. gov (last reviewed 2022)
63 'Female pain issues', International Association for the Study of Pain, iasp-pain.org
64 Ryan, R.M. and Deci, E.L., 'Self-determination theory and the facilitation of intrinsic motivation, social development, and well-being', *American Psychologist* 55:1 (2000), pp. 68–78
65 'Depression', World Health Organization, who.int
66 'Anxiety disorders', World Health Organization, who.int
67 'The facts and figures about global drug use', Russell Webster, russellwebster.com (2023)
68 Shapira, Y., Agmon-Levin, N. and Shoenfeld, Y., 'Defining and analyzing geoepidemiology and human autoimmunity', *Journal of Autoimmunity* 34:3 (2010), pp. 168–77
69 Dugan, A., 'Over 1 in 5 people worldwide feel lonely a lot', Gallup, newsgallup.com
70 'WHO Commission on Social Connection', World Health Organization, who.int

Chapter Two: Healing Your Relationship with Self

1 Brown, L.M. and Gilligan, C., *Meeting at the Crossroads* (Harvard University Press, 1992)
2 Damiano, S.R., Paxton, S.J., Wertheim, E.W., McLean, S.A. and Gregg, K.J., 'Dietary restraint of 5-year-old girls: Associations with internalization of the thin ideal and maternal, media, and peer influences', *International Journal of Eating Disorders* 48:8 (2015)
3 'VOA gender pay report 2024', Valuation Office Agency, gov. uk (2024)
4 'It's time to scrap the student loans motherhood penalty', The Conversation (2020)
5 Curtis, P. 'Women take longer to repay student loans', *Guardian* (2008)
6 'The gender pension gap report 2024', Now Pensions, nowpensions.com

7 Frederick, D.A., John, H.K.S., Garcia, J.R. et al. 'Differences in orgasm frequency among gay, lesbian, bisexual, and heterosexual men and women in a U.S. national sample', *Archives of Sexual Behavior* 47 (2018), pp. 273–88

8 Tedeschi, R.G., Calhoun, L.G., 'The posttraumatic growth inventory: measuring the positive legacy of trauma', *Journal of Traumatic Stress* 9:3 (1996), pp. 455–71

9 'No rest for the wicked', Dictionary.com (2018)

10 Kalu, M., 'What is the origin of "idle hands are the Devil's workshop"?', Christianity.com (2022)

11 Thank you Mandy Lehto for this gem – *Enough, the Podcast*, 'Episode 29: Do You Have Next-ies?'

12 Pollard, C. '"An insult to women": Holland & Barrett accused of "menowashing" with £3.79 chocolate-covered "menopause almond" bar that claims to ease hormonal changes', *Daily Mail* (2024)

Chapter Three: Breaking Free from Self-abandonment

1 'Prayer of Humble Access', Wikipedia.org

2 Ecclesiasticus 25:19, 24

3 Mongan, M.F., *HypnoBirthing: The Mongan Method* (Health Communications, 2005)

4 Kendath, T., 'Memories of an Orthodox youth' in S. Heschel (ed.), *On Being a Jewish Feminist*, New York (Schocken Books, 1983), pp. 96–7

5 Swidler, L.J., *Women in Judaism: The Status of Women in Formative Judaism* (Scarecrow Press, 1976), p. 115

6 Badshah, N., 'James Cleverley apologises for "appalling" date rape drug joke at No 10 event', *Guardian* (2023)

7 'How Starmer's cabinet stacks up', Datawrapper.de

8 Adu, A. and Goodier, M., 'Keir Starmer's cabinet will have most female ministers in history', *Guardian* (2024)

9 'Donald Trump's Cabinet, 2025', Ballotpedia (2025)

10 '100 years of women's work', DWP Digital, gov.uk

11 Willingham, A.J., 'What is no-fault divorce, and why do some conservatives want to get rid of it?', CNN (2023)

12 'Divorce laws and family violence', National Bureau of Economic Research, nber.org (2004)
13 'Dismissed, ignored, and belittled: The long road to endometriosis diagnosis in the UK', Endometriosis-uk.org (2024)
14 Haver, M.C., 'The no. 1 menopause doctor: they're lying to you about menopause!', *The Diary Of A CEO*, YouTube.com
15 'Domestic Abuse Statistics UK', National Centre for Domestic Violence, ncdv.org.uk (2023)
16 Radford, L. et al., 'Child abuse and neglect in the UK today', NSPCC (2011)
17 'Facts and Statistics', Refuge, refuge.org.uk
18 Femicide Census 2020, femicidecensus.org (2020)
19 'Facts and Statistics', Refuge, refuge.org.uk
20 'World Cup football is a risk factor for domestic violence', Lancaster University (2014)
21 Laws, C., 'The "Would you rather be trapped in the woods with a man or a bear" debate shows the reality of misogynistic violence', *Stylist* (2023)
22 Ng, K., Hancock, S. and Osborne, S., 'What happened to Sarah Everard? Timeline of 33-year-old's disappearance as Wayne Couzens report published', *Independent* (2024)
23 Dodd, V., 'Two Met police officers jailed over photos of murdered sisters', *Guardian* (2021)
24 Walker, P., 'Frances Andrade killed herself after being accused of lying, says husband', *Guardian* (2013)
25 'Rape: Levels of prosecutions', House of Lords Library, lordslibrary.parliament.uk (2025)

Step 1: I Reclaim My Mind

1 Adams, C.E. and Leary, M.R., 'Promoting self-compassionate attitudes toward eating among restrictive and guilty eaters', *Journal of Social and Clinical Psychology* 26:10 (2007), pp. 1120–44
2 Kross, E., Bruehlman-Senecal, E., Park, J., Burson, A., Dougherty, A., Shablack, H., Bremner, R., Moser, J. and Ayduk, O., 'Self-talk as

a regulatory mechanism: how you do it matters', *Journal of Personality and Social Psychology* 106:2 (2014), pp. 304–24

Step 2: I Reclaim My Attention

1 Ma, X., Yue, Z.-Q., Gong, Z.-Q., Zhang, H., Duan, N.-Y., Shi, Y.-T., Wei, G.-X. and Li, Y.-F., 'The Effect of Diaphragmatic Breathing on Attention, Negative Affect and Stress in Healthy Adults', *Frontiers in Psychology* 8 (2017)
2 Gupta, S. and Mittal, S., 'Yawning and its physiological significance', *International Journal of Applied and Basic Medical Research* 3:1 (2013), pp. 11–15
3 Pendolino, A.L., Lund, V.J., Nardello, E. and Ottaviano, G., 'The nasal cycle: A comprehensive review', *Rhinology Online* 1 (2018), pp. 67–76
4 Telles, S., Nagarathna, R. and Nagendra, H.R., 'Breathing through a particular nostril can alter metabolism and autonomic activities', *Indian Journal of Physiology and Pharmacology* 38:2 (1994), pp. 133–7

Step 3: I Reclaim My Body

1 Kraft, T.L. and Pressman, S.D., 'Grin and bear it: The influence of manipulated facial expression on the stress response', *Psychological Science* 23:11 (2012), pp. 1372–8
2 Porges, S., 'What's happening in the nervous system of patients who "please and appease" (or fawn) in response to trauma?', National Institute for the Clinical Application of Behavioural Medicine, nicabm.com
3 Arnsten, A., Mazure C.M. and Sinha, R., 'This is your brain in meltdown', *Scientific American* 306:4 (2012), pp. 48-53
4 Kaplan, J., Gimbel, S. and Harris, S., 'Neural correlates of maintaining one's political beliefs in the face of counterevidence', *Scientific Reports* 6 (2016)
5 Breit, S., Kupferberg, A., Rogler, G. and Hasler, G., 'Vagus nerve as modulator of the brain–gut axis in psychiatric and inflammatory disorders', *Frontiers in Psychiatry* 9 (2018)
6 Pellissier, S., Dantzer, C., Mondillon, L., Trocme, C., Gauchez, A.S., Ducros, V., Mathieu, N., Toussaint, B., Fournier, A., Canini, F. and

Bonaz, B., 'Relationship between vagal tone, cortisol, TNF-alpha, epinephrine and negative affects in Crohn's disease and irritable bowel syndrome', *PLOS One* 10:9 (2014)

7 Sessa, F., Anna, V., Messina, G., Cibelli, G., Monda, V., Marsala, G., Ruberto, M., Biondi, A., Cascio, O., Bertozzi, G., Pisanelli, D., Maglietta, F., Messina, A., Mollica, M.P. and Salerno, M., 'Heart rate variability as predictive factor for sudden cardiac death', *Aging* 10:2 (2018), pp. 166–77

8 Arneth, B.M., 'Gut–brain axis biochemical signalling from the gastrointestinal tract to the central nervous system: Gut dysbiosis and altered brain function', *Postgraduate Medical Journal* 94:1114 (2018), pp. 446–52

9 Ozel Asliyuce, Y., Berberoglu, U. and Ulger, O., 'Is cervical region tightness related to vagal function and stomach symptoms?', *Medical Hypotheses* 142 (2020)

10 Garcia-Rill, E., *Waking and the Reticular Activating System in Health and Disease* (Academic Press, 2015)

11 Moustafa, I.M., Youssef, A., Ahbouch, A., Tamim, M. and Harrison, D.E., 'Is forward head posture relevant to autonomic nervous system function and cervical sensorimotor control? Cross sectional study', *Gait Posture* 77 (2020), pp. 29–35

12 Dana, D., *The Polyvagal Theory in Therapy: Engaging the Rhythm of Regulation*, first edition (W.W. Norton & Company, 2018)

13 Golmakani, N., Zare, Z., Khadem, N., Shareh, H. and Shakeri, M.T., 'The effect of pelvic floor muscle exercises program on sexual self-efficacy in primiparous women after delivery', *Iranian Journal of Nursing and Midwifery Research* 20:3 (2015), pp. 347–53

14 Pfaus, J.G. and Tsarski, K., 'A case of female orgasm without genital stimulation', *Sexual Medicine* 10:2 (2022)

Step 4: I Reclaim My Right to Feel

1 Chapman, B.P., Fiscella, K., Kawachi, I., Duberstein, P. and Muennig, P., 'Emotion suppression and mortality risk over a 12-year follow-up', *Journal of Psychosomatic Research* 75:4 (2013), pp. 381–5

Acknowledgements

As I reflect on the process of writing this book, the word that comes to mind is *advocacy*. I am reminded of the many people who've opened doors for me, spoken up on my behalf when I wasn't in the room, championed me and my work, and nurtured my own belief in me. This book is a beautiful collective achievement, and I hope that via the fruits of your support, together we can help other people to know themselves, trust in themselves and advocate for themselves with confidence.

To my literary agent, Jane Graham Maw and the team at Graham Maw Christie, thank you for your impeccable support.

To Anya Hayes, my senior commissioning editor, deepest thanks for going in to bat for me and for your above-and-beyond skill in bringing the best of out my writing. You've been instrumental in my life and my career for the last decade, and I love that the culmination of those years of learning is this book.

To Jess Anderson, my editorial manager, and Fiona Robertson, my copy-editor/development editor, thank you for your insightful questions, gentle challenges, uplifting encouragement and your talent with words. You made this process truly joyful and together we have produced something we can all be proud of.

To Anna Bowen, my campaigns director, and Lucy Wingate, my senior campaigns manager, your enthusiasm for this book spurred me on. Thank you for galvanizing me and for creating so many opportunities to share my message.

To the clients I have had the honour of working with over the last 30 years, thank you for trusting me, letting me in, and sharing your pain, shame, hopes and dreams with me. You have shaped my work as a therapist and honed how I show up as a human being. Thank you for being such courageous teachers. Witnessing your personal evolution has been deeply inspiring.

To my readers, thank you for letting me know how my books are expediting your healing and for sharing my work with friends in need. Thank you for the love and care you bring to this world.

To my Instagram community, thank you for engaging with my daily love notes, for cheering me on and for the kind exchanges that are like rocket fuel for me.

To my dear friends Dr Mandy Lehto, Nicola Elliott, Louise Padmore, Toni Jones, Helen Marie, Nicky Denson-Elliott, Tamu Thomas, Dr Emma Hepburn, Harriet Inglis, and my film club crew: Nikki, Charlotte, Danielle, Emma and Clare, thank you for listening to me and for your incredible nurturing.

And to my ever-present mum, my darling husband Dave, and my sweet cherubs, Charlotte and Teddy, thank you for helping me stand tall and believe in me too.

About the Author

Suzy Reading is a chartered psychologist, yoga teacher, coach and mother of two. Suzy has over two decades of experience in the health and wellbeing industry, and draws from multiple modalities, together with psychology, to help people build sustainable healthy lifestyle habits. She is one of the top UK experts on self-care. Suzy is the Psychology Expert for Neom Organics, and a founding member of the Nourish app. She is the author of *The Little Book of Self-Care*, *The Self-Care Revolution*, *Stand Tall Like a Mountain*, *Self-Care for Tough Times*, *This Book Will (Help) Make You Happy*, *And Breathe*, *Sit to Get Fit* and *Rest to Reset*.